"Gary Noesner is a gripping story........, ...e stories. It's like watching an emotional bomb squad defuse explosive personalities. The big surprise is how recently the FBI learned the basic tenets of what makes a man put the gun down, a discovery story as captivating as the hostage standoffs that illuminate it."

—DAVE CULLEN, author of *Columbine*

"Gary Noesner has done something remarkable with this book, turning the murky process of hostage negotiations into a set of predictable and clear routes to bargaining success."

—ROBERT B. CIALDINI, bestselling author of *Influence: Science and Practice*

"Tortured people, desperate moments, dangerous solutions—*Stalling For Time* takes us deep into the lethal world of hostages, sieges, and terrorism. Gary Noesner, a thirty-year veteran of the Bureau, has written a landmark work that's both a nail-biting thriller and an expose of timely importance. This is a must-read not only for true crime fans but for every cop and G-man in the country."

—JOHN HUDDY, bestselling author of *Storming Las Vegas*

"*Stalling for Time* reads with the page-turning intensity of a first-rate thriller, only everything here is, remarkably, true. In finally opening up about his craft—about his thirty years spent reasoning with unreasonable people in situations that were literally life and death—Gary Noesner has written an essential book about the fine art of communication. For anyone who wants to know how to stay cool under fire, this book is indispensable."

—DOUGLAS STONE, bestselling co-author of *Difficult Conversations: How to Discuss What Matters Most*

"Gary Noesner has written an account of his decades-long career as a hostage negotiator that is so gripping it grabs the reader by the throat. It's a spectacular read, and every word of it is true."

—PETER BERGEN, author of *Holy War, Inc.* and *The Osama bin Laden I Know*

"The world doesn't need me to tell them that Gary Noesner has been there and done that. There are hundreds of living victims across the globe who are living testament to Noesner's abilities to successfully negotiate, or teach others effective crisis negotiation."

—LIEUTENANT TOM MONAHAN, Las Vegas Metropolitan Police Department, Director, Southern Nevada Counter-Terrorism Center

"Crisis negotiation requires experience, a cool head, and the ability to think on your feet in the face of extreme threat—and Noesner personified each and every element. It was an honor to work with him and to learn my skills from the very best."

—BYRON A. SAGE, retired FBI crisis negotiator

"Due to his effusive personality, ability to articulate his broad knowledge and experience, and renowned sense of humor, Gary Noesner is undoubtedly the foremost federal ambassador to American law enforcement in the field of critical incident management in general and crisis negotiation in particular. Experienced and knowledgeable crisis negotiators have learned that when Noesner speaks, we need to listen. It is in large part due to him and a very few others that crisis negotiation enjoys a noble position of respect and effectiveness both within and outside the United States."

—WILLIAM "BILL" KIDD, crisis negotiator, San Francisco Police Department and Sonoma County Sheriff's Office

"Gary Noesner's passion for the art of hostage/crisis negotiation has influenced hundreds, probably thousands, of police negotiators in the world. His enthusiasm for this highly perfected skill is contagious."

—BRUCE A. WIND, crisis negotiator, Seattle Police Department

STALLING
FOR TIME

STALLING

FOR TIME

My Life as an
FBI Hostage Negotiator

GARY NOESNER

RANDOM HOUSE
NEW YORK

2018 Random House Trade Paperback Edition

Copyright © 2010 by Gary Noesner

Published in the United States by Random House, an imprint and division of Penguin Random House LLC, New York.

RANDOM HOUSE and the HOUSE colophon are registered trademarks of Penguin Random House LLC.

Originally published in hardcover in the United States by Random House, an imprint and division of Penguin Random House LLC, in 2010.

Grateful acknowledgment is made to Cheryl Hart Frappier for permission to reprint the note on page 24. Reprinted by permission of Cheryl Hart Frappier.

LIBRARY OF CONGRESS CATALOGING-IN-PUBLICATION DATA
Noesner, Gary.
Stalling for time: my life as an FBI hostage negotiator / by Gary Noesner.
p. cm.
ISBN 978-0-525-51128-1
Ebook ISBN 978-0-679-60391-7
1. Noesner, Gary. 2. Hostage negotiations—United States. 3. United States. Federal Bureau of Investigation—Officials and employees—Biography. I. Title.
HV6598.N64 2010
363.25092—dc22
[B]
2010005888

Printed in the United States of America on acid-free paper

randomhousebooks.com

Text design by R. Bull

To Carol
For her love and support, particularly during the many times
I had to be away from home for the FBI

AUTHOR'S NOTE

The facts, dates, times, and direct quotations of dialogue are from official reports, personal notes, memos, and conversations as I recall them or as they were conveyed to me by those present. At all times, the recreation of events was done as accurately as possible. Hopefully, those depicted in this book will find their portrayals to be accurate and fair.

The opinions, observations, and comments expressed in this book are those of the author only and do not necessarily reflect those of the Federal Bureau of Investigation. Furthermore, they may not reflect those of the editors, endorsers, publisher, FBI Special Agents, or other persons who are described or mentioned in this book.

PREFACE

My line of work tends to inspire curiosity. The minute I tell people that I'm a hostage negotiator, they want to know what it's like to talk to people who have put themselves in truly desperate situations, who might at any moment kill themselves, their hostages, or the law enforcement officers attempting to bring an end to the crisis. Over the last several years, friends and colleagues encouraged me to write a book about these experiences, urging me to share the lessons I learned over years of convincing people to put down their weapons and surrender peacefully. Because I entered the field of hostage/crisis negotiations when it was still a new and evolving discipline, I've observed the process of trial and error that has transformed a rudimentary bargaining approach developed on the fly into a highly effective and flexible method. I've watched colleagues with no background in psychology or negotiation evolve in their tradecraft, many becoming functional street psychologists and crisis counselors, saving many lives and drastically reducing the number of police officers harmed during hostage, barricade, and suicide situations.

In the early years of the profession every negotiation seemed to involve two equally challenging components: managing the actual hostage situation, and managing leaders and colleagues captive to the entrenched law enforcement response to hostage events, which emphasized the use of force and viewed negotiators as do-gooder types who only got in the way of them doing their jobs. In those days, just when we had finally established a bond of trust with the perpetrator, moving closer to ending the crisis, we'd sometimes find that a fellow agent or police officer had thrown a rock through the window, ordered a military vehicle driven up on the lawn as a show of force, or turned off the power. This often produced violent resistance and injuries or deaths that might have been avoided. Of course there are times when you are forced to put down the phone and send in the SWAT team, but all too often in those early days, that decision was reached prematurely. I'm particularly proud of the degree to which we've been able to shift the balance toward the primary goal of any hostage negotiation, which is to resolve the crisis while avoiding loss of life. The results have been dramatic.

Hostage negotiation is about managing yourself and the people around you. And while the most important relationship may appear to be with the person you have on the other end of the phone, in fact this is often not the case. In the midst of trying to talk someone into giving up, you have to manage the people supporting you, to make sure that you have the help you need at hand to make split-second decisions. And you have to "manage up"—to make sure your commanding officer is paying attention to what you're doing, supporting your decisions, and fending off attempts to take actions that would undermine them. Throughout my career I worked a great many crisis incidents, most of which you've never heard about because they received little or no media attention. Others, like the sieges in Waco, Texas, and Jordan, Montana, were covered feverishly by the national and even international media. Each of these experiences, whether success or failure, taught me valuable lessons about human behavior, interpersonal communication, and conflict resolution, and each helped me to understand how to influence people away from violent courses of action.

The observations and lessons that I discuss in this book may be derived from specific hostage negotiations, but many of them apply equally to the kinds of negotiations we face in everyday life, from hammering out contracts to tense interpersonal conflicts with intransigent colleagues or hostile neighbors, not to mention with friends and family. I know my own life relationships have benefited from what I've learned along the way, and I believe that the skills discussed in this book can help anyone to become a better person, a more engaged spouse, a more attentive parent, a better friend, and a more effective leader. Before we can influence others we must first listen and understand.

Listening is the cheapest concession we can ever make.

STALLING
FOR TIME

CHAPTER ONE

IT'S TIME TO DIE

*Time cools, time clarifies; no mood can be maintained
quite unaltered through the course of hours.*
—MARK TWAIN

There it was, hard and direct. "You going to shoot me when I come out?" Charlie said.

"No," I responded. "That's not going to happen. You said you wouldn't hurt anyone. You said you'd drop off the pilot somewhere in the mountains. So there's no reason for anyone to get hurt."

The logic of this formulation appeared to work for Charlie, perhaps because this was his only chance to go on living with Cheryl and their son, little Charlie.

But what I knew that he didn't was that somewhere out in the fields surrounding us, FBI marksmen were poised, waiting to take his life.

A large part of a negotiator's job is to establish trust, yet there are fundamental contradictions in that. In order to convince someone that despite all appearances to the contrary, everything will be okay, you have to project sincerity. You have to make him believe that what you are saying is honest and aboveboard. You have to address his primal need for safety and security by establishing a bond. And on rare occasions, you have to lie.

"Have you ever been on a helicopter before?" I asked.

"No," he said.

"You'll enjoy it. The view over the mountains will be spectacular." Of course, I knew that he would never take that ride or experience that view. Once again, the contradiction: he was hearing what he wanted to hear.

"Charlie," I said, "I need to ask you an important question."

"What?"

"The helicopter pilot is an old friend of mine. His name is Tom Kelly. I've known and worked with Tom for many years, so I need your absolute promise that you won't harm him in any way. If anything happens to Tom, I would never be able to live with myself."

"I won't hurt him," Charlie said.

About ten days before, Charlie Leaf had abducted his estranged former common-law wife, Cheryl Hart, and their young son from her parents' home in Connecticut. After a seven-year relationship, Charlie and Cheryl had separated two years ago. When Cheryl had finally left him, she said she saw him snap. She moved in with her parents, trying to get on with her life, but Charlie, like so many men in such situations, was not willing to let her go. The way he saw it, Cheryl and little Charlie were his possessions, and he wanted them back. Over the next two years he threatened her and physically abused her whenever he found her. He had once even abducted little Charlie for six months, and gave up the boy only when the police intervened. Cheryl had sought and obtained a restraining order a year ago. The next day, right before he had to go to court, Charlie came to kill her.

It was on Friday, April 1, 1988, that Charlie cashed his paycheck and purchased a carbine rifle, sawing off the gunstock in order to conceal it. Then he drove to Cheryl's parents' house—they were away for the weekend—and pried open a door leading into the garage. He kicked in the door to Cheryl's bedroom with the rifle in his hand. He beat her and raped her before telling her to pack things for little Charlie. He told her that she could go or die.

Fortunately, Cheryl had the instincts of a survivor. She remained calm and said she would come; she convinced Charlie that he didn't have to kill her.

"We can go away," she said. "We can start a new life together with little Charlie."

Cheryl had made it clear by now that she wanted no part of Charlie, yet he wanted so much to believe her that this gleam of hope obscured his judgment. He gave her a few moments to get the boy out of bed and to gather up some clothes. Then they took off in Charlie's car.

Cheryl had no plan other than to try to stay alive. Charlie's plan, to the extent that he had one, was to avoid being caught. Both knew that Cheryl's parents would call the police the moment they discovered she was gone. Both were simply stalling for time.

Charlie drove south through the night along the eastern seaboard, and somewhere near the Washington, D.C., area headed west into the mountains of Virginia. Charlie liked mountains. When little Charlie was still an infant, he started to build a log cabin, which remained unfinished when Cheryl left him. Cheryl had grown tired of him, of the idea of living in a remote cabin, and of their relationship, and so she left.

On Saturday, April 2, about an hour and a half due west of Washington, D.C., Charlie's car ran out of gas. They abandoned it near Sperryville, Virginia, a scenic little town on the eastern slopes of the Blue Ridge Mountains.

The Virginia authorities found Charlie's car on Sunday. By this time, Cheryl's sister had reported her missing when she didn't show up to a planned dinner, so when the police ran the plates, they quickly connected this vehicle with the story of the abduction in Connecticut, then launched an all-out search.

Just outside Sperryville, a sleepy country village where tourists came in season to buy apples and view the fall colors, Charlie took his family once again into the woods. This time, he built a simple lean-to. They made their way to a nearby country store, where they purchased food and drinks and a few other supplies. Meanwhile, all around them, a search went on involving the local police, the Virginia State Police, and the FBI. Helicopters flew over the ridges and valleys, while teams on foot searched the woods with tracking dogs.

This went on for almost a week, by which time the authorities were ready to give up. Then on Friday the eighth, Charlie waited until after dark, then broke in to the same country store he had visited before and stole additional supplies. This confirmed for the police that their fugitive was still in the area, and the next morning they renewed their search. Investigating the burglary, the authorities showed photographs of Charlie, Cheryl, and little Charlie to the store owner, who made a positive identification.

The FBI's efforts in tracking down Charlie and his victims would be led by the Richmond, Virginia, SWAT team, with an assist from members of the SWAT team from the FBI Washington Field Office (WFO). Both groups are tactical operations specialists, that is, the ones who subdue the perpetrators if and when negotiations fail to bring an end to the crisis. In other words, their jobs do not involve establishing trust or empathy, or the contradictions attendant therein.

They made a house-to-house search of the area, and late in the afternoon on April 9, Special Agent Barry Subelsky and his team from the WFO SWAT approached a two-story farmhouse, a weekend getaway place for a successful Washington couple, less than a mile off the main road. The sunlight was fading fast, so they wanted to get this done as quickly as possible.

Barry conferred with Wayne Waddell, SWAT leader for the Richmond FBI office. These two experienced agents, both Vietnam combat veterans, decided that Barry's team would search the ground floor of the farmhouse and Wayne's team would then take the upstairs. Before they moved in, however, they saw something that made them cautious. The electric meter on the outside of the house was humming along at a brisk pace, more active than what one would expect in an unoccupied dwelling.

They summoned an FBI helicopter for support, and it landed in a field some hundred yards away, just as a local sheriff arrived with keys to the house.

Barry's team searched for signs of forced entry but found none. They came up on the rickety porch outside the kitchen and went in through the back door, then fanned out to secure the ground floor. Wayne and his team followed in single file up on the porch, through the kitchen and then the family room, turning the corner near the front entryway, then advancing, slowly and carefully, up the creaking main stairs to the second floor.

When Wayne got upstairs he found Charlie on the floor of the bedroom holding Cheryl and little Charlie in front of him, a gun to her head.

"Back off!" he yelled. "Back off or I'll kill her."

Wayne Waddell had spent hours training for situations just like this, and he knew exactly what to do.

"We're backing off," he said. "Nobody's going to get hurt."

He and the agents moved back down and clustered at the foot of the stairs.

Law enforcement often overreacts to threats of the kind that Charlie made, even though in most cases such threats are merely defensive, designed to keep the police at bay. Some law officers hear only the threatened action, "I'll kill this lady," while failing to hear the conditions under which that action will be taken: "if you try to come in here." That is one reason why the most critical skills of a negotiator are self-control and the ability to help those around you keep their cool.

Wayne had a lot on his mind as law enforcement settled in for the long haul. Mere chance had made him the group's primary negotiator, and his immediate task was to deescalate the confrontation, and then to convince Charlie that he was here to help him. But he also had to lead the SWAT team and coordinate the actions of the roughly twenty FBI personnel on the scene, as well as communicate all of this to his superiors.

Back in Sperryville, other agents and local police officials were setting up a command post at the local firehouse, from which all efforts would be coordinated. State police brought in an armored vehicle, one of those old Brink's trucks that had been converted to a forward command post, which they positioned about a hundred yards away from the farmhouse on the long drive leading to it. Sniper/observer teams took up positions in the nearby woods, and the men inside the house began to wait.

As dusk settled in, Wayne and his team decided to turn on the lights. Charlie didn't like this. In response he fired several shots at the lightbulb in the ceiling above the second-floor landing, shattering the bulb and sending shards of glass in all directions.

"Relax! Relax!" Wayne yelled. He kept his guys cool, avoiding what could have been a bloodbath right there and then. It was going to be a long night.

Wayne now realized he would need a trained negotiator to talk to Charlie. He called in another agent from the Richmond FBI office, Gray Hill, who soon arrived, still in civilian clothes, and assumed the task of talking to Charlie from the bottom of the stairs. Their conversations over the next couple of hours were sporadic, and in the few exchanges that took place Charlie remained adamant: he was not going to give up without hurting Cheryl and the boy. Hill was a veteran agent and had taken the FBI's two-week hostage-negotiation training course, but this was his first actual hostage situation. His job at this point was to relieve Wayne and hold the fort until a resolution strategy was in place. An hour went by, maybe two. Then Charlie called down with his first demand. "We need our clothes out of the dryer. We need you to get the clothes and bring them up here."

It actually had been Cheryl's idea to break in to the farmhouse, with clean clothes as the objective. There had been some wet weather in the mountains and she and the boy had been cold and miserable. She had convinced Charlie that they needed to take a warm bath and wash their clothes, which were still in the dryer when Wayne and his crew entered the house.

Gray was nothing if not cautious, a negotiator who would play it by the book, and the book says that you do not give a hostage taker anything without getting something in return. His answer to the request for the clothing was no. He did not want to empower Charlie by making concessions to him without getting something in return. But at the same time, he continued to emphasize the themes that Wayne had established: No one had been hurt. The charges that might be brought against Charlie at this point were not that serious. The FBI didn't want to see anyone hurt.

These are all standard tactics of hostage negotiation: to minimize the consequences the perpetrator will face once the siege is over, and to assure him that he won't be hurt if he surrenders. The other essential part of the message is that harming someone will only make matters worse. Even so, there are times when playing it by the book won't get the job done, and when a more experienced negotiator might be more willing to improvise. This would prove to be one of those times.

It was after one in the morning when the phone rang on the nightstand next to my bed in my home in Fairfax, Virginia. I heard a voice telling me that it was FBI headquarters, calling to tell me about what was going on in Sperryville and asking me to report to the command post there as soon as possible to assist with negotiations and eventually take over direct communication with Charlie. As the negotiation coordinator for the Washington Field Office, I'd been involved with previous such incidents and I knew the drill.

While I would have preferred this call at a more convenient hour, I felt the usual charge of excitement that comes with responding to cases of this kind. I quickly jumped out of bed, threw on my clothes, and told my wife, Carol, that I would call her when I could. This was my job, like it or not. I had just come back from an assignment overseas and my FBI car—my "G-ride"—was still parked at the office, which meant that I would have to take the family station wagon. As I got in the car and backed out of the driveway, the absolute calm of the quiet suburban street once again reminded me how different my life was from that of my neighbors.

The trip would normally take about ninety minutes, driving out of Fairfax through Warrenton. My family and I had been to Sperryville the previous year to pick apples, so I knew the way. There was almost no traffic at this time of night, and, not having my light and siren, I edged over the speed limit cautiously and made it in about an hour. When I reached the command post at the fire station in town I was given directions to the farmhouse a little ways up the road. I was told to speak to the Assistant Special Agent in Charge (ASAC), Virgil Young.

I showed my identification to the trooper on the scene, parked near the armored truck serving as the forward command post, and approached the small group of men standing out in the cold. It was 2:30 a.m. I shook hands with Special Agent Young and also met Wayne Waddell, whose welcome consisted of tossing me a bulletproof vest.

The two agents quickly brought me up to speed. When you first come into a situation you want all the information you can get. The agents you are relieving mostly want to go home, so sometimes you have to push a bit to tease out the facts. As I listened to them, I could barely see their faces, but I could tell from his weary voice that Wayne was especially tired. He and his team had been out all day searching when their late-afternoon decision to check out one last house had hit the jackpot. He told me that he and his team had stood down a couple of hours earlier, and that Gray Hill and the group from the Washington Field Office SWAT team were now on shift inside the house. I had worked and trained with this team and knew them well. My job was going to be to relieve Gray right away, although he would stay on as my backup negotiator, or coach, until a replacement arrived. Before I left home I'd called another experienced negotiator, Steve Romano; he and Agent Bill Wang would join me shortly.

Wayne Waddell led me toward the farmhouse, which was about a hundred yards off the road at the end of a long, straight driveway edged with tall junipers and shrubs, though in the dark of night I couldn't see it or much of anything else. I was feeling somewhat optimistic because the situation appeared to be stable: Charlie had abducted Cheryl and little Charlie more than a week ago, and he had not yet killed her. The standoff itself had gone on for hours now, and again, Charlie had not gone over the edge. My best guess was that if I could keep him calm until daylight, we might be able to get him to surrender.

When we reached the farmhouse we went around to the back, climbed the two or three steps onto the porch, and entered the kitchen door. All the lights were turned off, so Wayne used his flashlight to guide us. I followed close behind as we made our way into the family room.

In the flashlight's beam I caught glimpses of photographs on the walls, books on the shelves, and the carpets, drapes, and other furnishings that made this a nice, cozy place for a weekend getaway. But right now it wasn't cozy at all. It was actually colder inside than it had been out on the lawn, and I could see my breath condensing in the air as I spoke. I wished I had brought along a heavier coat and gloves. At least I had the Kevlar vest for a bit of insulation.

The SWAT team was clustered near the door where the family room opened onto the entryway at the foot of the stairs. They looked particularly ghoulish in the flashlight beam, each wearing a dark uniform, bulletproof vest, and Kevlar helmet, and each armed with a 9 mm MP5 submachine gun. With them was Barry Subelsky, my squad partner and a guy with whom I'd spent all too many hours in scenes just like this, who greeted me with the respect to which I'd become accustomed: "Now look what the cat dragged in."

I wondered, not for the first time, why these guys seemed to enjoy SWAT duty, which usually involved being cold, wet, and hungry, not to mention spending a good deal of time in the direct line of fire. Negotiators usually had a warmer, drier place to work from, a ready supply of coffee, and less likelihood of being shot. The telephone was our usual mode of contact with the perpetrator, and one of the truisms of the profession is that no negotiator has ever been killed over the telephone. Unfortunately, tonight I would not be on the phone. Charlie and his carbine were right upstairs, just a few feet away.

Standing with the SWAT team, just beyond the door, was Gray Hill, the negotiator I would be relieving. Wayne took him by the arm and tugged him back into the family room to introduce us.

Gray and I shook hands, and then he leaned forward as he gave me the update, speaking in low, confidential tones.

"Very quiet for the last hour or so," he told me. "Charlie hasn't been saying very much, though I've tried to keep him engaged. Overall, tense but calm."

"Seems like a good sign," I said. "The man's calmed down. No new threats and no one's been hurt. So maybe he'll come to his senses."

"Then again," Gray said, "he did blow out the lights the minute we turned them on." We glanced at each other. "Charlie definitely has an edge to him."

Gray told me about the clothes in the dryer that Charlie had requested. He told me that he had said no, and asked me what I thought.

"Well," I said, "the usual deal is quid pro quo. We give the perpetrator something tangible only in exchange for releasing a hostage. But Charlie isn't holding Cheryl and little Charlie with a clear goal in mind. When a subject doesn't want or need anything from us, the only real tool we have is to show him some respect. So I think it would be a good idea to give him the clothes. If we can create a relationship of trust, we have a better chance of influencing his behavior."

Among negotiators, this process of trust building is called the "behavioral change stairway." You listen to show interest, then respond empathetically, which leads to rapport building, which then leads to influence. But influence does not accrue automatically. We can suggest alternatives to violence, but we must first earn the right to be of influence.

Would Charlie see us bringing him the clothes from the dryer as a sign of weakness on our part? I didn't think so. I believed that the gesture, without any preconditions, would make us appear less threatening. By appearing more willing to help, we would appear more worthy of respect in his eyes.

Gray went down to the basement and brought back up the bag of clothes. "You come, too," he suggested. "I'll introduce you to Charlie."

"I think it's better if I give him the clothes," I said. As the new negotiator, I needed to demonstrate that I was here to help. "It'll build trust," I said. Wayne nodded.

It was almost 4:00 a.m. when Gray introduced me to Charlie. Standing at the bottom of the stairs, I began with a simple hello.

Silence.

I tried again. "Hello, my name is Gary and I'm here to help," I said, before adding, "Can you hear me?"

"Yeah. I hear you."

"Good. That's good, Charlie. You know, we really mean you and your family no harm." I used the word *family* very deliberately, in an effort to remind Charlie what Cheryl and the boy meant to him. I repeated the standard lines that he had already heard from Wayne and Gray. It is not only what you say that counts, but how you say it. Being sincere and genuine are powerful tools to gain influence. "We don't want to see anyone get hurt, you know. This is just a domestic dispute. If you'll just put down your weapon and come downstairs, I guarantee you that no harm will come to you."

I waited, and then in the darkness I heard a single word. "No."

I didn't expect him to give up so easily. I just wanted to keep reinforcing the thought that a peaceful ending was still possible.

It stood to reason that Charlie would be exhausted. Also hungry. "Charlie," I said, "you need anything? Anything I can do for you?"

As I anticipated, he asked if I could get their clothes from downstairs. "Sure, Charlie," I said. "I can do that for you."

I had the bag of clothes at my side, but I waited a bit, as if we were just then going down to the dryer. After a while I said, "Charlie, I've got the bag. You want me to throw it up to the top of the stairs?" He told me to go ahead.

I threw the bag and it dropped onto the landing. A moment later Cheryl Hart darted into view, wrapped in a blanket, looking terrified. She glanced at me for a split second, then grabbed the bag and disappeared.

"It's cold in here," I said to Charlie. "I didn't want you or your family to be uncomfortable."

I waited again.

"You need anything else?"

"I'm good," he said. Then a moment later he added, "Little Charlie's sleeping ... so if you guys could keep it down ..."

"Sure," I said.

I wanted to comply with his request. On the other hand, keeping big Charlie awake might encourage him to surrender sooner rather than later. But exhaustion can also make people more impulsive and unpredictable.

I waited about forty-five minutes before I reestablished contact.

"Everything okay, Charlie?"

"Yeah."

He sounded half asleep. Most likely he hadn't had any real rest since this whole thing began. "Got some good news for you," I said. By this time we had an army field telephone wired up from the forward command post to the house. I had just heard back from Max Thiel, the FBI agent in New England who was interviewing people back in Trumbull, Connecticut, for us. "Your boss won't lose the bail money he posted for you." Charlie had been charged earlier with failure to appear in court. "Your boss sounds like a good guy. He says he's holding your job for you." Again the message was, *You have a future.*

But there was no response from Charlie, so I left him alone with his thoughts.

I rubbed my hands together and killed time by talking with the SWAT guys. The weather was always a good topic. It just wasn't supposed to be this cold in April. But I also took the time to ask various members of the team how they sized up the situation. It brought them more into the process, but I also genuinely wanted to know what they had to say. Everyone seemed to think that what we had was as good as it was going to get, at least for now. Early that morning the WFO SWAT team had been relieved by members of the FBI's elite Hostage Rescue Team (HRT). Each FBI office has a SWAT team, but HRT was the FBI's full-time domestic counterterrorism and tactical response unit, stationed at the FBI academy. Just before daybreak, I felt it was time to begin to ramp it up a bit.

"Charlie! Good morning. Hope you got some rest."

He muttered something unintelligible, so I went on. "I hope we've made it clear that we don't want to hurt you, Charlie." I then reminded him that our agents had not responded when he fired shots at the light-bulb. We had given him the clothes he had asked for, and, before I arrived, we had even provided some food. I later learned that Charlie told Cheryl he was going to kill her after that breakfast. I restated our position that this was simply a domestic dispute between him and Cheryl, once again downplaying the seriousness of the kidnapping. There was no reason for anyone to get hurt. No serious crime had been committed, I said, although that did not mean that we could just walk away.

No response from Charlie. I knew that he could hear me, but I had no sense that I was having any effect.

For the next two hours I continued this kind of running commentary. In the negotiation business we call this a "one-way dialogue," where the goal is to address concerns that may not have been articulated, and answer questions that haven't been asked. I suspected that Charlie could see the logic in what I was saying, but people who are cornered often fall into a kind of paralysis, so no decision becomes the de facto decision.

Fully awake now, Charlie yelled out, "Just get the fuck out of here and leave us alone!"

This sudden shift caused me concern. Again, exhaustion could be taking its toll, adding a wild card to his already erratic behavior of late.

I asked him if he was considering harming himself. I knew that there was plenty of evidence that bringing up the issue of suicide was not going to plant the thought. And if he was really thinking of considering suicide, I needed to know so I could focus my efforts on suicide intervention.

"I'm not going to kill myself," Charlie said. His voice became more intense. "You're going to have to kill me."

"We're not going to do that," I said. "There's no reason to do that."

His voice continued to rise in intensity. He was now angry. "I'll give you a reason. You're going to have to kill me after I kill Cheryl."

My heart sank. I had hoped his prior threats against Cheryl were simply intended to keep the police at bay. But his increasingly angry tone, and the fact that it came after several hours in which we'd demonstrated that we didn't want to hurt him, gave me great concern. Charlie continued to work himself up into a frenzy.

"Right now I'm sitting on a chair with Cheryl on the floor beside me," he said. "I have the gun against her head and I am about to pull the fucking trigger!"

His voice went up several decibels as he enunciated those last syllables, which were punctuated with what sounded like a choking noise from Cheryl. The two HRT agents closest to me moved in, actually nudging me out of the way as they readied themselves to make an emergency assault. If Charlie fired, they would charge up the stairs to try to save the little boy. I couldn't figure out what had gone wrong. Things had seemed stable just moments before, and now they were slipping out of control. I needed to buy some time.

"Don't do it, Charlie," I blurted out. This wasn't inspired or subtle, but I had to say something. I couldn't just wait for the sound of the gun. "Don't kill Cheryl. Don't kill her in front of your son."

Charlie started shouting again, calling Cheryl a no-good whore. His voice grew louder and angrier as he spewed out a litany of complaints. She had cheated on him. She had done this, she had done that. Each outburst and accusation seemed to make him more agitated.

The HRT operators were locked and ready. It looked like this was going to be it for Cheryl. The only question remaining was whether we could get to the boy before Charlie killed him as well.

But then Charlie stopped yelling. There was silence for a moment, and then I heard him whispering, "Charlie, come sit in Daddy's lap."

It's hard to explain the experience of that moment. I was absolutely convinced that the next sound I would hear was the gun going off and Cheryl being killed. But for the moment I was out of ideas. I desperately tried to conjure something to stop him.

"Charlie, if you really love your son, you won't do this. A boy should not see his mother being killed."

"He'll be okay," he said. "I was raised without a mother. My son can get by without a mother." In truth, Charlie's mother had died only a few years earlier of stomach cancer.

I took another tack. "You don't want to see your son hurt, do you?"

"The only way he's gonna be hurt is if you come up here after I kill Cheryl."

"Talk to me instead of hurting her," I said.

"I'm going to shoot her in one minute."

Then I heard him whisper to Cheryl, "I'm going to blow your fucking head off."

"Charlie, is there anything, anything at all, that I can do to keep you from doing this?"

"Can't you get us out of here?" Cheryl yelled. She was more desperate than I was—her life was on the line—and her fear had produced an inspired response. Charlie had narrowed his vision to the dynamic going on within this house. Cheryl's question suddenly widened it again. Charlie followed up immediately.

"Yeah," Charlie said. "We want to get to that helicopter outside."

Suddenly it appeared that we might have a chance after all. At least this was a demand that could be bargained for, another way of stalling for time.

I signaled for the HRT operators to step back from the stairs to give me a little room. "Charlie," I said, "this is the first time you've mentioned wanting to leave the house. You know, this is something I could work on. I don't have the authority myself, but I could get on the phone and talk to my boss to get his approval."

I waited, knowing that the next time Charlie spiraled out of control, it would probably mean the end for Cheryl.

"I'm going to speak with my boss, Charlie. Can I have your promise that you won't hurt Cheryl while I'm talking to him?"

"Hurry up."

"Is that a promise?"

"Just hurry up."

When I had communicated with the command post about an hour before, the situation had been stable and the prognosis for an eventual peaceful outcome seemed good. How was I going to explain what we had just experienced? How could I convey how close we'd come to having the situation blow up in our faces? I rang them up on the mobile phone and, standing in the far corner of the family room, speaking in a hushed voice, I explained the situation to Virgil Young, the on-scene forward commander. I told him that the only reason Cheryl was alive was that she had blurted out a desire to get out of the house, and that Charlie had seen the helicopter. Now our subject had this notion that he could fly away. "If I give Charlie a negative response," I said, "there's no doubt in my mind that he'll carry out his threat."

Agent Young listened carefully and thoughtfully, accepting nothing at face value. "What exactly did he say?" he asked. "How angry did he appear?" He challenged me to back up each and every one of my recommendations.

I asked his express permission to engage in a dialogue with Charlie about going to the helicopter. Getting his approval was important, because if later he said we couldn't make the offer, I would be caught in a lie. Not only would that destroy my credibility with Charlie, but it would probably trigger the murder we all wanted to avoid.

I then did something that is extremely rare in the negotiation business. I recommended that I be given permission to lure Charlie out of the house by negotiating with him for access to the helicopter, and that we prepare to have a sniper take him out as he left the house.

I could see the look of surprise on some of the SWAT team members' faces, but I really had no other choice. I am not a self-questioning kind of guy. This was an explosive situation and mollification had just about run its course. I saw no other way to keep Cheryl alive.

I also knew that commanders don't like deadlines, and that this was a serious request that would require some time to consider. Still, I added, "I need a response very quickly."

Waiting for an answer, I went back and reengaged Charlie in discussion. I told him that I had made the request and that I was waiting for the answer from the boss. Again I asked him not to hurt Cheryl. Again, no reply. Yet I sensed I had purchased some time.

There was nothing to do now but wait. I tried to maintain a calm appearance, but inside my mind was running at full speed. I was trying to pull a rabbit out of a hat, and the lives of a young woman and her son depended on making the trick work.

A half hour later the field telephone rang; it was Virgil Young. He told me that his boss, Special Agent in Charge Terry O'Connor of the Richmond Field Office, had given us the green light. His wording was characteristically dispassionate. "The Special Agent in Charge has authorized you to proceed with the plan you have recommended," he said.

He told me nothing about the specifics of the plan HRT had worked out for dealing with Charlie; I didn't need to know. My job was simply to get the subject out of the house and walking toward that helicopter. I walked back to the stairway and directed my voice upstairs.

"Charlie," I said, "this is Gary again. I told my boss about you wanting the helicopter. He didn't understand why you don't just put your weapon down and come out. But I also told him you wouldn't take no for an answer. Based on that, my boss has agreed for you to take the helicopter. He didn't like it, but he'll go along if it will keep people from getting hurt."

Once again I was trying to establish myself in Charlie's mind as his advocate. I was also trying to make our position seem credible. If I just blithely said okay, Charlie might think we had given in too easily and might become suspicious.

This is when I asked Charlie if he had ever flown in a helicopter before. The question seemed to brighten his mood, so I followed up by asking where he wanted to go. He said he would tell the pilot to fly them over the mountains and they would land when he spotted a place that looked good to him.

It was then that I asked him not to harm my friend Tom Kelly, the pilot.

The tension seemed to be easing as time passed by, enough so that after an hour or so Charlie and I began to talk more casually, first about the farmhouse. Though relieved that we had stepped back from the brink, I was aware that any misstep could set him off. He told me that he had seen the beams down in the basement when they had gone downstairs to use the washer and dryer. He told me how much he admired that kind of solid construction, far better than what was built these days. I asked Charlie about the cabin he had built in Connecticut, and he seemed to take pride in talking about his craftsmanship. We then moved on to talking about camping and the outdoors. I told him that I had an old motor home and that I wanted to take my family camping in New England this coming summer. I asked him about some places we might go, and he gave me some recommendations. Our conversations were becoming more relaxed.

For the first time I also mentioned to Charlie that I also had a four-year-old son. We talked about how fascinating it is to watch kids grow. Again I tried to push Charlie toward thinking about the future in a positive way. I reminded him how important it was for a father to show his son the woods and outdoors, to help him grow to be a man.

Suddenly he said, "I've got some stuff in the lean-to. Some favorite toys for the boy . . . and some other stuff. I want to take it on the helicopter with us."

This was a complication we could do without, but I had to play along. "Can you tell us where the shelter is in relation to the farmhouse?" I said. "We'll go get your stuff."

Charlie's directions were a bit vague, but we dispatched agents to recover the items.

"You must be a pretty good woodsman," I said, "to have gone so long in the mountains without being found, especially with so many people looking for you."

He seemed to relish the compliment. "Nobody's going to find me if I don't want them to," he said.

When I got back on the phone with the command post, they described a four-phase plan that I would have to sell to Charlie. First, two FBI agents would carry the recovered personal items out to the helicopter. They would place black garbage bags filled with these items at the foot of the helicopter and walk away. Phase two called for the helicopter pilot, Tom Kelly, to walk to the aircraft, load the bags onto the copilot's seat, get in, and start the engine. Phase three would have those of us on the ground floor exit the house. Phase four would have Charlie, Cheryl, and little Charlie exit, walk to the helicopter, board it, and fly away as previously agreed. At least that was phase four as we would describe it to Charlie.

I went back to my position at the foot of the stairs, and for the rest of the morning, Charlie and I went back and forth over the plan. I wanted to make sure that he fully understood what to expect. I also wanted to reinforce his belief that he was really going to fly away. If he sensed betrayal, this whole thing could blow up in our faces.

After a couple of hours our guys came back from their search for Charlie's shelter in the woods and said they still couldn't find it. Charlie tried to explain again, but even after a second try our agents still came up empty. I was growing concerned that Charlie might lose faith in this whole plan, so I asked him to really spell out the directions for us. He drew a crude map on a coloring book and threw it down the stairs. I gave the map to our agents and they went off to try again.

"We're hungry," Charlie said.

We sent a police cruiser to the closest McDonald's, and when the food arrived the HRT guys covered me as I placed it halfway up the steps. A moment later, Cheryl came down to pick up the food. This was the first time she and I had a chance to look clearly at each other. She was a pretty girl, but frail and terrified. Earlier, the command post and I had discussed whether or not we should ever try to grab her. We weren't sure if she would cooperate if it meant leaving her child, so we'd decided the most we could do was to hold up a sign asking if she was okay, then stand ready to sweep her out of the way if she appeared to want to flee down the stairs. I held up the sign—*Are you okay?*—and she looked at it, but she made no response. She knew Charlie was watching her every move.

An hour or so later our agents returned. They had located the shelter and brought back the Easter candy and other items Charlie had requested.

Our four-phase plan was ready to begin. Then the command post called. FBI legal personnel wanted to clearly document that we had given Charlie every opportunity to surrender. They told me that I needed to ask Charlie one more time if he would come out. I explained that this might raise his suspicions and mess up our agreement. Still, I had to do it.

I gathered Bill Wang, who had relieved Gray hours earlier, and the HRT operators close around me and quietly explained what I was about to do. I told them they needed to listen carefully to my request for Charlie to surrender, because they needed to be able to describe in court not only what I said but what Charlie said in reply.

I wasn't sure how to raise the issue, so I just forged ahead. "Charlie, we're about ready to begin the process, but before we start, my boss wants me to ask you one more time if you'll just put down your weapon and come down."

"No way," he said.

Then I uttered the dumbest thing I have ever said as a negotiator.

"Okay," I said, "I won't kick that dead horse anymore."

I could almost see the words drifting up the stairway, and I wanted to reach up after them and pull them back.

Charlie didn't miss a beat. "Dead horse? Is that what's going to happen?"

"No, Charlie, it's just a figure of speech. What I mean is that if you've made up your mind, then that's the way it is, nothing more."

The tension eased again, and I reported back to the command post this final attempt to get Charlie to surrender. We were now ready. The command post wanted to know from what door of the house they would exit.

"Charlie," I said, "what door are you going to come out of?"

"Why do you want to know? So you can shoot me?"

"No. It's just that we're going to go out the back door and we'll be waiting behind the house. I don't want you to come out and trip over us." Charlie never answered me.

On the phone, the command center asked where I thought he would exit. I said I was pretty sure he would come out the front.

Phase one began with the two agents carrying the bags of personal items to the helicopter. A short time later the helicopter engine revved up and the big rotor began to whirl.

"Charlie," I said, "we're leaving the house now. Remember, you said you wouldn't harm the pilot."

Silence.

"Good luck, Charlie. I hope you and Cheryl will be okay."

There was another moment of silence. Then I heard him say, "Good-bye."

The six or seven of us who had been on the ground floor now moved through the back door to the outside and hung close to the rear wall. We could not see the area in front where the helicopter was waiting. A tactical radio was within earshot, though, and I heard someone say that Charlie and his family had come out the front door. Minutes passed, then I heard an explosion. I edged to the corner of the house and looked cautiously around it. I saw Cheryl standing alone in the middle of the field, screaming. Lying at her feet were big Charlie and little Charlie. I feared the worst.

Someone yelled for her to start running, and Wayne Waddell went after her. Another agent, Terry Neist, picked up little Charlie and cradled him in his arms.

Before leaving the house, Charlie had tied the boy onto his back with the cloth belt from a bathrobe. Little Charlie's head had been only inches behind his father's—not much room for a marksman to find a target. Charlie had held Cheryl close in front of him, the carbine pushed into her back. The distance from the house to the helicopter had been about a hundred yards, perhaps a bit more. As Charlie moved forward, shielded by his captives, the snipers had called out over their radios, one after the other. They never had a clear shot. Then, when Charlie was about halfway to the chopper, the machine suddenly lifted off the ground. At that moment, agents tossed flash-bang diversion grenades at Charlie's feet. The noise and bright light must have disoriented him, because he fell to one knee. He said to Cheryl, "This is it, Kitten." But the fall had shifted little Charlie's weight, opening up a space between father and son, and in that split second an FBI marksman fired a shot that entered Charlie's right cheek and exited the rear of his head.

I hurried over to Terry and little Charlie and put my hand on the boy's head.

"How you doing, Charlie?" I hoped the boy would recognize my voice and find it reassuring. He was shaking and very scared. Cheryl was brought over and took him in her arms. She looked toward the FBI emergency medical technicians, who were frantically trying to revive Charlie.

"My God, they're going to bring him back and he's going to do this to us again." But this would not turn out to be the case—the shot proved fatal.

My wife later asked me if I'd formed any kind of bond with Charlie, and indeed I had. The moment of going so close to the brink was a kind of shared event, and I think it helped set up the positive interaction that followed. I don't think Charlie ever would have walked out of that house if we hadn't established some sense of trust in this moment. But despite this I felt no remorse about my recommendation that we use deadly force. I was convinced it was the only way to save Cheryl and little Charlie.

I realized I had left my jacket in the house and started walking back to get it; Steve Romano joined me and asked me if I was okay with what had happened.

"I'm fine," I said. Then I added, "But I'm mad at that son of a bitch for making us do it." It felt like such a waste of life.

By the time I reported to the main command post in Sperryville, Cheryl was sitting there calmly with little Charlie in her lap. She rose to greet me, then, with tears streaming down her face, gave me a hug. I did not, could not, say a word. Everyone in the command post was watching. It was a long time before my voice worked. I don't remember what we said or what thoughts we shared. I remember only the incredible sense of relief I felt in seeing them both alive.

When I drove home late that afternoon, our neighborhood was as calm and serene as it had been when I left, only this time Carol was standing on the front porch. I parked the car in our driveway and got out, heavy with fatigue. She had been watching the television news and knew how the incident had turned out. With a big smile on her face she said, "Welcome home, Batman. Now take out the garbage."

The following Christmas I received a card from Connecticut. It was from Cheryl, and this is what she wrote:

Thank you so much for all you did for little Charlie, big Charlie, and myself. Lil Charlie has grown so much since April. He seems to be doing very well with everything. He goes to counseling every six weeks just so they can keep an eye on him. I'd like to thank you for all you did in Virginia. When you kept on talking, even when Charlie wouldn't talk or let me talk, your voice was so soothing to hear for me and for big Charlie. At one time Charlie was a very nice person and I know he ended up liking you and he had wished you could have met under different terms. I know for myself I will never forget your voice or you, for all your caring and help we hope you and your family have a great holiday season and that God will be with you always.

> *Thank you,*
> *Cheryl Hart and LiL Charlie.*

CHAPTER TWO

MY START

*People grow through experience if they meet life honestly and
courageously. This is how character is built.*
—ELEANOR ROOSEVELT

I could not have had a more quintessentially American childhood. I
was blessed with loving and supportive parents. I grew up three
blocks from the ocean in Atlantic Beach, Florida, near Jacksonville. I
spent my summers swimming in the ocean, rafting in a nearby lagoon,
building forts in the adjacent woods with my buddies, and later taking
up surfing as that craze moved east from California.

I was a typical clean-cut child of the fifties and early sixties. At
Fletcher High School I was captain of both the track and cross-country
teams; I also worked afternoons and Saturdays at an office supply store
and mowed lawns for extra money. At the age of twelve, I had an experience that would give me a sense of focus and a goal that I would pursue for the rest of my childhood. Believe it or not, it came while
watching *The Mickey Mouse Club*.

For those too young to remember, *The Mickey Mouse Club* was a
variety show with cartoons and skits involving a group of wholesome
young boys and girls known as the Mouseketeers. I'd often watch it after
school. One day not long after my twelfth birthday, the program went to
Washington, D.C., to visit the headquarters of the FBI.

Those who didn't live through the 1950s and early 1960s would have a hard time understanding the respect with which most Americans treated their government institutions at this time. This was well before campus protests and counterculture movements dominated the news, an era in which rock-and-roll stars such as Elvis Presley and the Everly Brothers were in uniform, Jimmy Stewart starred as an FBI agent fighting the Ku Klux Klan in *The FBI Story,* and the Bureau was revered as our society's first line of defense against both crime and subversion.

The Mickey Mouse Club's producers reflected this, approaching the FBI with palpable, almost worshipful respect. What I remember most from that show was a segment in which a Mouseketeer spoke with J. Edgar Hoover, the legendary director who had headed the Bureau since 1924. Seated on the steel-framed butterfly chair in our family room, I was utterly transfixed. Hoover looked the young host firmly in the eye and spoke about the FBI's mission; he talked about the high caliber of its agents and told stories of these agents chasing gangsters during the Roaring Twenties and tracking down German spies during World War II. It was like a boy's adventure novel come to life! But what really sealed the deal was when the host was taken to a firing range and allowed to shoot a Thompson submachine gun, the weapon of choice for both G-men and Al Capone. I was hooked.

When my mom came home from work that day, I could speak of nothing else. Being a good mom, she went out and got me a kids' book about the FBI, which amplified and further dramatized all the stories of derring-do that Hoover had only hinted at. The book contained stories of agents tracking down dangerous fugitives, arresting bank robbers, and securing the release of kidnap victims. From that time forward I never wanted to do anything else.

Of course, life was not as simple and sweet as it was portrayed on television, particularly if you lived in the segregated South, as I did. Throughout my childhood I would be reminded regularly that there were people who lived near me in Florida who had a very different kind of life. My first memory of this came on a shoe-buying expedition to Jacksonville, when I first noticed the omnipresent signs indicating separate water fountains, building entrances, and the like. I had never really appreciated the ugly face of discrimination before then, and I didn't like what I saw. I remember my parents sitting me down and telling me that segregation was not right, and emphasizing that we had a responsibility to look out for others less fortunate than us, regardless of their skin color.

During my senior year at Florida Southern College, I took secondary education courses and did a teaching internship in history and sociology at Lakeland High School. This was 1972. School busing was causing protests as far north as Boston, and down in Florida, when Lakeland's all-black high school was closed and its students merged into two formerly all-white schools, it did not sit well with many people. During my internship at Lakeland High School, there were frequent altercations in the hallways between white and black students. Whenever the school siren rang at an unscheduled time, all the male teachers were expected to rush out to break up those fights. I had always been a kind of mediator and peacemaker among my friends, but this was my first exposure to crisis containment as an adult. These were kids, technically, but not long after I started on the job, as I stepped between two football players, one black and one white, to create a physical barrier, I realized that they were easily as big as I was, and half crazy with anger. I'm almost six foot two, but they were bigger and stronger than I was. I don't remember what I said, but I was able to use words to calm them down and keep them apart until some of their anger had subsided. I knew intuitively that once the fists started flying, it was all over.

For some Americans during this period, the stark contrast between the inspiring goals of the civil rights movement and the reality of everyday life caused them to revolt to varying degrees against America's institutions, including the FBI. But I was raised more traditionally, and I never really embraced the counterculture movement. I continued to dream of being an agent; for me, the FBI still represented justice, something American society seemed to need more than ever.

And so when I graduated in the spring of 1972, there was only one job I really wanted. I didn't want to run a business or be a banker. I wanted to be an FBI agent. Problem was, you needed to be twenty-three and have three years of other work experience. I had enjoyed teaching in spite of the time I spent breaking up fights, and thought this would be a great way to gain the required work experience, but full-time positions were scarce, and so I became a substitute. I also met with a recruiter at the local FBI office in Jacksonville. He suggested an idea I hadn't considered before, which was to start as a clerical employee at FBI headquarters, something I could do right away. So I filled out an application, sent it in, and was eventually accepted. A few months later I found myself loading up the 1954 Ford I had purchased from my grandfather and driving up to Washington, D.C.

The FBI I joined in 1972 was in a kind of time warp. Even though J. Edgar Hoover had died a few months before I came on board, his presence was still felt, largely in the straitlaced conservatism of the Bureau. No matter how much the world had changed since the Beatles and Bob Dylan had shaken up American culture, agents at the FBI still wore white shirts only; some still even wore fedoras. Not long after I joined, one agent was given a special commendation for nabbing a Top 10 Most Wanted fugitive. But he was also reprimanded when a photograph during the collar showed him wearing a sports jacket rather than a dark suit.

This conservative atmosphere didn't dull my wish to be an agent; the only trouble was that I wasn't one yet. I immediately discovered that, far from being thought of as agents in training, clerks were members of a different caste altogether, one whose purpose was to do the entirely unglamorous work of supporting the field agents. I found myself engaged in mundane tasks such as delivering mail and filing paperwork. There was a seemingly endless pile of documents. To say that I was demoralized would not do the experience justice. I hung in, though, and after a few months, I got to know an agent named Jim Sherman, who became a kind of mentor for me. He knew how much I wanted to become an agent, and while he couldn't make that happen any sooner, he did arrange for me to get an interesting assignment assisting him on the Foreign Counterintelligence Squad, collating data on the movement of foreign spies in Washington. It sounds more exciting than it was— but it was certainly a huge improvement over pushing the mail cart.

During my time working for Jim I had another stroke of good fortune. One night, about three months after I'd started working for the FBI, I went out with other people from the office and found myself seated across from an attractive young woman in our group. Her name was Carol Drolsbaugh, and I plucked up the courage to introduce myself. She had joined the FBI as a stenographer just a few months earlier, right out of high school. I was immediately attracted to her irreverent wit, which distinguished her from many of the more traditional, restrained southern girls I'd grown up with. I didn't have much money to date in those days (Carol made more as a stenographer than I did as a clerk), but we began to see each other regularly.

In the fall of 1973 my dad began having serious back problems, so I requested a transfer from Washington to the FBI Field Office in Jacksonville, Florida, just a few miles from home. This meant being apart from Carol, and we missed each other so much that when she came down for a visit in December we got engaged. We were married in August 1974 and eventually moved in to a great little apartment near the ocean in Neptune Beach.

In 1976, after three and a half years as a clerical employee, I received the formal letter appointing me to join the incoming class of special agents for training at the FBI academy in Quantico, Virginia. For the next seventeen weeks, I studied hard for each exam, concentrated on my shooting skills, and got in great physical condition. I scored near the top of my class in every category, and, thanks to my years running track in high school, I also won every distance-running challenge.

After graduation in 1976, I was assigned to the fugitive squad of the FBI Field Office in Columbia, South Carolina. Many agents begin their careers doing tedious background investigations, but within two weeks I was apprehending criminals. A few weeks into the job, our office received an alert about a South Carolinian wanted for murder in California. He was on the run, and the thought was that the most likely place for him to be was back home in our area. Relying on the standard gumshoe work of contacting the fugitive's family members and every other known associate, eventually my partner and I tracked him down to a crumbling white frame apartment building surrounded by palm trees and azalea bushes. This was late August, and when the landlord let us in the front door, it was so hot inside I nearly fainted, but I rushed on through the apartment and found the man in bed, reaching for his gun in a holster on the nightstand. Fortunately, he stopped before I had to fire my weapon in self-defense. For a young guy who'd always wanted to be a G-man, this was very exciting indeed.

One of my training agents in South Carolina was named Jimmy Calhoon. Jimmy looked the way I'd always thought an agent should look: with dark hair and a square jaw on a rugged face, he was a dead ringer for the cartoon police detective Dick Tracy. He was a tough guy who had played football at Florida State, and he exuded a confidence and authority that I'd never seen before. One night we were looking for a fugitive, a guy who had murdered someone in another state, and we walked into the toughest bar in town, a dark smoke-filled place filled with tough guys. Jimmy moved into the room and slowly stared down each person, to see if the guy we were looking for was there. Not one of them dared to make eye contact with him.

But Jimmy wasn't just a tough guy. Over the next two years he would teach me his own kind of street psychology: how to speak with witnesses, victims, and criminals and gain their cooperation. When we were out trying to develop leads, he could adapt his approach for a big-city lawyer or a farmer down at the feed store in a small town. He could tell jokes, and he seemed to be able to talk to anyone about anything, whether it was crops, fishing, dove hunting, or taxes. He was as tough as anyone in the Bureau, but what he showed me was that good law enforcement wasn't just about using a gun or a nightstick; it was also about communication.

As much as Jimmy was a positive role model, there were others whose actions taught me what not to do. There were a couple of guys in the office who constantly took unnecessarily confrontational approaches, arrogantly asserting their authority as FBI agents. In one bank robbery case another agent and I were interviewing a guy who we were pretty certain could help us locate the robber. Practically before he had sat down, the agent was accusing him of lying and covering for his friend. I felt my frustration rise as the witness clammed up—I was certain I could have gotten what we needed from him with a more subtle approach.

Carol and I enjoyed our two years in South Carolina and even bought our first house there, but "first office" agents get transferred, and in

1978, the FBI summoned me back to the Washington Field Office and assigned me to the Foreign Counterintelligence Squad. It was great to return as an agent, though I made sure to treat the clerks with the respect that they deserved. I began my new Washington life as an agent developing evidence in espionage cases, while also working contacts to recruit defectors from hostile nations as counterspies for us. But the previous years had seen the challenges facing the FBI evolve. A series of crises would awaken it to the threat of international terrorism and to the need for a more rigorous approach toward handling major incidents. Both of these things would become the focus of my work in the years to come.

During the Munich Olympics in the summer of 1972, eight members of the Palestinian Black September terrorist organization seized and ultimately killed eleven Israeli athletes. Despite the tensions rising in the Middle East since the 1967 Six-Day War between Egypt and Israel—and the fact that at least one West German forensic psychologist had predicted this hostage event almost exactly as it played out—there was no armed security for the Munich games, no checkpoints. When the hostage taking began, there was no federal authority in place to deal with it, which left local and regional police to make do as best they could. They had no radios, woefully inadequate firepower, and too few snipers to be effective, and they relied on flawed tactics that put police forces in danger from their own cross fire. Once the action began, decision making was mostly ad hoc and cumbersome, with one tactician sharing responsibility with two politicians. For many law enforcement officials, the Munich siege of 1972 was a wake-up call. Before that time, when subjects took hostages, responding police would simply demand that the perpetrator come out and surrender. If the hostage taker refused, the police would then mount an assault. Sadly, that rigid and inflexible approach often resulted in loss of life. Even when it did not, the outcomes depended more on luck than on the application of a well-established set of procedures. In New York City, just one week before the events in Munich, police had bumbled through the botched bank robbery and hostage taking that was later depicted in the Al Pacino film *Dog Day Afternoon*. The actual fourteen-hour siege became a spectacle on live television, and it drew a crowd of three thousand people to the street corner in Brooklyn where the bank was located. Fortunately, the hostages were eventually rescued, and loss of life was limited to one of the perpetrators. But to all observers, it was clear that the NYPD and assisting FBI lacked an effective response. A more egregious example of the state of police crisis procedures (demand compliance, go in if your demand is refused) had been the Attica prison riot, also in New York State, which had taken place only one year earlier. When negotiations failed to bring results, the State Police moved in with tear gas and shotguns, the net result of which was the death of ten inmates and twenty-eight correctional officers. A Special Commission of the State of New York later described it as "the bloodiest one-day encounter between Americans since the Civil War," excepting perhaps the Indian massacres of the late nineteenth century.

The New York police would lead the way as law enforcement sought to respond to these kinds of crises. Shortly after the Munich and *Dog Day Afternoon* events, New York police commissioner Patrick Murphy established a committee to explore ways to respond to crises in a more organized and effective fashion. The committee's conclusions led the NYPD to create a full-time unit—the Emergency Services Unit—that would be responsible for responding to crisis events. No longer would the response to and management of the incident be left in the hands of whoever showed up first. They also established protocols emphasizing proper containment of the situation as well as nonviolent approaches, in contrast to what had previously taken place.

In January 1973, the Emergency Services Unit had its first opportunity to apply this new, more restrained approach when officers responded to a robbery in progress at John and Al's Sporting Goods Store in Brooklyn. A group of perpetrators held nine hostages, and an immediate exchange of gunfire resulted in the death of one officer and the wounding of two others. Nonetheless, forty-seven hours later, the situation was resolved with all hostages released and all four perpetrators in custody.

A post-incident review concluded that restraint had succeeded far better than earlier, more aggressive approaches. One flaw that the review commented on was that communication with the subjects inside had been uncontrolled and uncoordinated. This prompted NYPD Lt.

Frank Bolz and Officer Harvey Schlossberg, a trained psychologist, to be assigned to build the nation's first dedicated hostage negotiation team, selecting and training a group of officers specifically for this purpose.

In 1974, the FBI recognized that the NYPD was on to something, and developed its own formal hostage-negotiation training program at its Quantico training academy. This course was designed for use by FBI agents as well as police officers. Those who volunteered for negotiation training, selected from each of the FBI field offices around the country, tended to be mature and experienced agents, known in their offices as solid, effective, and successful. Many had shown a knack for developing informants or gaining confessions from otherwise uncooperative criminals. The negotiation skills they learned during the course further enhanced their ability to communicate with citizens on the street and avoid verbal confrontations.

After training, these agents would then work with FBI SWAT teams in regional field offices around the country to help resolve hostage and barricade situations. Then as now, FBI agents were assigned to a SWAT team or field negotiation unit on a part-time basis only. An agent might spend most of his time hunting down mobsters and get called in every now and again when a siege occurred. The original concept developed by NYPD and adopted by the FBI focused primarily on bargaining skills, among them reciprocity; negotiators would in essence say, "If you cooperate with me and do this, I'll cooperate with you and do that." This gave rise to the principle we saw applied early on in Sperryville: never give a hostage taker anything unless he gives you something in return.

During my initial training to become an FBI agent, I had made a mental note to try to become involved in this new specialty at the earliest opportunity. In 1978 I mentioned this interest to my partner Ken Schiffer, a very experienced senior agent who knew the WFO training coordinator, the person who decided who got to attend the negotiation training program at Quantico. With Ken's support, two years later, in 1980, I was given the opportunity to attend the FBI two-week negotiation course. During the course I learned the mechanics of the negotiation process, studied abnormal psychology, heard case studies, and participated in role-playing exercises. I was deeply impressed by the power of the simple communication techniques being taught. I was also impressed by the insight of the man teaching these new skills, Agent Fred Lanceley. Fred's great skill was his ability to break down incidents into their component parts and glean the dos and don'ts. He also had a unique ability to draw out stories from the agents and police officers he trained and use this information to build a base of knowledge.

Fred taught us that the key to successful negotiation was to discern the subject's motivation, goals, and emotional needs and to make use of that knowledge strategically. Once we understood the hostage taker's real purpose, we had a better chance of convincing him that killing the hostages would not serve that purpose and would only make an already bad situation worse.

One of our most effective tools for negotiation is to offer the hostage taker something he wants in exchange for something we want—ideally, the release of at least one hostage. (In the Charlie Leaf situation, as I've said, this didn't work—he didn't want anything from us—so we had to try a different strategy.) Often we'll say something like, "Why don't you help me help you? Give me something to work with, and let's see what we can accomplish working together." If the subject resists making a trade, the negotiator might say, "I'd like to help you, but my boss just won't let me send in what you want until you send someone out in return." By making the subject work hard for everything gained, we wear down his resolve. He realizes he doesn't have as much power or control over the situation as he thought he had.

We can not-so-subtly reinforce that realization by showing a visible tactical force capability. This can also be a leverage point in moving negotiations along. For instance, we'll suggest to the hostage taker that we won't kill him as long as he behaves reasonably.

Dr. Mike Webster, a Canadian psychologist who has worked with the Royal Canadian Mounted Police and FBI negotiation programs, describes this as the "parallel approach" to crisis resolution, in which we contrast the benefits of cooperation with the risks of resistance. Authorities negotiate in good faith, while simultaneously preparing for and showing their ability to undertake tactical action. Limited demonstration of tactical capability can help the negotiation process along by encouraging dialogue. Too little action can make the subject feel confident and secure, thus less likely to negotiate in earnest. Too much action might trigger a firefight, which is what Webster calls the "paradox of power"—the harder we push the more likely we are to be met with resistance. Law enforcement officials who have become angry and agitated owing to a lack of progress are more inclined to use force in a nonincremental way.

Most hostage takers do not begin their day planning to kill someone and then die in a hail of bullets. They are usually focused on getting their demands met. In a small number of cases, a suicidal individual purposefully holds hostages and seeks a confrontation with the clear intention of dying at the hands of the police. These rare cases are classified as "suicides by cop." But most hostage takers want to live; even many who seem bent on self-destruction are, at most, ambivalent. That ambivalence serves as the access point to insert the wedge of negotiation.

The duration of most such incidents is usually only a few hours or less, with surrender achieved well over 90 percent of the time when a proper negotiation approach is used. Very few activities in law enforcement yield success rates that high.

Even so, it can be a complex and timely process to move the hostage taker to a point where he realizes he won't achieve his goals, and that's why we think about much of our work as stalling for time. After a few hours, days, or even weeks, things may not look as bad as they did at first, both for the hostage taker and for the authorities. Alternatives to violence begin to emerge, and our goal is to move the hostage taker away from the tunnel vision that prevents him from seeing those alternatives.

One example from these early days came during a domestic hijacking when a young man brandished a weapon and demanded to be flown to Cuba. The FBI and local authorities surrounded the plane and negotiations began. At some point during the dialogue, the hijacker forcefully demanded that the negotiator send him in a hot cup of coffee with cream and two sugars. The negotiator replied that it would be difficult to get coffee out to the plane, but that he would do his best. Several hours later the coffee showed up. It was black with no cream, very cold, and it contained no sugar at all. A short time afterward the young hijacker surrendered. With the man in custody, the FBI agent asked what had made him decide to give up. He responded: "I figured if I couldn't even get a decent cup of coffee, I certainly wasn't going to be able to fly to Cuba."

Few case studies so succinctly illustrate the value of the negotiation process: Contain. Open communications to deescalate tension. Stall for time. Lower expectations. Make him bargain for everything.

I came away from the training course excited by what I had learned and anxious to spread the word. Even though I was a brand-new negotiator, I immediately began to run occasional negotiation training courses for officers in the D.C. area, and I became negotiation coordinator for the WFO—all of this in addition to my day job hunting down foreign spies. I really enjoyed those training courses, and they were hugely helpful in developing my own knowledge of the field. I'd travel to a local police station and put on a daylong seminar for fifteen or twenty guys. I'd say, "I don't have a lot of practical experience, but here are the things I've learned from the FBI academy, and here's what they've learned from around the world." In those days the FBI had a rep for taking and not giving, and so the police really appreciated getting this information. In return, they told me about the hostage incidents in which they'd been involved, and we talked about how the FBI methods could've been applied to them.

In 1982, as global terrorism became an increasing threat, I transferred to the WFO Terrorism Squad, identifying and arresting suspected terrorists, developing informants to penetrate groups we were concerned about, and monitoring individuals in the United States who we believed were supporting terrorist organizations in the Middle East. In those days, there were probably only a dozen or so FBI agents who knew the difference between Iraq and Iran, or between Sunni and Shi'ite. But I made it a point to learn everything I could about the Muslim world and its troubled politics, as well as the threats presented by Islamic extremists. For the next eight years I would travel the globe working terrorism cases, often applying communications lessons from the FBI negotiation course to the task of recruiting informants and investigating terrorist incidents.

One early case for the WFO Terrorism Squad occurred close to home. I was called to assist with the investigation of the kidnapping of Clelia Quinonez, the wife of a former Salvadoran ambassador to the United States. Mrs. Quinonez had been abducted from her home in Miami. FBI teams responded to the Quinonez residence and set up technical support and provided assistance to Roberto Quinonez, who was negotiating for the release of his wife. The first task was to figure out where the kidnappers were.

As just about anyone knows who has ever seen a cop movie from this period, in those days law enforcement could trap and trace telephone calls, but it took a while. Digital technology, of course, now makes this process instantaneous. But at the time, the information available immediately was limited to the region of the country a call was coming from. The longer a caller stayed on the line, however, the more specific technicians could be in identifying the town, the neighborhood, and ultimately the precise telephone where a call originated. Sophisticated criminals knew to limit the length of their calls, but the men who had abducted Mrs. Quinonez were not sophisticated. One of them had done odd jobs at the Quinonez house, and he and his partner had seen this contact with a wealthy family as a chance to make some easy money.

FBI agents coached Ambassador Quinonez on maintaining just the right degree of cooperation while drawing out the conversation with questions. Again, this was a stalling-for-time strategy to give the perpetrators an incentive to keep talking, while also stretching out the discussion in order to keep them on the phone longer each time. When the abductors made a demand, we instructed the ambassador to break it down and address it in tiny increments, which necessitated additional phone calls. With each phone call, the technical team was able to zero in more closely on where the calls were coming from. Eventually, they narrowed it down to a few square miles in the Washington, D.C., area.

We were getting close. The ambassador agreed to a ransom of $1.5 million but insisted on receiving proof that his wife was still alive before making the payment. As we'd expected, the kidnappers agreed, and they told him they would have Mrs. Quinonez herself make the next call so that he could hear her voice. Armed with that information, as well as knowledge of an approximate location, we stood at the ready to respond, rescue, and arrest. We hoped they would bring her to a phone booth.

I led a six-person team assigned to a rough part of northwest Washington, ready to respond the moment the technicians identified the specific location from which the call was being made. Additional agent teams from WFO were spread out to cover other parts of the city. Usually, in such a situation, the agents will locate the suspect making the call, then follow him back to the location where the victim is being held. In this case, the perpetrators saved us a step.

Four days into the crisis, Agent John Heieck and I had set up shop in a crime-ridden part of town and were sitting in an unmarked FBI car parked on a dark street near the Pitts Hotel, a run-down place whose name seemed entirely apt. We were across the street from the entrance, about fifty feet down the block. Nearby was a phone booth that we suspected might be used by the kidnappers, since we thought earlier calls might have originated from this block. The two other teams I was responsible for were parked at similar locations not far away. Our attention was focused on the radio as we watched the comings and goings of those on the street. The idea was simply to be spread out in this neighborhood, ready to move in quickly when we determined the location the call was being made from.

We sat there for the rest of the afternoon and into the evening. In this mostly black neighborhood, two white men sitting in a sedan was a fairly obvious giveaway that we didn't belong, but no one seemed to care. We exhausted all manner of small talk as we endured the tedium of a stakeout.

At 9:40 p.m. the radio finally crackled to life with the news we'd been waiting for. Mrs. Quinonez was at that moment talking with her husband from a pay phone, which had been traced to a street location just outside the Pitts Hotel. John and I could see a white woman standing at a phone booth, with a young black man on either side of her. We had a photograph of the victim, and we had binoculars. A closer look confirmed that this was indeed Mrs. Quinonez.

We radioed for backup, got out of the car, and drew our weapons as we approached them.

When we got twenty yards away, we shouted, "FBI!," flashing ID and pointing our revolvers. "Hands on your heads! Get on the ground! On the ground now!"

John moved to handcuff one of the subjects and I moved to handcuff the other. Meanwhile, the other members of our team pulled up, got out of their cars, and grabbed Mrs. Quinonez. She simply dropped the phone, which was now dangling at the end of its cord a few feet away from me.

As I moved to handcuff one of the subjects now lying facedown on the ground, later identified as Craig Blas, I noticed his body rise slightly off the ground and his hand move toward his waistband. I saw the butt of a revolver. "He's got a gun," I yelled. Then I pounced on his back and jammed the barrel of my revolver directly into his ear. "Move another inch and I'm going to blow your fucking head off," I said. Then I reached down and confiscated his revolver. Mr. Hoover would not have approved of my language, but it certainly got Blas's attention.

With the handcuffs on Blas, I raised him to his feet and quickly frisked him for additional weapons. I then turned him over to two other agents, who took him back to my vehicle for transport. That's when I noticed that the telephone receiver was still dangling, presumably with Mr. Quinonez in Miami still on the other end. I picked up the phone and said, "This is Gary Noesner up here at WFO. We got both subjects and the victim. She's safe." I could hear a loud cheer come over the line from Miami.

As I continued to hold frequent training sessions for police officers in Washington, I have to admit that, like any other highly trained professional, I was curious to see how my expertise would hold up in a major hostage crisis. In those early days, I often worked closely with the Washington Metropolitan Police negotiation team and assisted in several of their hostage or barricade incidents. But the siege that would first really put my negotiation skills to the test occurred 240 miles to the south, in Raleigh, North Carolina, in 1982.

CHAPTER THREE

MY FIRST MAJOR SIEGE

When the conduct of men is designed to be influenced, persuasion,
kind, unassuming persuasion, should ever be adopted.
—ABRAHAM LINCOLN

It all began on October 7, 1982, when a passenger listed as W. Rodriquez boarded the 10:40 p.m. Amtrak Silver Star out of Jacksonville, Florida, bound for New York. Accompanied by his sister, Maria, and her two children, Julie, four, and Juan, nine months, he entered the sleeping car they'd reserved and handed the porter a three-dollar tip for carrying his luggage, which instead of clothes and other personal items held a Browning semiautomatic pistol and a fully automatic MAC-10 submachine gun.

"W. Rodriquez" was, in fact, one of many aliases used by twenty-nine-year-old Evangelista Navas Villabona. Nicknamed Mario, he was a native of Colombia who had entered the United States illegally and set up shop trafficking drugs into New York.

All was quiet on the Silver Star until 5:45 the next morning, when passengers in the adjacent sleeping berth awoke to the sound of children crying and a man and woman arguing loudly in Spanish. The argument grew increasingly heated for the next hour, gaining intensity until, shortly before the train arrived in Raleigh, North Carolina, shots rang out. The conductor radioed ahead for help, and local police were waiting when the train arrived in Raleigh.

In charge of managing the incident was Raleigh police chief Frederick K. Heineman, a retired NYPD official, easily identified by his crisp big-city accent amid the southern drawls. Chief Heineman was an experienced and thoughtful law enforcement leader and well aware of the dangers associated with this type of situation. The FBI offered our resources and deployed personnel to the scene. We also went about the task of fully identifying Mario Navas and learning all we could about his criminal and mental-health history, as well as his connections in both Florida and New York. We discovered that in 1976 Mario had been convicted of conspiracy and possession with intent to deliver a narcotic in New York. He had been sentenced to fifteen years and had served time at three prisons before being paroled in 1980 on condition that he return to his home in Colombia. His prison record also indicated that he had an explosive temper and was given to fits of rage.

During the next couple of hours, Amtrak officials and police evacuated the other passengers and detached the train car holding Mario, its windows curtained, onto a side track about fifty yards to the right when viewed from the station. There was one empty car immediately adjacent on either side. Responding police officers, shielded by the steel girders of the station, attempted to communicate with the Colombian via loudspeaker, but their overtures were met with silence. Next, a tactical officer under heavy cover crept up to Mario's train car and attached a listening device as well as a speaker. As he worked to set up this means of communication, he noticed a hole where a bullet had exited the compartment door.

At around 9:00 a.m., the Raleigh officers on the scene heard another shot ring out from inside the compartment. At this point they considered the option of storming the train, but they simply did not know enough about what was going on inside and who was at risk.

At 10:20 a.m., the portion of the train not isolated by the police pulled out of the station to continue with the journey to New York.

Based on the few facts available at the time, neither the FBI nor local police had any reason to assume that Mario had boarded a train in Jacksonville with the intention of shooting off his weapons just before arriving in Raleigh. The loud argument reported by witnesses suggested that a domestic dispute had triggered the violence. It made sense that the subject inside had acted spontaneously, was now scared, and probably had no clear plan on what to do next or how to extricate himself.

About an hour after the other train cars left the station, several more gunshots rang out from inside the compartment. Once again, the police had done nothing to provoke Mario. Was he killing his captives one by one? Had he killed himself? The police simply didn't know.

Chief Heineman knew he had three options. The first was to mount a rescue attempt. The second was to establish a dialogue with Mario to convince him to surrender. The third was to wait and do nothing, and see if he would come out on his own, what the NYPD's Harvey Schlossberg used to call "dynamic inactivity."

Heineman questioned Amtrak officials to try to pick up any insights that might help him devise a strategy. He learned that railroad passenger cars are made with heavy-gauge steel in order to survive derailments, which makes them almost impenetrable. He also learned that the thick glass windows were built to withstand gunshots coming in from the outside, which meant that a rescue attempt was not a viable option. He knew it wouldn't be like trying to kick in a wood-framed door in a tenement building; Mario would have plenty of time to kill the children if he was so inclined. And Heineman couldn't simply wait, because the children were at risk. So he was going to have to establish a dialogue with Mario.

Unfortunately, the Raleigh Police Department did not have a Spanish-speaking negotiator. Fortunately, one of the EMTs deployed to the scene was Jorge Oliva, a Cuban native. Heineman recruited him on the spot and installed him in another sleeping compartment about fifteen feet away. He took over the effort via bullhorn to elicit a response from Mario.

At around 12:30 p.m. officers heard four more shots fired from inside the compartment. So Mario had not killed himself earlier. But what was going on? Was he simply firing off rounds to keep the police at bay? Most of all, were his captives still alive?

Throughout that afternoon and early evening, Jorge conveyed to Mario offers of food and drink, with special concern for the children. No response. Then the listening device attached to the compartment door picked up the sound of the children crying. Okay, the kids were still alive. But this only increased the urgency of establishing communication; they were clearly in distress and in danger.

At 8:00 p.m. Mario fired another shot. Then silence returned.

Four hours later, almost nineteen hours into the standoff, Mario suddenly and inexplicably yelled out to the police in Spanish, "Everything is okay." He told the police to leave him alone. At least he was now communicating with words rather than gunfire. With some coaching by officers on the scene, Jorge stepped up efforts to open a dialogue, throwing out questions like "What's going on? How can we help?" But shortly after midnight, Mario stopped communicating just as abruptly as he had started.

At 9:55 a.m. Saturday, Mario broke the silence once again, blurting out that he was holding a gun to the head of one of the children. Again, the police had done nothing to provoke this action or this announcement.

Chief Heineman's frustration was growing, along with the pressure on him. He was in command of all of the personnel on hand, a job that included making sure that officers on the perimeter protected the scene from unwanted intrusion. He had to coordinate all of the assisting agency representatives, ensure that sniper/observers were relieved and allowed to get food and rest, speak to the press, and try to come up with a strategy to resolve this situation without loss of life.

At 11:00 a.m., Heineman brought in a medical doctor to try to assess the condition of the children, based on the sounds they were or were not making. During the evening it had gotten very cold, but temperatures rose again during the day, which must have made the compartment hot, stuffy, and uncomfortable. Officers attached a better listening device, almost like a large-scale stethoscope, outside the compartment door so that the doctor could listen in. He heard Julie asking her mother to wake up, but nothing else that would indicate the child's own condition or that of her baby brother.

At 11:37 a.m., two shots were fired in a rapid burst, the first indication that Mario had a machine gun—yet another fact weighing against a tactical assault.

At 1:00 p.m., Mario shouted out again, threatening to kill himself and the children. He also demanded that orange juice and matches be sent in. Jorge offered water, but only if Mario would let the children go. Through the listening device, the officers on hand could hear Julie saying, "Agua, agua." Then they heard Mario telling her to be quiet. Jorge continued to offer food and water, but Mario's only response was to yell obscenities at the police.

It was a Saturday and I was at home in Virginia when I received a call from Fred Lanceley, my primary negotiation instructor at Quantico, who had become a good friend. Fred told me he had been asked to help with an incident on an Amtrak train; some shots had been fired and they were trying to negotiate with the guy, but he spoke only Spanish. Did I have someone on my team at WFO who spoke Spanish? I thought immediately of Ray Arras, a thirty-nine-year-old El Paso native who had just recently completed the FBI hostage-negotiation training course. He had come to the FBI at a relatively late age after running the El Paso Zoo. I had been impressed by his confidence and easygoing manner; he would be great in a tense situation like this. Fred told me to have Ray come to Davidson Army Airfield, located at nearby Fort Belvoir, where he would be picked up by an FBI plane and flown directly to Raleigh.

This sounded like the kind of challenging case I had been hoping to be involved in. I had handled other crisis situations—someone holed up and threatening suicide, domestic disturbances that turned into barricades—but this was a chance to work a major standoff. And so I asked Fred if he could use my help in Raleigh. He agreed and told me to meet him and Ray at Fort Belvoir.

In a couple of hours a four-seat Cessna took the three of us from Virginia to the Raleigh airport, where an FBI sedan ferried us directly to the Amtrak station. Just as we were arriving, at around 6:00 p.m., Mario fired two more shots through the compartment door. Tactical officers had been attempting to deliver the matches that Mario had asked for earlier, and apparently this movement had spooked him.

The station in Raleigh is about the size of a typical suburban home, ranch style, with a portico out front facing a small parking lot. Fred, Ray, and I found Chief Heineman inside, looking understandably tired and beleaguered. He was a tall man with salt-and-pepper hair and a mustache; he wore a tie and tweed jacket.

I had talked to my share of southern sheriffs over the previous couple of years, and I'd noticed that when meeting an FBI agent, they usually spent time on the slow exchange of pleasantries before getting down to business. In all likelihood they were meeting the federal agent for the first time, and they wanted to get a sense of whom they were dealing with. Heineman, though, got right down to business. His accent told me that he was a New Yorker, and it was obvious that he had a big problem on his hands and needed our help.

"Thanks for coming down," he said, directing us to the station manager's office behind a snack bar. He and a couple of other officers briefed us on the situation, focusing on Mario's actions up to this point. Heineman told us that he thought Mario's sister, Maria, was dead. The listening devices were picking up only the voices of Mario, Julie, and the crying baby, Juan. The implications of those three people trapped inside a small train compartment with a decaying corpse under the hot North Carolina sun were not pleasant to think about. He told us about their inability to get Mario to respond, and asked our advice.

Fred and I described a strategy to get him to start talking with us. The key in situations of this kind is to vocalize the fears and concerns likely driving the perpetrator's refusal to talk. "I know you're afraid and concerned that we want to hurt you," the negotiator might say. "I want to assure you that no one out here wishes to harm you in any way." Or "I know you're confused about what to say or do. I want you to know that I'm here to help you get safely out of this situation, but I need to be able to speak with you in order to help." We told Chief Heineman that even if the communication is all one-way, the calm and controlled voice of the negotiator can lower tension and create a more comfortable environment that encourages the subject to speak. Even though Mario might not be talking, he was probably listening.

Chief Heineman responded that he viewed us as the experts; he would follow our advice. We suggested that Ray be the primary contact with Mario and that we have him take over as soon as possible. I would assist him as a coach, using Jorge to translate what was being said to me so I could in turn provide Ray with suggestions in real time. Fred would be nearby to provide strategic guidance, concentrating most of his efforts on gathering more of a criminal and psychological history on

Mario in hopes of uncovering important personality clues that would help us get him to communicate.

Also assisting would be FBI agent Lathell Thomas, from the Charlotte FBI Field Office. He was fluent in Spanish—previously he had been assigned to the field office in San Juan, Puerto Rico—and he would be able to help Jorge provide me with instantaneous interpretation of the dialogue between Ray and Mario so I could coach.

While we were still inside the station, we received confirmation of what we had dreaded all along: Mario shouted out that his sister Maria was dead.

We knew that when one person dies in an incident, the chances of there being additional loss of life greatly increase. What had been the worst-case scenario all along was now more likely than ever: facing a homicide conviction, Mario might decide to kill the children and then kill himself rather than surrender.

Ray, Fred, and I walked back out the station's front door, on the side opposite the platform, then circled around through the parking lot, coming back to the rail lines at a point just beyond where Mario's compartment was stranded. We took up a position behind a steel girder supporting the roof over the platform. This put us about a hundred feet from Mario's compartment, just alongside one of the other cars attached to it. The only problem with this location was that Mario stood between us and the command post, back inside the train station proper. This meant that anytime we needed to consult with the chief, or even use the restrooms, we had to follow the same circuitous route through the parking lot to stay outside the potential range of Mario's weapons. Fred in particular made many, many trips, serving as liaison and information source. Still, sniper/observer teams were there, hidden from view, both to protect us and to use force if Mario suddenly came out with guns blazing.

As darkness fell, the warmer daytime temperatures dropped precipitously, and Ray and I appropriated blankets from the passenger car sitting on the track next to us. Even wrapped in a blanket, I was still standing on the cold cement train platform in loafers. Then it began to rain, a steady drizzle that would continue through the night.

The SWAT team had set up transmitters with microphones and

speakers that would allow us to hear Mario and him to hear us. We now put on headphones, and Ray took a deep breath and purposefully picked up the microphone.

Ray's an incredibly affable and outgoing guy, one of the more upbeat people I've ever met. As he launched into his monologue he projected a sense of calm and kindness. "Este es Ray," he said. Then, continuing in Spanish, he said, "I'm here to help you. How are the children?"

No answer. Ray continued along the lines we'd suggested to Heineman. No one wanted to hurt Mario; he should speak with us so that we could help him. Again, no response, but Ray kept up the patter, which is more difficult than you might imagine. It can be counterproductive to keep saying the same things over and over—as well as torturous for both speaker and listener alike—so I tried to help Ray come up with fresh ways to make the representations that we thought would be most effective. "Think about the children. You don't want them to suffer." "Let us get you some food and some drinks. Those kids need to eat." "Think about yourself. Life is still worth living."

I was struck by Ray's ability to come off as entirely genuine, speaking to Mario as if they were brothers. He carefully avoided the stereotypical "voice of authority" so often associated with law enforcement personnel. The cold monotone of Sergeant Joe Friday from *Dragnet* is not what you need when you're trying to convey empathy and establish rapport. It's also true that individuals likely to engage in a standoff usually have a negative view of the police already. They expect law enforcement to be autocratic, demanding, and stern, so when someone like Ray projects real understanding, it disarms the subject and can help win his cooperation. As my psychologist friend Dr. Mike Webster says, "People want to work with, cooperate with, and trust people that they like." It's hard to like someone who is threatening you or challenging you.

Ray had attended the FBI negotiation course at Quantico fifteen months earlier, and now he was getting his initiation by fire—this was in fact his first negotiation. Knowing this, I tried to help as much as I could, first sorting through the translation of all that was said, then whispering or jotting down my suggestions on a yellow legal pad and holding them up for him to see: "Mario, we know you must be scared, but nobody wants to hurt you.... We're really concerned about the children and want to make sure that they have something to eat and drink.... Help us to help you." We soon fell into a comfortable pace that enabled us to keep the monologue going.

After two solid hours, Mario finally responded to a comment about the children. He began to shout at Ray: "You no-good son of a bitch. Stop talking to me. You're a no-good bastard. You don't care about the children. You're lying." I looked over to Ray to see his reaction to this outburst, but his demeanor hadn't changed.

We had achieved our initial goal of getting him to respond. But we were aware that time, normally on our side, was less available because of the children. We had to keep Mario talking and listen for clues that would help us quickly determine his psychological state and concerns.

Ray responded quickly that he did in fact care about the children, and he spent the next twenty minutes explaining this and trying to keep Mario engaged. Again, Mario responded.

"If you really want to help the children, I need some IV fluids." He explained that he wanted us to pass a tube through one of the many bullet holes in the compartment door. Even though officers had been shot at the previous day when trying to deliver matches, we desperately wanted to comply with Mario's request. We had to demonstrate good faith.

Chief Heineman agreed, and a short time later, he dispatched the SWAT team to undertake the task. We were all incredibly tense as the men entered the train, moving defensively and covering each other as they went. This guy had already fired his gun several times in response to perceived noises. Would he do it again? Ray explained carefully to Mario what we were doing, and as the men drew near Mario's compartment, the chief and I made our way to the other side of the train. We drew our guns and watched through the open window facing the door to Mario's compartment as the SWAT team tried to push the tube through the bullet holes, but apparently the outgoing bullets had taken a zigzag course, and the tube would not pass through. Ray explained the problem to Mario and suggested that he try to gouge out the holes to make them larger. Mario didn't believe us and soon became impatient and agitated, shouting out that we were dishonorable. Then he went silent again.

Twelve of the most bleak and tedious hours I've experienced on the job followed. It was freezing cold, and we stood the entire night on the exposed platform, stomping our feet occasionally to try to stay warm. Periodically we heard the kids crying out. Mario's request for an IV had left us more worried about them than ever. Sandwiches or perhaps baby food is what you ask for to deal with hunger. An IV is what you ask for when a life is at risk. We continued to try to engage him throughout the night, but to no avail.

When dawn arrived, the rain stopped and the sun came out. It was at that point that we began to notice the stench. At first we thought it might be the toilets on the train, but gradually it became clear that this was something different and an indication of what we had feared all along— Mario's sister was indeed dead and her body was starting to decompose. As the morning progressed the smell got worse. One of the police officers brought us some Vicks VapoRub, which we rubbed under our noses to mask the odor. I could only imagine how bad it must have been inside the compartment. I thought about the young children trapped in that six-by-ten-foot space, their volatile uncle pacing back and forth and firing off weapons, their mother dead on the floor. I quickly pushed those thoughts aside. Finding a way to get them out was a much better use of my time and energy than thinking about what they were going through.

Later that morning we summoned a pediatrician to the scene. He warned us that we were very close to the point where the children might die from dehydration. Baby Juan might last another twelve hours without water, the doctor said. The older sister, Julie, could last perhaps another day.

Now we had our deadline, but that still didn't give us a plan. We continued to try to get Mario to talk with us, without success.

At 2:40 p.m., a shirtless Mario suddenly pushed back the curtains and threw open the window of the compartment. After a fifty-hour siege, and with the North Carolina sun creating sweltering temperatures inside, that train compartment must have been intolerable. Was Mario finally weakening? He stuck his head out and waved, then quickly ducked back in. Moments later, he strung a bedsheet out of the still-open compartment window. He told Ray that he wanted containers of food and water tied to it so that he could pull them in.

According to the protocols described earlier, a negotiator typically would demand the release of a hostage in exchange. In this case, I knew that we simply had to seize any opportunity we had to keep the children alive.

We conveyed the request to Chief Heineman, and within an hour, police officers had brought doughnuts, sandwiches, and drinks to the station. With Mario's window now open, exposing them to fire, the SWAT team members crawled under the train from the far side and tied the drinks and food up in the sheet. We watched as Mario hauled the sheet up through the window and into the compartment.

We had finally been able to demonstrate our desire to take care of him and the children, and Ray immediately emphasized this. "Eat. Drink. Feed the children." He continued with this theme, using what negotiators refer to as "positive police actions," in which we reiterate all the good things we've done. The list also includes all the threatening things we purposely haven't done. For example, he reminded Mario that we had not fired at him when he opened the window.

We could hear some movement in the cabin, and after a while Mario spoke up again. "Gracias, Ray." Ray continued to do most of the talking, asking about Julie, the little girl, and about the baby, Juan. Mario now opened up slightly; he gave only brief, noncommittal responses, but he seemed less agitated. He also began to call Ray "señor," a sign of respect. This felt like a major breakthrough after the events of the previous day.

Ray continued to develop his rapport with Mario, and early that evening convinced him to surrender one of his weapons in exchange for some cigarettes and soft drinks. Mario wrapped the handgun in the sheet that had been used to deliver the food and lowered it to the ground. It turned out to be a 9 mm automatic pistol that was jammed and unworkable. Still, it represented a step in the right direction.

We decided that this was the moment to press Mario to surrender. Ray told Mario that it was time for him and the kids to come out.

Mario responded, "Only if my *padrino* is here."

Ray glanced at me and translated, "Godfather."

"Who is your godfather, Mario?"

He gave us the name of Paul E. Warburgh, a New York attorney who had defended Mario in a prior drug-smuggling case. He wanted Warburgh on the scene to guarantee his safety.

The FBI office in New York quickly located Warburgh and spoke with him, and he agreed to help. Even so, I knew it would take time to fly the lawyer down to North Carolina on an FBI plane. We continued to press Mario to release the children.

"Señor, what about Julie and the baby? Let's get them out of there, yes?"

No response. Ray continued. "Send the kids out now and you can come when your lawyer arrives." He continued along these lines periodically over the next hour. Suddenly I heard Mario speak again, his tone matter-of-fact.

I listened for the translation.

"The baby is dead. Don't worry about the baby, Ray."

Nothing in the way he uttered this sentence could have prepared me for the translation. He spoke as if telling us to get over something, with no hint of remorse. I looked at Ray and saw pure anguish. Mario continued. "I woke up this morning and he was blue and stiff." He blamed us for not having delivered the IV through the holes in the door, as he had demanded earlier.

I looked again at Ray and could tell he was devastated. He turned and walked farther down the train platform. Then he knelt down and prayed.

Every negotiator handles the loss of a hostage differently. I tend to focus on what needs to be done now rather than what went wrong. But I was afraid Ray would feel responsible for the child's death—that somehow he would think he'd done something wrong. I gave him a minute and then made my way down the platform and placed my hand on his shoulder.

"It's not your fault," I said. "You're not the one responsible for this death."

Ray lifted his head, but he kept his eyes closed.

"We've got to think about Julie now. We still have to get her out alive."

This reminder of the mission still before us seemed to give him a new resolve. He stood up, walked back to our position, and picked up the microphone.

"I have just made my peace with the Lord," Ray said. "I will not carry the responsibility of the death of that baby. The responsibility is yours."

Ray sounded like a new man, a little angry and much more forceful. "I have just gotten up from my knees praying for the soul of that little boy. Also I'm praying for the girl because she's going to die." He was like a father talking sternly to his son.

"Julie is fine," Mario protested. His tone also had changed; he seemed defensive and stung by Ray's reality check.

"Are you absolutely sure?" Ray asked. "I do not want that little girl to die."

"No, Señor Ray, she has eaten and drunk. She's all right." Mario sounded as if he was pleading, trying to convince Ray that he was not such a bad guy. The microphone attached to the train car was sensitive enough that we could hear Julie in the background, complaining to Mario about her stomach. Ray seized on this opportunity and immediately jumped in.

"You see? The girl is getting sick. This means that she, too, is going to die from dehydration. Julie needs immediate medical attention."

Lathell and I watched as Ray paused for a moment, the microphone to his lips. Then he became increasingly bold, saying to Mario in a manner that invoked a sense of honor, "Will you meet me at the window now and give me Julie? I will come unarmed."

Lathell was still interpreting that last statement for me as I saw Ray take the blanket that had been around his shoulders and drape it over his extended arms. He was already moving toward Mario's compartment. My head was racing a million miles an hour, but all I could say was, "Wait a minute."

I turned to tell Lathell to radio to command and SWAT and let them know what was going on. I didn't want someone to shoot at Ray by mistake. As I did this I saw Ray remove his revolver from his holster and put it in his hand, hidden from sight by the outstretched blanket. I unholstered my own revolver, the pitifully small five-shot .38 caliber Chiefs Special I had brought with me, and followed a few feet behind him. As he walked forward I followed a few feet behind, hugging as close as I could to the railroad car to stay out of Mario's sight. This situation was moving way too fast, and I knew Ray and I were engaging in a tactical role that had not been planned or coordinated, a big no-no. As negotiators, we shouldn't have been doing this at all. Still, Ray needed some backup in case something went wrong, and I wasn't going to let him go out there alone.

Ray stood just below and directly facing the compartment window. His arms outstretched to receive Julie, he was completely vulnerable. Pressed against the train itself, I had some room to roll under if shooting started, but Ray didn't. He simply stood waiting for the child. Back then the FBI didn't give out medals for bravery as they do today, but if anyone ever deserved one, it was Ray. What he did was one of the most courageous things I have ever witnessed an agent do.

It seemed like an eternity, waiting for the unknown, but in a few seconds the window opened and Mario reached out to shake Ray's hand. Luckily, Ray was left-handed, and it was in that left hand that he carried his revolver.

From my position wedged between the platform and the train I could see Mario for the first time; he was tall and thin and sweating profusely. After shaking Ray's hand he disappeared again into the train and emerged a moment later with Julie's little body cradled in his arms. Ray wrapped her up in the blanket, thanked Mario, and headed toward the station. I turned and walked back the other way toward our protective girder, staying close to the train. Ray walked up to the surprised officers at the command post and handed Julie to an EMT, who then rushed her to the hospital.

When Ray got back to our negotiation position he seemed oblivious to what he had just done. I gave him a big hug and said, "You stupid son of a bitch, don't ever surprise me like that again." We laughed together, but I could see the sadness on his face. I looked him in the eye and said, "You aren't God. All you can do is your best to save every life that you can. That's the measure of our success or failure as negotiators. You just saved that little girl."

On Monday, very early, Paul Warburgh arrived, escorted by FBI agents. Fred Lanceley made it clear to the attorney that we did not want to turn him into a negotiator and move discussions into legal or other matters that might cause further delay in the surrender.

"I get it," Warburgh said. "Let's just wrap this thing up peacefully."

We took him down to the train and he said a few words to Mario. "I'm here, my friend. You're going to be safe."

Now it was the moment of truth. Ray got back on the speaker and asked Mario to surrender any remaining weapons.

Moments later, Mario lowered the sheet, which now contained his MAC-10 submachine gun.

"Time to come out," Ray said.

At 5:45 a.m., Mario slid back the door to his compartment, raised his hands, and surrendered to the SWAT team. As he emerged from the train, Ray stepped forward and offered him a cigarette.

Leaning toward the flame from Ray's lighter, Mario looked him in the eye and said, "I didn't want to hurt anybody."

Chief Heineman would later tell the press that his primary concern throughout the seventy-two-hour ordeal—the longest nonprison siege in U.S. history up to that time—was the safety of the children. A more aggressive approach might have led to Julie losing her life and would have placed his officers in clear jeopardy. In a press conference, Chief Heineman said, "I feel good that we didn't fire a single shot. We were all saddened by the loss of the baby, but I felt we got all we could possibly get out of this." He was right. The chief also graciously acknowledged the assistance of the FBI, saying that he had benefited immensely from our expertise.

The entire Raleigh community had been closely watching this situation, and the hospital where Julie was in good condition received more than fifty calls from people who said they were willing to be her foster parents. Her relatives soon arrived from Colombia to take her home. Mario would eventually be convicted of first-degree murder and given a life sentence.

A few days after the siege ended, *The Washington Post* ran an editorial titled "Freeing Hostages Safely." It spoke about the Amtrak siege, as well as another hostage incident that had been handled successfully at the same time in New York City by NYPD lieutenant Robert Louden: "Impressive work was done by specially trained hostage negotiating teams, a relatively new phenomenon in law enforcement." After summarizing these two incidents, the editorial concluded: "Such person-to-person bridge-building, psychologists tell us, is just what's needed when dealing with a dangerous person who feels trapped. The objective is to set up voice communication—through a wall or window or over the phone—and keep talking until the gunman has established a trusting relationship with at least one lawman. It takes time, but in almost every case it's far more sensible than attempting to rescue the hostages with force."

Our methods were bearing fruit, and we were thrilled that the press and public were beginning to take notice. Unfortunately, many of our law enforcement colleagues still viewed negotiation with skepticism. That, combined with the fact that we all had day jobs doing other things, meant that it would be a while before we could fully consolidate the respect we'd earned in Raleigh.

CHAPTER FOUR

TROUBLE ABROAD

*There is no den in the wide world to hide a rogue. Commit a crime
and the earth is made of glass.*
—RALPH WALDO EMERSON

Though I found myself increasingly drawn to negotiation work, my primary posting in the early 1980s was still with the Terrorism Squad, a job that suddenly was to become much more demanding.

In 1985, a series of violent hijackings across the globe made nearly constant front-page headlines both in the United States and overseas. The first I was involved with directly was the June 14 hijacking of TWA Flight 847 out of Athens, Greece, by Lebanese terrorists. During a standoff that ultimately would last until June 30 and unfold over multiple locations from Algiers to Beirut, U.S. Navy diver Robert Dean Stethem was murdered and his body thrown onto the tarmac at the Beirut airport. Because of a recent U.S. law that had made it illegal to take an American citizen hostage anywhere in the world, I was assigned to lead the case, the first extraterritorial hostage situation investigated by the FBI. Over the next five years I would travel extensively in connection with this and other cases, developing evidence, interviewing U.S. citizens who had been victims, and in the case of TWA 847, coordinating witness testimony for the trial of one of the hijackers, Mohammed Ali Hamadei, who was arrested in Germany, convicted in

May 1989, and sentenced to life in prison (though he was paroled in late 2005).

In October 1985, only a few months after the TWA hijacking, Palestinian terrorists hijacked an Italian cruise ship, the *Achille Lauro*, in the Mediterranean Sea. Aboard were a number of Americans, including wheelchair-bound Leon Klinghoffer. The hijackers shot and killed him, then threw his body into the sea off the coast of Syria.

Egyptian authorities intervened, working out a deal on their own for the passengers to be released and the four hijackers to be flown to Libya aboard an Egypt Air commercial plane. The U.S. government had its own ideas, and U.S. Navy F-14 jets intercepted the plane over the Mediterranean and forced it to land in Sigonella, Sicily, where the four hijackers were arrested.

Based on my experience handling the TWA case, I was initially assigned as the FBI lead agent for this new investigation as well. I traveled to Italy with other agents to conduct interviews aboard the returned cruise ship and to interrogate the four hijackers, now in Italian custody. The Italian authorities at first resisted our efforts to question the hijackers, apparently because they hadn't secured confessions and didn't want us to get them first. Eventually, though, political pressure prevailed. We soon found ourselves escorted to a stark prison in Turin, where we would interrogate the four terrorists, including Majed al-Mulqi.

A guard led me and my partner/interpreter down a corridor to a large interview room. We seated ourselves at a table, and Mulqi was brought in, wearing a khaki prison uniform and handcuffs. As he sat down, he gave us a look of such unadulterated hatred that I was momentarily concerned that he might try to jump across the table and kill us. I could feel myself tense in readiness and observed a similar involuntary reaction in my partner; we were now focused and alert. I thought, *There's no way we can get a meaningful statement from this guy.*

We began by explaining who we were and telling him that we wanted to ask him about the hijacking. Taking a page from my hostage-negotiation training, I had planned to approach him in an open and unthreatening manner. I assumed the Italians had been more direct and confrontational with him, to say the least, and I thought this would allow us to assume the role of "good cop."

I began asking simple questions about his background, which my colleague would frame in the Palestinian-inflected Arabic that Mulqi spoke. His command of the dialect—like Mulqi, he had been raised in Palestine—and his nonthreatening delivery of the questions really surprised Mulqi. Initially, Mulqi said little, but after an hour he became less tense and began to open up. My partner would pose my question and Mulqi would respond, often with a long stream of words, after which my partner would render it in English for me. I periodically glanced at the Italian policemen standing outside the door, and I could tell they were surprised that Mulqi was talking to us for so long.

We appealed to his vanity, praising the efficiency of the operation and telling him it was among the boldest and most well-executed hijackings we'd ever seen. As we did this, we embedded questions that encouraged him to give us important details such as who had been in charge. After one exchange, my partner suddenly turned to me and translated a key admission: "I was the leader." Without missing a beat, I asked, "How were you able to keep control of the entire ship and your comrades?" Mulqi seemed to sit up straighter with this acknowledgment of his abilities as a terrorist team leader.

A little later I sought to find out why they had targeted one disabled older American. "We're very interested to know what brought about Mr. Klinghoffer's death."

Mulqi told us that at one point the ship had been surrounded by news helicopters. He didn't like them flying so close, and so he'd threatened to harm people if the copters didn't move farther away. The helicopters didn't withdraw, so to show that he was serious, Mulqi moved the passengers up on the deck below the bridge and surrounded them with cans of fuel as a warning. But he and his fellow hijackers couldn't move Klinghoffer because of his wheelchair. What followed was a confession that we hadn't expected.

"So I wheeled him to the side of the ship and shot him, then threw him overboard for all to see."

Few law enforcement officers had ever even talked to a terrorist at this point, and we were momentarily stunned by what had just happened. A hardened terrorist who had refused to reveal this information under prior relentless interrogation had just opened up. This was an important moment for me, when I began to think about the distinction between interrogation and interviewing. The former, at least at face value, seemed the appropriate way to handle someone who had committed the kind of atrocious crimes that Mulqi had. And yet if the goal was to find out useful information, there were at least times when it made more sense to use a nonthreatening and relaxed manner and try to project some sense that we were trying to understand him. Even a hardened terrorist, when handled the right way, might be encouraged to provide important information.

One month after the *Achille Lauro* tragedy the terrorists struck again, when operatives for Abu Nidal, a terrorist organization committed to the destruction of Israel, hijacked Egypt Air Flight 648, again out of Athens. When the three hijackers took over the plane it prompted a shoot-out with an Egyptian sky marshal, who managed to kill one of them. During the shoot-out, the plane's fuselage was pierced by a bullet, leading to cabin decompression and forcing the pilot to fly low. The decompression and a declining fuel supply eventually led the pilot to perform an emergency landing in Malta. Once on the ground, the two surviving hijackers demanded that the plane be refueled so that they could fly it to Libya, but the authorities refused. And so one by one, over several hours, they marched five of the passengers, two Israelis and three Americans, to the open doorway and shot each of them in the head. Amazingly, three of these victims would survive their wounds.

The Maltese government had no structured crisis management apparatus or any trained hostage negotiators. The Maltese president and other officials assembled in the airport control tower, but had little idea of how to effectively communicate with the hijackers on the plane. In fact, a big part of their strategy seemed to be to avoid communicating with them altogether and instead await the arrival of Egyptian commandos. A skilled negotiation team might have been able to fully engage and occupy the hijackers, thereby preventing them from feeling compelled to execute hostages in order to have their demands addressed by the authorities.

There was no serious attempt to negotiate a nonviolent resolution;

instead, Egyptian commandos stormed the aircraft in what would prove to be an exceptionally ill-conceived and poorly executed rescue attempt. As a diversion for a tactical assault, they planted an excessively high-powered explosive charge in the luggage compartment near the rear of the aircraft. When it detonated it killed one of the two remaining hijackers and dozens of hostages. The resulting fire and indiscriminate shooting from the tactical teams resulted in more than sixty-five deaths. I would later assist in debriefing the two surviving Americans from Flight 648, since the FBI investigated this crime against American citizens. I could not help thinking that skillful negotiation might have delivered a better outcome.

In addition to the TWA Flight 847 and *Achille Lauro* incidents, the terrorism squad at WFO (which became known as the extra-territorial terrorism squad) worked an ongoing hostage ordeal in Lebanon involving several Americans who had been taken prisoner by Hezbollah terrorists over a long period of time, including journalist Terry Anderson, who would be held for seven years. I assisted case agent Tom Kelly (the helicopter pilot from Sperryville) in debriefing Reverend Benjamin Weir, the first American to be released from captivity.

I also assisted case agent Tom Hansen during the investigation of Royal Jordanian Flight 402, which was hijacked from Beirut by the Amal militia on June 11, 1985. As we investigated the TWA Flight 847 hijacking that happened three days later, we learned that two American citizens had been aboard this other aircraft, giving the FBI investigative jurisdiction. We eventually hatched an operation to lure the hijack's leader, Fawaz Younis, to the Mediterranean Sea; he was arrested by undercover FBI agents, returned to the United States, and eventually convicted. His apprehension on the high seas and return to the United States to face justice was a historic first in the war against terrorism.

These were indeed busy times for the very few of us who were working these matters. All the major investigations were intense and time-consuming, and we were up to our necks in work. I would spend five years on the TWA Flight 847 investigation alone, not only helping successfully prosecute Mohammed Ali Hamadei in Germany but pursuing the apprehension of the other two hijackers, Hasan Izz-al-Din and Ali Atwa, both of whom are sadly still at large. All this, and I was still teaching negotiation courses and responding to callouts such as the incident in Sperryville.

This wave of international terrorism (which included attacks on the Rome and Vienna airports in December 1985) marked a turning point for the FBI and for the United States; it was the first time that any nation had aggressively gone after terrorists beyond its shores in order to bring them to justice, rather than just target them for assassination, as the Israelis had done to the Munich Olympics terrorists. We were blazing new ground, which was exciting, but because we had limited manpower (in 1985 the WFO terrorism squad, which handled all international hijackings for the FBI, had only six or seven agents; after the tragic events of September 11, 2001, literally thousands of FBI agents began to work terrorism cases), I was called on virtually every time a terrorist incident involving Americans took place. From 1985 to 1990 I was probably on the road at least six months out of the year, and when I was home I was working nights and weekends. After several years of this high-stress, globe-trotting routine, I began to get worn out. I had a ten-year-old, an eight-year-old, and a six-year-old; I missed them; and I felt I needed to be there coaching soccer games and going to piano recitals and swim meets. There were times when good friends had to shovel snow from my driveway because I was out of town. The FBI always said that families came first, but that was not true. The needs of the Bureau always took precedence over family. I recalled speaking to my kids on brief phone calls from overseas, hearing them ask, "Daddy, when are you coming home?" My work was exciting and stimulating, but my family was suffering as a consequence.

I had barely returned from spending the summer and fall of 1988 in Germany for the Hamadei trial—where I had been off and on for eight months, testifying twenty times—when Pan Am Flight 103 was bombed over Lockerbie, Scotland, on December 21. The FBI was slow to realize just how much manpower and resources were required to do this kind of work effectively. As soon as we received word of the Lockerbie incident, I was called into my boss's office and told I would be taking the lead on this major terrorism case. But I had reached my breaking point and was in no mood to be brusquely informed that I was being deployed yet again, this time to Scotland. I was tired of being taken advantage of, and we argued. Not getting the understanding I felt I deserved, I left his office, walked down the hall to see his boss, and said, "Enough already." I felt righteously angry at being told I would once more have to work around the clock with limited support, all because the Bureau didn't have the foresight to adequately staff this crucial squad. I suppose that in a way I was being complimented; after all, Lockerbie was the largest single homicide in the history of the United States at the time, and my boss wanted me to head up the investigation. But I had made up my mind. I did later deploy to Lockerbie for a short time to provide an assessment of the investigation, but by then other agents had been brought in to manage the case.

After I came back from Lockerbie, I met with my senior Assistant Special Agent in Charge, Nick Walsh, and told him I really needed to get away from terrorism for a while and wanted to transfer off the squad as soon as possible. Nick acknowledged that, as the longest-serving agent on the extra-territorial terrorism squad, I deserved a break, and he said that wherever I wanted to go within WFO, he would see to it that I got there. I had been working terrorism for eight years and a change of pace would be welcome.

CHAPTER FIVE

CRISIS INTERVENTION: LISTEN AND LEARN

*To listen closely and reply well is the highest perfection we are able
to obtain in the art of conversation.*
—FRANÇOIS DE LA ROCHEFOUCAULD

For the next six months I held a quiet job investigating corrupt politicians from the Bureau's Tyson's Corner, Virginia, office, twenty minutes from my home. Life was good. Then an unexpected opportunity arose. One of three full-time positions on the negotiation staff at Quantico came open. I had been asked on previous occasions to transfer to Quantico to become a full-time hostage negotiator, but had declined the offers due to my demanding terrorism work. This time I agreed to apply for the position, and I was selected for the job. I would assume responsibility for the two-week training course and provide operational support during hostage crises. This meant a promotion, as well as a transfer down to Quantico. Finally I'd be able to devote myself to what by then felt like a calling.

As one of the three agents assigned to the hostage negotiation program, I was part of the Special Operations and Research Unit (SOARU), which was configured to support tactical, hostage negotiation, and crisis management research, training, and operations for the entire FBI. Those of us on the staff were in a position to greatly influence the direction of the FBI's policy and operational guidelines for these programs. The SOARU was purposefully set up to better coordinate the often conflicting and sometimes contradictory approaches historically practiced by the FBI's SWAT teams and field hostage negotiators.

Behind closed doors, our crew was not above jokingly referring to the SWAT guys as Neanderthals and knuckle-draggers. But experience had shown us time and again that hostage negotiators were less likely to achieve a desired surrender when there was no visible show of force and a lack of tactical containment. Conversely, we had also learned that tactical entry was almost always safer and more successful *after* negotiators had bought time for necessary planning, practice, and implementation.

It wasn't that we didn't appreciate the SWAT teams—we knew that we depended on them just as much as they depended on us. I also had my own reasons to appreciate them: while I had been in Germany for the Hamadei trial, information surfaced that terrorists might be targeting me for reprisal. In response, the FBI had dispatched members of the Hostage Rescue Team to my house to guard my family, even accompanying my wife and kids on outings and daily errands.

As distinguished from the fifty-six part-time SWAT teams in FBI field offices around the country, HRT was a dedicated national counterterrorism tactical response unit. HRT was located, like SOARU, at the FBI academy, and was staffed by over sixty-five full-time tactical operators who were always either engaged in training rotations or operationally deployed on unique missions anywhere in the United States that required their unique skill sets. Protecting my family became one of those missions.

When I wasn't traveling to conduct law enforcement training programs or speaking at law enforcement conferences, my time was spent developing new negotiation instructional training blocks or researching and writing articles for the *FBI Law Enforcement Bulletin*. The objective was to gather information, assess its value, identify the key learning points, and then pass that information to negotiation practitioners.

In addition to the intensive two-week hostage-negotiation training courses we conducted four to six times each year at the FBI academy, we also conducted regional training programs for local police departments in the field. The basic negotiation course in Quantico provided essential training for all new FBI negotiators, but we also kept open several slots for domestic and foreign officers.

Practically every significant law enforcement leader in the free world cycled through the FBI academy at some point or another. Many of these officials would take time to stop by our unit to learn about the negotiation program, and to tap into our experience and expertise. They collected copies of our training materials and often requested that we travel to their jurisdictions to conduct field negotiation schools for their personnel.

During the six months I spent at the Tyson's Corner resident agency, I hardly left the zip code. I remember telling my wife, Carol, that this new assignment at Quantico would be less disruptive to our family life, and that I would not be traveling nearly as much or to such faraway destinations as I had when working overseas hijacking cases. Little did I know that by becoming a full-time negotiator, I was setting myself up not only for continuing worldwide travel but also for round-the-clock duty as a consultant to on-scene negotiators, taking those urgent phone calls seeking advice on nights, weekends, and holidays.

The FBI has worked kidnap cases since 1932, when the abduction and murder of the two-year-old son of aviator Charles Lindbergh stirred public outrage. In response, Congress passed a law making it a federal crime to kidnap and transport a victim across state lines. From that point forward the FBI aggressively investigated kidnapping for ransom in the United States and did much to make this a fairly rare crime today. Through the years the FBI developed significant expertise and capabilities in working these cases. Sophisticated electronic, airborne, and ground surveillance and tracking make this a crime with small prospects for success. As a result, while kidnapping for ransom has become a scourge overseas, for the most part criminals in the United States have moved on to different crimes. (Of course, women and children continue to be abducted by sexual predators, not as hostages but as "homicides to be.")

When I arrived at Quantico the FBI's negotiation training tended to focus largely on classic hostage situations, in which a perpetrator holds someone against their will in order to compel a third party, usually the police, to do something (or abstain from doing something). During a class Fred Lanceley and I led in Oakland, California, for local, state, and federal law enforcement officers, Fred asked our group of thirty-five experienced hostage negotiators how many had dealt with such a classic bargaining situation. Not one hand went up.

Then he asked how many students had negotiated an incident in which a hostage taker was in emotional crisis and had no clear demands, and every hand went up.

We were both surprised, though we had felt all along that such emotionally driven incidents, not bargaining interactions, constituted the bulk of what most police negotiators had to deal with. Right then, Fred and I realized that the need was not so much for training in quid pro quo bargaining but for the skills needed in crisis intervention situations, with a heavy dose of active listening. Our students needed to learn the slow and patient communication skills that could defuse the kinds of situations they were most likely to face. When we returned to Quantico, I pitched my boss on revamping our negotiation training curriculum. He agreed, and I set out to redo the program, putting more emphasis on how to deal with individuals under extreme emotional stress.

The core of the new curriculum consisted of specific active listening skills first developed by the counseling profession. In brief, this entails creating positive relationships with people by demonstrating an understanding of what they're going through and how they feel about it. By applying this approach, the negotiator can demonstrate empathy and show a sincere desire to better understand what the individual is experiencing. We know that people want to be shown respect, and they want to be understood. Listening is the cheapest, yet most effective concession we can make. The positive relationship achieved through this interaction then sets the stage for the negotiator to exert a positive influence over others' behavior, steering them away from violence. The skills boil down to restatement of contact and reflection of the captor's feelings. Increased use of these techniques would have dramatic results.

I sent my new ideas to the fifty-six field offices for input, and incorporated their feedback into the final product, an extensive binder filled with hundreds of new and improved slides. This was probably the most impactful thing I did at the FBI. In those days your local police department depended on its local FBI office for training, which occurred on an entirely ad hoc basis. Now, for the first time, there was a precise, standardized, detailed approach to handling emotionally driven cases. The manual also covered every other aspect of the negotiation process. If you had a siege situation and the media became involved, you could find out what to do. It provided guidance for dealing with family members outside the crisis site. Most important, the manual identified specific active listening skills that could be easily learned and applied to most negotiation situations.

The new training slides provided specific guidance, for example, on recognizing a "suicide by cop" situation, in which the subject purposefully engages with the police to bring about his own demise. It also contained a list of indications of progress and a similar list to help identify incidents that were becoming more dangerous. Specific active listening skills were provided, with examples of how they could be incorporated into dialogue to create a relationship of trust with an individual in crisis. The response to these new training materials was enthusiastic and overwhelmingly positive. The number of field-training requests quadrupled; more and more police began to look to the FBI for guidance in this area.

On one Fourth of July, I was sitting on a blanket on the Washington Mall, having a picnic with my family and looking forward to the start of the fireworks show, when my beeper sounded. I pulled out my cell phone, punched in the number on the display, and soon reached Mike Duke, an FBI negotiator assigned to South Carolina. He was calling to tell me that a gunman had taken over the USS *Yorktown,* a decommissioned Navy aircraft carrier and museum in Charleston. According to the best information Mike had, the subject was a Vietnam vet with emotional problems. He had taken a high-powered rifle on board the ship and fired off some rounds, but he was not believed to be holding any hostages.

It does not take Sigmund Freud to connect the dots that might link a symbolic U.S. Navy ship, the Fourth of July, and a Vietnam veteran suffering from post-traumatic stress disorder (PTSD). I told Mike that this was probably a classic crisis intervention situation where the gunman had no clear substantive demands, and advised him to suggest to the police our standard approach of establishing rapport with active listening skills and talking this man through his crisis. I then asked him to call me again once he arrived at the command post and had gathered additional information. He said he would, and I returned to my family picnic.

About an hour later my beeper went off again, but this time it displayed a different number. When I dialed the number, my call was answered by a voice I didn't recognize. I asked to speak with Mike Duke, but the man on the phone said he didn't know a Mike Duke. I then asked if this was the command post; the man said it was not. I next asked if this was the negotiation team room, and again the man said no. Then he asked me who I was. I told him my name and said that I was a negotiator with the FBI, calling from Washington, D.C. In response, he said, "I guess I'm in bigger trouble than I thought."

Dumbfounded, I asked: "Are you by any chance the man with the gun?"

"Yes, I am," he said.

I learned later that the phone number Mike had sent me was for the souvenir shop where the command post and negotiation team had been set up. What Mike didn't know was that this same number also rang on the ship's bridge, where the gunman was.

Now that I had been thrust into the dialogue, I didn't want to just hang up on him. I needed to do what I could to keep him calm, then extricate myself as diplomatically as possible.

"What's your name?" I asked him.

"Jim."

"You okay, Jim?"

"I'm okay."

"Well, you know that no one wishes you harm. We all want you to come off that ship safe and sound, with nobody getting hurt, either."

I didn't want to cross wires with the local police's strategy, but with this basic civility I thought I was on pretty safe ground.

"What happened today, Jim?"

He responded, "I'm a Vietnam vet and I'm not getting the help I need. I served my country, but nobody cares about me or wants to hire me. I've got nothing to look forward to."

He projected hopelessness and helplessness, the most important suicide warning signs. He seemed to be saying that life wasn't worth living, and I was worried that he might take his own life.

As I started to acknowledge his feelings, he suddenly interrupted me.

"What the fuck was that?" he said. I heard the sound of his phone receiver banging against something—he must have stepped away.

Then he picked up the receiver again and said, "You tell those fuckers that nobody better try to come up here. I see anybody coming at me and I'm going to start firing this weapon."

I was worried now, and at a serious disadvantage, because for all I knew, whatever sound he'd heard was indeed the SWAT team moving in. But I had to try to contain him.

"Jim, no one wants to hurt you. They're there to try to help you."

I could hear him breathing heavily, but after a bit he seemed to calm down.

"Everything's going to be okay, Jim."

"Yeah. So long as nobody tries to come in here." He was silent for a moment. Then he said, "I gotta go...."

I could hear the receiver banging around again, but he hadn't hung up. I stayed on the line and waited, hoping for the best.

A moment later my beeper went off again and displayed yet another number. I grabbed my wife's cell phone and quickly punched it in, hoping that it was Mike and I'd be able to explain that I had Jim on the other line.

My call was answered, but the voice that said hello wasn't Mike's.

"Hi," I said. "Is this . . . Jim?"

"Yeah."

"Oh my gosh, this is Gary again."

I couldn't believe this. This was one of the more ridiculous moments of my career. The command post had given me yet another number that Jim was able to intercept, so I was now speaking to him on one line and on hold with him on another. Meanwhile, I was five hundred miles away on the Washington Mall with my family, holding a plate of potato salad on my lap.

"Jim, tell you what. I'm going to hang up on this line, but let's keep talking on the other. Is that okay with you?"

The line went dead. I went back to my own cell phone again, and Jim picked up the other receiver at his end. But even before we could speak I heard the second line at his location starting to ring again. I had no idea what kind of circus this was going to turn into.

"Jim," I said, "if that's the news media, I'd like you to hang up on them and come back and talk some more with me. But if it's the police, the negotiator down where you are, just let me know and I'll hang up."

Jim took the call, then came back on the line with me. "It's the cops," he said.

"Good. Listen, they want to help you, not hurt you. They're good guys. You just talk it through with them, and they're going to get you out of there safe and sound, okay?"

"Yeah. Sure," he said.

Whether that was a sincere response or sarcasm I couldn't tell. Still, I was somewhat optimistic he could be talked out.

For the next thirty hours the local police negotiators stayed on the phone with Jim, employing the techniques set forth in our manual, listening to and acknowledging his problems and frustrations. They eventually convinced him that he shouldn't harm himself, and he surrendered. This case was emblematic of something I would see often in the years to come: a guy feels hopeless and acts out in a cry for help. While his depression may lead him to suicide, this attention-seeking behavior indicates that at least part of him wants to live. This creates an opening for the negotiator, who, by the act of listening to him and acknowledging his difficulties, can make him realize that there is hope after all.

There are of course cases when the subjects are a great deal more desperate than Jim and have no intention of turning back. Maybe they've already committed a murder or some other serious criminal offense. In situations like this, all the signs point to disaster. But even at times like this it often proves possible to avoid further loss of life. In one instance in Houma, Louisiana, a uniformed police officer named Chad Roy Louviere, driving a marked cruiser, stopped a woman for a purported traffic violation, raped her, and then handed her his business card. Clearly, this was not a man working with any objective other than to act out and to sever his ties with humanity. Information we received later indicated that he was an obsessively controlling husband and that his wife had recoiled from his demands. She insisted on a separation, which had sent him over the edge.

At 11:00 a.m., immediately after the rape, Louviere went directly to the small-town bank where his wife worked. When he entered the building, his wife was there along with five other employees and two customers. Waving his gun and shouting orders, he forced the two customers to leave, then lined up his victims and went down the line. "I know you," he said to the first. Then he went on to the next person in line and then the next, saying, "I know you," until he reached a sobbing teller named Pamela Duplantis. "I don't know you," he said, and shot her in the head, killing her instantly.

After this, it seemed more likely than ever that neither of the Louvieres would leave the bank alive. This looked to be a classic homicide followed by a suicide.

By this time, the building was surrounded by squad cars from local, county, and state authorities. As the Houma police began the painful process of trying to negotiate with one of their own, the chief called on an untrained officer to be their primary negotiator because he was a friend of Chad Roy Louviere's. But what inexperienced crisis managers don't realize is that if it was that easy for troubled individuals to open up to friends, many of these situations would never happen in the first place. It is often easier for a well-trained stranger to develop the necessary relationship with an emotionally troubled subject.

A store across the street became the de facto command center, and from there, this officer called the bank repeatedly to plead with Louviere to give up and come out. "No way," Louviere responded again and again.

Other friends of Louviere's from the force were brought to the phone across the street, but every one of them focused on the same practical objective—getting the man to surrender. After several hours of his friends saying "Just come on out, Chad," Louviere became so frustrated that he simply refused to answer the phone. Fortunately, he let his hostages answer when the police continued to call.

Louviere was known to be a man of few words, but amid his taciturn refusals, his friends never picked up on the one clear message he was trying to send. Several times, as he refused to surrender, he muttered, "I just want to talk to somebody."

Shortly after Louviere broke off communication, the Houma police chief and local sheriff called me and asked for my advice. Right away I leveled with them: this situation did not hold out a great deal of promise. The initial rape and the subsequent murder of a random teller at the bank appeared to be the work of a man determined to push himself until there was no way of turning back. Our only hope was to get inside his head and begin to probe what had triggered his rage so that we could disarm it. But because the situation had reached a crisis point, with the hostages' lives as well as the gunman's a trigger pull away from being obliterated, we had to be extremely cautious.

As he briefed me, at one point the chief almost offhandedly mentioned Louvier's desire to just talk. I seized on this as a glimmer of hope. Then the chief also mentioned that Gloria Newport, an experienced FBI agent assigned to the New Orleans field office, had just arrived at the scene. I knew Gloria to be a skilled negotiator—I had trained her myself at our course at Quantico. "Make Agent Newport your primary negotiator," I told the chief. "I think he'll open up more with a woman."

The chief was taken aback, to say the least, by my suggestion.

"This man just raped one woman and murdered another," he said. "What makes you think he wants to talk with a woman? Looks to me like he hates women. I think the last person he'd want to talk to is a woman."

"Sometimes a man has an easier time talking with a woman about his emotional life," I said. "I think we need someone who can appear non-threatening and nonjudgmental, someone who can project a sense of understanding. I think a soothing female voice is what we need to get Louviere back from the edge."

"We'll think about it," the chief told me. But he went back to the strategy of calling in more of Louviere's friends from the police force. Finally, when it became clear they were making no progress in the negotiations, the chief relented and put Gloria on the phone.

At first, she was able to speak only with the hostages. Louviere's wife reiterated her husband's need to talk.

"Do you think he'd talk to me?" Gloria said.

"Let me see," she said. And a moment later Louviere picked up the phone.

"Chad," Gloria said, "I've heard that you want to talk to somebody. I'm here to listen." Her voice was soft, soothing, and nonconfrontational.

In the pause that followed, Gloria heard a loud exhalation. She told me later that it was like a dam bursting, after which Louviere began to talk about his issues. He was an extreme case of a controlling husband who couldn't accept the fact that his wife had a mind of her own. Gloria was the perfect listener, and her ability to deliver basic empathetic responses with absolute sincerity almost immediately calmed him down: "I'm worried about you. Tell me what happened. Tell me all about it." She validated his emotions, often just by naming them. "You sound so angry and frustrated," she said to him. "What do you think your wife would do if you just told her how you feel?" She gave him an attentive ear and, most important, hope.

Once Gloria had established a relationship with Chad, she began to lay a foundation that would help her convince him to end the standoff with no further loss of life, suggesting to him that there might be opportunities to fix his relationship with his wife. Chad was a police officer and he knew full well the implications of what he had done. Still, the idea of reconciling with his wife was compelling. And when he was finally given an opportunity to express his hurt, anger, and frustration, this helped to relieve the pressure cooker of his emotions that was about to burst. His rage dissipated significantly. Gloria was finally able to convince him that the best course of action was for him to come out peacefully and not hurt anyone else. She gently encouraged and coaxed him to do the right thing. She had gained influence with him, and because of this, and this alone, he soon surrendered without incident. As of this writing he is still awaiting execution.

A small-town police chief might face one situation like this in his career. Working on a national, even global scale, my colleagues and I saw these situations every week, and we'd learned that part of effective resolution is pulling back from the end objective and focusing on how to establish a relationship with this guy, right now, at this moment. I felt Gloria had the right communication skills to make her effective with

Chad. Part of Louviere hated his wife, but some other part of him still loved her as well. He simply didn't have the capacity to express that love except as a wish to dominate and control.

And it takes nothing away from Gloria's ability to say that she might also have entered the game at an opportune moment. Often, the first negotiator to work with someone gets nothing but incoherent rage. But then, after the subject has vented and calmed down with the passage of time, he can become more willing to engage in a more substantive dialogue. Sometimes it's the change in personnel that triggers the shift. I just knew they were getting nowhere with the approach being taken prior to Gloria's involvement.

In the Louviere case, we averted a larger tragedy because police gave the perpetrator time to cool off. This was not the case on July 11, 1993, in Antioch, California, when a man named Joel Souza drove into a parking lot with his five-year-old daughter in his lap, holding a gun to her head. His eight-year-old son was sitting in the backseat.

Souza pulled up beside his estranged wife's car.

"Get in the car," he told Jennifer Souza. "Do it or I'll blow her head off."

She got into Joel's car and they drove to the house they had once shared. There, Joel held her at gunpoint for an hour while he raged at her and peppered her with personal questions. Whom had she been out with? Why hadn't she returned his telephone calls? Like Chad Louviere, he was a controlling ex-husband who seemed to consider family members to be his personal property.

After Souza's frightening diatribe was over, he let Jennifer go but kept the children. He warned her: "Tell anybody about this, and I'll shoot the kids."

Terrified but not intimidated, she ran to a neighbor's house and called the police. During the phone call she told them that her husband owned at least five different guns.

According to court testimony, Officer Michael Schneider was one of the first members of the Antioch Police Department to arrive on the scene. When he asked to speak to Joel and to see the children, Souza retreated with them to an upstairs bedroom and locked the door. Schneider, a trained hostage negotiator, took up a position at the head of the stairs.

"Joel, come on out now. I know you don't want to hurt your kids."

"It's none of your business," Souza yelled back. "Get out of my house or somebody's going to get hurt."

Outside, the SWAT team arrived and established a perimeter downstairs. Their presence made it even more imperative that Schneider keep Souza calm.

"Don't worry about those guys," Schneider said. "We're going to stay cool and everything's going to be fine. They are definitely not going to force their way in unless you do something really stupid. But you're not going to do anything stupid, are you, Joel? Because you love your kids, right? It's going to be easy does it."

Schneider, who had been trained in one of our regional programs, had thirteen years of negotiation experience. Unfortunately, some members of the Antioch police were less sophisticated in their thinking about how to deal with subjects who chose to barricade themselves against the cops. Taking the old-school approach, they immediately began to eliminate creature comforts. They disconnected the phone, electricity, and water, then, with the house already warm on a hot day, turned up the heating system full blast.

As the temperature in the bedroom began to rise, Souza became enraged and began to yell obscenities at Schneider. When he threatened to start shooting, the police turned the heat back down. The only quid pro quo was a promise Schneider extracted from Joel that something would be worked out.

Schneider worked to establish and then maintain a dialogue with the subject, relying on the standard approaches of building empathy through active listening. He also tried to get Souza to try to think about what he wanted to happen. How could this situation be resolved so that nobody got hurt?

After a while, Joel said that he wanted to exchange notes with his wife. Schneider agreed to deliver one note to Jennifer for every gun lowered by a rope out of the bedroom window. Over the next five hours, four rifles came out this way. Progress was being made, albeit slowly.

It was at the five-hour mark in the standoff that an off-duty police captain arrived to take over command of the incident. Here was a clear case of hierarchical authority taking precedence over knowledge and experience—a classic law enforcement mistake when negotiation expertise is not given its due. To make matters worse, this captain immediately suggested setting a time limit. This, of course, violated a basic premise of negotiation, which is that time can be a tool that allows anger to dissipate and better options to enter into the mind of the subject. We never put a deadline on ourselves. Time limits force a decision, yes, but it may be the wrong decision. The whole point of skilled negotiation is to provide the time and encouragement for subjects to make the right decision. The difference of a few hours can be, literally, a matter of life or death.

Schneider strongly resisted this imposition, and he continued to work on building rapport with Joel. At times it seemed as if the suspect was close to surrendering. He and Schneider began to discuss the process in detail. "When you come out, Joel, I want you to take your shirt off, okay? That way the SWAT guys will know you're unarmed. Will you do that for me?" This was all good stuff.

There was no response.

"I can stand in front of you when you come out," Schneider said. "Would that be good? That way you know that nobody's going to take a shot at you."

Again, no response from Joel, but no resistance, either.

Schneider called out to Joel's son. "Is your dad okay, Danny? Is he listening?"

"Yes, sir. He's listening," the boy said.

Schneider promised not to handcuff Joel in front of the children, and also to give them some time together. "You know, you haven't really hurt anybody. You haven't even fired any rounds. This whole thing can be worked out, Joel. It's really not so bad."

Unfortunately, Joel needed more time to make up his mind. He had not yet gotten over the hurdle of his ambivalence.

About four hours after taking command, the captain ran out of patience. "I'm tired of this shit," he said. Then he told Schneider, "Give him ten minutes—then we're coming in."

Once again Schneider argued that this was totally inappropriate, but this time the "suggestion" was an order.

Reluctantly, Schneider gave in. "Joel, you really have to come out now. It's time to do the right thing. You've got ten minutes."

Nine minutes later, three shots rang out. The SWAT team charged into the bedroom to find Joel and the two children dead. As a tragic indicator of how the pendulum can swing either way, Joel Souza was shirtless, just the way Schneider had told him to be when he was ready to surrender.

Jennifer Souza would later file a successful lawsuit claiming that the police had been responsible for the "negligent wrongful death" of her children. In his testimony at the trial, the captain said that he'd intended the ten-minute warning as a "bluff," not as an ultimatum. He said that he'd expected the warning to prompt Souza to surrender or to at least participate more fully in the negotiation process. But experience teaches us never to bluff with an armed man forced into a desperate situation.

The tragic error in handling Joel Souza was grounded in the captain's inexperience. He failed to appreciate how very different someone else's mental processes can be. Because the captain believed there was no way on earth that he would ever shoot his own children, he assumed the same was true for Joel Souza.

Oddly enough, though, the captain and Joel Souza may have had more in common that the captain imagined. The psychological makeup of traditional law enforcement officers tends to include a fair amount of classic controlling behavior, though they may not be self-aware enough to realize it on any conscious level. That typical law enforcement profile can also include a fair amount of arrogance.

In the years ahead, the FBI would confront an increasingly diverse array of citizens barricading themselves against the police. In addition to tortured, solitary individuals such as Joel Souza or Chad Louviere, there would be large groups of disaffected people linked together by political or religious conviction. In these cases, the dangers inherent in emotional instability would be compounded by weapons caches and the potential for quasi-military action by tightly bound groups hostile to the government.

In the face of these challenges, the FBI was becoming increasingly sophisticated in its negotiation strategies as well as in its tactical operations. But a large problem remained: how could these two aspects of the FBI's role be brought together effectively? Starting in 1991, the FBI would face a series of cases that would expose a fundamental divide between proponents of force and proponents of negotiation. Over this period, I would face the greatest challenge of my career, defending our role to skeptical colleagues increasingly convinced that they didn't need us.

It all began with two seemingly separate events: a prison riot in Talladega, Alabama, and an incident involving a right-wing separatist who lived with his family on a ridge in Idaho.

CHAPTER SIX

FROM SUCCESS TO HUBRIS

A man must be big enough to admit his mistakes, smart enough to profit from them, and strong enough to correct them.
—JOHN C. MAXWELL

When prisoners take hostages, there is great potential for things to spiral out of control. For one thing, prisons, while designed to keep people in, can also be effective in keeping them out. And your average prisoner has a fair amount of pent-up anger and rage over real and perceived mistreatment. Add to this the euphoria of suddenly having power when you've had none, and things can get out of hand quickly.

On the morning of August 21, 1991, a group of detainees awaiting repatriation to Cuba rioted and took control of their unit at the Talladega Federal Correctional Institution in Alabama. They seized eight Bureau of Prisons (BOP) employees and three from the Immigration and Naturalization Service (INS). The FBI has jurisdiction over serious crimes at federal prisons, and so I was immediately sent to Alabama.

This was not the first time that the FBI had confronted angry Cuban detainees. In November and December 1987, Cuban inmates had seized the Atlanta Penitentiary and the Federal Detention Center in Oakdale, Louisiana. The combined uprisings threatened more than a hundred hostages, lasted more than eleven days, and required protracted negotiations to resolve.

Many of the Cubans involved in those prison riots had been arrested after the infamous 1980 Mariel boatlift in which Fidel Castro had emptied his prisons and mental health wards, dumping their residents on an unsuspecting United States. Reports suggest that up to 16 percent of the 125,000 individuals entering the United States in that armada had spent time in Cuban prisons. The INS had detained about 2,500 of these, declaring them "excludable" or unfit to remain in the United States. These individuals were moved to over a dozen federal facilities around the country until their situations were resolved. Cuba initially refused to accept these inmates back, and American authorities could not simply release them. Those with violent criminal records were in perpetual limbo, and their frustrations led to the Atlanta and Oakdale riots. In both cases, peace was restored after a Cuban bishop from Miami was brought in as a mediator, but not before the riots cost the U.S. government more than $100 million and destroyed significant portions of the prison facilities.

The U.S. government eventually persuaded Cuba to take back more than 2,500 of the 3,800 Mariel refugees, and Talladega was the last stop for those being deported after their appeals had been exhausted. The Talladega uprising began one day before thirty-four detainees were scheduled to be shipped back to Cuba. Some of these were resigned to going back home, where they awaited an uncertain future in the Cuban legal system. Some were adamantly opposed to their repatriation. Others, who had served their sentences for criminal offenses committed here in the United States, simply wanted to be set free. All felt betrayed by the "agreements" for immediate resolution they thought they had reached at Oakdale or Atlanta.

At Talladega, our negotiation team consisted of local and regional FBI negotiators, including several Spanish-speakers who had helped resolve the earlier prison uprisings.

We formed two teams staffed with FBI and BOP negotiators, with native Spanish-speakers assigned to each team, and each team on duty for twelve-hour stints. I was the negotiation team leader for the evening shift, with FBI negotiator Pedro Toledo on hand as one of those chosen to communicate with the inmates directly in Spanish. The FBI's Hostage Rescue Team was also on hand, preparing an emergency assault plan in case violence erupted.

At a glance, Talladega might be mistaken for a large community college campus. A dozen or so modern, no-nonsense buildings in gray concrete were connected by walkways crossing grassy courtyards. The only indications of this institution's real purpose were the exceptionally small windows and the substantial perimeter fences. Those features clearly marked this as a prison, as did the fact that the BOP had correctional officers in full riot gear—helmets, body armor, weapons—surrounding Alpha Unit, the building the detainees had taken over.

Our teams had set up shop in the prison administration building across the courtyard, about a hundred yards away. We had captured the phone lines in and out of Alpha, but when we called in, either the detainees would refuse to answer or they would answer and immediately hang up. They knew that the FBI and prison authorities had outsmarted them last time, so now they were in no mood to talk. The situations in Atlanta and Oakdale had taught them what every negotiator knows: protracted discussion usually works to the advantage of the authorities. Now they wanted their demands met, plain and simple, end of story. Some were willing to return to Cuba; some were dead set against it. But none of them wanted to linger indefinitely in an American jail with no prospect of release.

It worked in our favor that inmates here had taken over only a single unit, rather than an entire prison, as had been the case in Atlanta and Oakdale. Modern prisons are highly modular so that problems like this can be contained. Alpha Unit consisted of rows of cells on two levels overlooking common areas, but the traditional bars beloved by the directors of old prison movies had been replaced by electronically operated steel doors with narrow slits for windows. Inside this prison within a prison, the detainees had created makeshift weapons and erected barricades behind which they held their eleven hostages.

We had every reason to be concerned about the safety of these abductees. Already, as is usual in a prison uprising, some inmates had used the chaos and confusion to carry out vendettas, with several stabbings as the result. We knew that among the group were dangerous, desperate men who might now reasonably conclude that there was no turning back.

It's much easier to gather information on hostage takers when the subjects in question are already prisoners. We had ready access to mental health records, criminal history records, and personal insights and observations from correctional officers who had daily contact with the subjects. We used these data to try to identify potential leaders as well as those most likely to carry out violent acts.

In Atlanta, there had been one prisoner so crazy that the Cubans tied him up with duct tape and put him outside. He had been known to throw his own feces at guards, and at one point he actually chewed off one of his own fingers.

There appeared to be no one quite that far gone at Talladega, but several inmates had very violent histories, including murder and rape. When an uprising is opportunistic, as this one seemed to have been— there was no evidence of significant advance planning, and inmates appeared to have spontaneously overpowered officers during prisoner recreation—it usually takes several days before a clear leadership structure emerges. This is not entirely surprising, given that few inmates have meaningful organizational skills or leadership abilities. Their normal behavior for working out differences is not consensus and cooperation but threats, intimidation, and violence. In our negotiations, we would try to encourage the reasonable people, but as of yet, no one would communicate except through banners hung from the rooftop asking the press to get involved and advocate on their behalf. The banners said, *We are not hungry for food but for freedom. Give it to us.*

On the second day, using the information gleaned from correctional officers, I prepared an assessment for the on-scene commander, Special Agent in Charge Al Whitaker, a man who seemed new to siege management, but who at least had surrounded himself with good people.

In my opinion, the inmates' refusal to engage in substantive negotiations reflected their lack of clear purpose and goals, as well as their conflicting agendas, which varied according to the status of each prisoner's case. The point of access I suggested was based on the fact that prisoners are like most people—they get used to creature comforts and a set routine, even if it's simply watching TV or working out in the gym. They don't like it when those simple pleasures are withdrawn, least of all food. At Talladega, inmate cooks prepared food in a central facility, after which meals were brought over to each unit. With no kitchen of their own, the Cuban detainees had gone for days now without food. In every brief conversation they demanded that we send in something for them to eat, but we had made it clear that they had to give us something in return. So far this had not led to anything positive, but I judged that hunger, properly manipulated, provided our best opportunity for leverage.

What prisoners want on day one of an incident, or even on day two, is often much different from what they are willing to accept only a few days later, after they come to see that they are not in as much control as they'd initially thought. It's no surprise, then, that a number of significant prison incidents have lasted around ten days or less, with the inmates ultimately accepting on the final day the deal that they could have had on day one. Simply put, inmates are more likely to make concessions or act reasonably when they get hungry, bored, and tired.

I suggested that prison employees begin frying bacon and brewing coffee, the smells of which would provide a powerful incentive for the inmates to come out from behind their barricades. This concept of "aromatic warfare," as I called it, had been used effectively by the NYPD in the 1970s, when Frank Bolz once fried bacon in the hallway of a house where he knew the barricaded subject was hungry.

The next day, at lunchtime, correctional officers set up a large outdoor grill not far from the front of Alpha Unit. Ostensibly, the grill was there to cook hamburgers for the officers in their riot gear, standing as a visible containment line around the facility. They tried not to obviously flaunt the food, but clearly inmates would be able to see and smell the grill.

That night, our Spanish-speaking negotiator, Pedro Toledo, continued to call in, and at last his persistence paid off. An inmate picked up the phone and said, "We want to talk. Outside. Right now."

This was our first real breakthrough in days, so Pedro and I immediately left the administration building and started walking across the courtyard. Correctional officers had erected mobile units with floodlights that shone on the walls of Alpha Unit. We could see the inmates in their blue denim prison uniforms emerging from the steel inner door of the unit and gathering against the heavy bars of the outer door. With their tattoos, head scarves, and occasional missing teeth, they looked the part of hardened criminals. Many of them had improvised weapons in their hands, shanks fashioned from scraps of wood or metal.

No data show that exposed face-to-face negotiations produce a better result—and all of the dozen or more U.S. negotiators who have been killed performing their duties over the years died in face-to-face situations. In this case, however, the potential payoff appeared to outweigh the risk.

With our snipers on alert, Pedro approached the men and began a dialogue; I followed about ten feet behind. Because a negotiator can easily get caught up in the dialogue and inadvertently put himself at risk, part of my job as his coach was to ride herd on him. Sure enough, in the intensity of his conversation, Pedro kept inching forward, and I kept reminding him to step back. After a while I was actually hanging on to the back of his jacket, tugging on it now and then to remind him not to get too close. I kept him at least thirty feet away from the inmates behind the bars at all times.

My Spanish is limited, but I could hear him saying the kinds of things we always say: "I hear you. We'll work on it. We need to get on the phone and talk."

Their most immediate demand was for food, but there were also heated denunciations of U.S. policy and rambling diatribes about what were seen as the injustices of each man's specific case. Despite Pedro's best efforts, what we emerged with was a grab bag of complaints rather than a coherent list of demands.

The next morning we handed off our shift to the other team, briefing them on the exchange we'd had the night before. I told the day shift about the weapons we'd seen, and reminded them to keep their distance if they decided to move forward, as we had. But when we returned twelve hours later to relieve them, I saw surveillance photographs lying on the desk showing my colleague Clint Van Zandt, the other negotiation team leader from SOARU, and one of the other Spanish-speaking negotiators leaning on the bars while speaking to some of the same Cubans. They were within inches of one another. In the photographs you could see the makeshift weapons the prisoners were brandishing.

We had a meeting later to discuss this incident, and tempers flared. Van Zandt said that his proximity had been necessary to show the

Cuban inmates that we were not afraid of them. He felt that this was important culturally. I didn't agree with his rationale then and I still don't. In my mind, while some risks are unavoidable, safety should always be the primary consideration when negotiating. Thankfully this unnecessary safety breach didn't happen again.

Despite these forays and the limited rapport they created, our engagement with the inmates remained more of a running argument than a true negotiation. All in all, however, we were fortunate to be in a stalemate rather than an escalating crisis. The question of when we might need to take decisive action—an assault—was always on our minds, but so far things had remained sufficiently calm for us to pursue our measured course.

On Wednesday, August 28, seven days into the standoff, the inmates suddenly asked to meet with Cynthia Corzo, a reporter from *El Nuevo Herald,* the Spanish-language edition of the *Miami Herald.*

Corzo proved willing, and we agreed to the dialogue, demanding in exchange that the inmates release one hostage. A few hours later, Kitty Suddeth, a twenty-four-year-old prison secretary, appeared at the gate looking like death warmed over. For seven days she had lived in the same clothes, without food, without the chance to wash, and in fear for her life. Correctional officers rushed to support her as she came out into the courtyard. Her ordeal had been so terrifying that she would never return to prison work.

We told the inmates that they could send several representatives to meet with Corzo. Correctional officers put a table and chairs outside the main door to Alpha Unit and set up a canopy overhead to block the sun. Corzo met with them in three separate sessions, allowing the men to tell their side of the story.

Meanwhile, Kitty Suddeth had provided important information that changed our view of the gravity of the situation. She warned us that whatever fragile leadership had once existed was now losing control. The inmates had begun to fight among themselves, and in her opinion, the more dangerous individuals were gaining influence.

Our negotiators continued to hold out the promise of food in exchange for hostages being released. We did achieve one concession when the inmates next agreed to allow prison doctors to assist one of the hostages, a correctional officer with high blood pressure. He came to the front gate, and a medic—actually an FBI agent—checked his blood pressure and provided him with necessary medications. This agent was then allowed to converse briefly with and provide first aid to the rest of the hostages at the front entrance, one at a time. During this exchange, some managed to slip notes to our agent expressing their belief that they were about to die and that this might be their last opportunity to communicate with their loved ones. The grim evidence they cited was that they had been ordered to place their identification cards in a pillowcase. They were told that one card would be drawn and that person would be killed.

Agent Whitaker took this as a sign that it was time to move in with a tactical assault, and I concurred. I still felt that the long-term prospects for surrender were good, but I also felt that it was highly probable that at least one hostage would die before we would be able to bring the inmates to the point of standing down. Given this very real threat, it was time to move.

One of the advantages in dealing with a siege in a prison is the availability of detailed plans of the facility. HRT and BOP tactical officers had removed inmates from another unit within the prison that was identical to Alpha, and they had used it to practice each step of how they would enter, secure the hostages, and subdue the inmates. Then again, prisons are made to keep inmates from getting out, which means that they are none too easy for tactical officers to breach.

A half dozen FBI and BOP officials met in the warden's conference room to go over the plan. HRT had already assembled all the equipment and personnel required, including several FBI field SWAT teams. They were under the command of Special Agent Dick Rogers, the new commander of the HRT. Tall, with ramrod-straight posture and red hair clipped in a military style, Rogers had served as a noncommissioned officer in the military. He was clearly type A; I noticed that his jaw seemed perpetually tense, as if he was ready to spring on someone at any moment. His nickname, I would come to find out later, was "Sergeant Severe."

Though a tactical operation was in the works, I emphasized to the others that our job as negotiators was not over yet. Crisis management works most effectively when both elements, tactical and negotiation, work in close coordination. Given the challenges of breaking in to a prison, our job would be to soften up the inmates to minimize their ability to resist and maximize the chances that all the hostages would come out unharmed.

During an assault, hostage takers' first instinct is to preserve their own lives rather than to harm hostages, but the longer an assault drags on, the greater the possibility of hostage execution. Thus the circumstances placed a premium on quick and decisive action.

For our part, the negotiation team developed a plan to lull the inmates into complacency, a plan that I admit sounds like something out of an old folk tale. We recommended that we pretend to give in to their demand for food with no preconditions. We felt that such an apparent victory would make them lower their guard. The risk with this plan was that if for some reason the assault had to be postponed, our having provided them food without getting something in return would weaken our bargaining position. But that was a risk worth taking.

At a more biochemical level, the rest of the plan called for the food to be as rich and plentiful as the prison kitchens could manage. We ordered up steaks and potatoes with gravy, as well as cakes and pies. We really went over the top, assuming that these famished men, accustomed in the best of times to a limited prison diet, would gorge themselves at the first sight of this high-calorie feast.

That evening Pedro got on the phone and delivered what appeared to the inmates to be a major concession. "Okay, you get your food. We're going to feed you, so don't hurt anyone. Stay cool."

In the bright glare of the mobile floodlights, correctional officers brought the food over on heavy aluminum carts. From our vantage point in the administration building, we watched through binoculars as the men came to the gate and immediately began to grab the food, even before the carts were rolled inside.

We waited about an hour, and then Pedro called again. Apparently the food had begun to work as we had hoped. There were sounds of celebration in the background, and the inmates who spoke sounded arrogant and cocky. "We want more and better food tomorrow," they said. "You cocksuckers better deliver some real Cuban food this time."

It appeared that the inmates had taken our bait and literally swallowed it, hook, line, and sinker.

HRT waited until well after midnight, then began to move their men into ready position. Pedro stayed by the phone, but I stepped outside to see two lines of big black SUVs slowly and deliberately roll across the campus toward Alpha Unit. The trucks stopped, and two agents in full armor ran ahead to the front gate, bent down for a moment, then ran back. At precisely 3:43 a.m., ten days after the siege had begun, a series of explosions blew open the front entrance of Alpha Unit and lit up the sky.

HRT and SWAT members piled out of the SUVs and stormed the building. They carried ladders, saws that could cut through steel, and additional explosives. Following the plan they had practiced, they fanned out through the building, quickly located the three separate rooms where hostages were being held, and secured their safety. Other teams of HRT and SWAT personnel then moved to their assigned sections and took control of all of the inmates. Despite the risks they faced, these tactical teams performed brilliantly and secured the prisoners and the prison without firing a single shot.

All the evidence suggested that our two-part plan had worked like a charm and that the rich feast, combined with a sense of victory, had lulled the inmates into a complacent slumber.

All hostages were freed unharmed, and the next day, thirty-one of the Talladega detainees were boarded onto an aircraft and flown back to Cuba.

This was a great moment for the FBI, compelling validation—as if more were needed—of the wisdom of the Bureau's standard approach to crisis management, an approach that integrates negotiation and tactical operations as two parts of the same whole. From the beginning of the special operations units in the late seventies, authority for balancing the role to be played by each unit was in the hands of the on-scene commander, usually the Special Agent in Charge for that location. As I saw it, Talladega was a textbook case of how negotiation and tactical operations can work hand in glove to bring a dangerous situation to closure without bloodshed. Here negotiation had worked like an artillery barrage to soften up the opposition and gain critical intelligence information from a released hostage, enabling the tactical forces to move in with far greater chances of success. But as the after-action review took place I began to wonder whether the Bureau fully appreciated the negotiation team's role in the successful rescue. Our negotiation staff at Quantico consisted of three people; HRT had sixty-five and had a budget and training time to match. Negotiation wasn't even really thought of in the same light.

Unfortunately, it would soon become clear that in fact negotiators were considered by some as subservient to the tactical team. After Talladega, the balance would shift more toward tactics, giving those in charge of tactical assaults far more power and influence. The limited lesson that some officials took away from the Talladega success would have escalating and tragic consequences.

America in the early 1990s saw a series of antigovernment and cult-like groups, driven by extreme religious and political sentiments, retreating into psychological bunkers, as well as actual compounds where they chose to isolate themselves from mainstream society. These groups would provide one of the thorniest problems ever to confront the FBI. First, dealing with these groups would directly expose the unresolved tension within the Bureau that pitted negotiation advocates against those who favored hard-line tactics. Second, FBI missteps would quickly add fuel to the brushfire of separatist antigovernment movements.

The flash point for that brushfire was a confrontation involving a former army soldier and Iowa factory worker named Randy Weaver. He and his wife, Vicki, had sought to escape what they saw as a corrupt world by squatting on twenty acres of land in Idaho. Vicki, especially, was deeply religious. She saw the "end times" approaching, the apocalyptical battle described in the book of Revelation between God's chosen few and the forces of evil. The Weavers hoped that they and their children could ride out the turmoil in their cabin on Ruby Ridge, near the town of Naples, in Boundary County, Idaho.

In 1984, a series of disputes over trespassing onto a neighbor's property and frequent gunfire brought Randy Weaver to the attention of local authorities. In 1986, Weaver attended a meeting of the Aryan Nations, a right-wing separatist group, where he got to know a man serving as an informant for the Bureau of Alcohol, Tobacco, and Firearms (ATF). In 1989, the informant claimed that Weaver sold him two sawed-off shotguns, weapons that federal law prohibits. In 1990, a grand jury indicted Weaver for making and distributing illegal weapons. Weaver was arrested and released on bail, but he failed to show up for his trial date. At that point, relations between Weaver and the government went from bad to worse.

To avoid further exposure to arrest, Weaver stayed holed up in his remote cabin on Ruby Ridge and he never left the property. On August 21, 1992, a surveillance team of six U.S. marshals carrying M16 rifles and wearing night vision goggles climbed up Ruby Ridge to scout out areas where they might arrest Weaver away from his cabin. Their movement and scent alerted Weaver's dogs, which began to bark. Weaver, his fourteen-year-old son, Sammy, and Kevin Harris, a family friend, armed themselves, let the dogs go, and followed along to investigate.

How exactly it began is not entirely clear, but an exchange of fire broke out on Ruby Ridge, and within a brief while, Deputy Marshal William Degan lay dead, as did Sammy Weaver and one of the dogs. Randy Weaver and Harris retreated into the cabin, along with Weaver's wife, Vicki, and the other Weaver children. The standoff that ensued would last for ten days.

I was in Bermuda with Carol at the time, celebrating our eighteenth wedding anniversary and attempting to get away from it all in a small guesthouse with no telephone or television. It was one of the few times in my career that I've been fully isolated. Nonetheless, I found a newspaper in a local store, and spread across the page above the fold was an article about the siege.

I used the phone at a nearby hotel and immediately called my boss, Charlie Prouty, back at Quantico. Charlie briefed me on what he knew and told me to continue with my vacation for now, but to be prepared to respond when I returned.

Already en route to Idaho was my partner, Fred Lanceley. With him on a military C-141 aircraft was Dick Rogers, who was in charge of HRT and had led the successful assault at Talladega. His HRT and my team were both at Quantico and we saw each other in the gym daily. He was cordial but a bit of a loner, and we hadn't really gotten to know each other after Talladega. After joining the FBI, Rogers had been a field agent in Arizona, and he had also worked in the bomb tech section at FBI headquarters in Washington. True to his "Sergeant Severe" moniker, he epitomized the tough-guy school of law enforcement. As a grade 15 Assistant Special Agent in Charge (ASAC), the equivalent of a colonel in the army, Dick was one rank higher than either Fred or me. While FBI protocol was that the negotiation and tactical programs were to be given equal weight during any incident, the reality was the HRT had more than sixty-five agents, millions of dollars of equipment, and a more senior manager who, especially after the success at Talladega, had greater access to and influence with key FBI decision makers. The FBI's historical desire to be tough on criminals naturally favored tactics over talk.

When they arrived in Idaho, Dick briefed his team on the current situation and issued the rules of engagement. It became clear to Fred that Dick had already decided that this was a tactical situation only, and there would be no negotiation. Despite this, Fred said he would help develop information in the command post and be available if needed for negotiations.

Perhaps the death of a U.S. marshal had pushed Rogers immediately into action mode. But those of us who dealt with him could not escape the feeling that he also never appreciated the important supportive role negotiators had played in softening up the Talladega inmates, thus clearing the way for a successful assault. As would become obvious as events unfolded, Rogers had no interest in dealing with Randy Weaver through any means other than force. And in the absence of any other experienced, countervailing FBI command leadership on the ground in Idaho, Dick Rogers would literally call the shots.

Almost immediately upon arrival at Ruby Ridge on August 22, Rogers sent FBI HRT snipers and observers up the mountain to reconnoiter the Weaver cabin. He did so with rules of engagement that were substantially less restrictive than those customarily employed. The normal rules state that FBI agents may use their weapons only to protect their own lives or the lives of others, or if they feel they are in danger of serious bodily harm. But according to a Justice Department task force that subsequently investigated the incident, Dick Rogers's rules "instructed the snipers that before a surrender announcement was made they could and should shoot all armed adult males appearing outside the cabin." These rules not only contradicted long-standing FBI policy, they were later found to be unconstitutional.

This was a self-fulfilling approach, and it led quickly to disaster. Hearing the noise of an FBI helicopter, Weaver, his sixteen-year-old daughter, and his friend Kevin Harris stepped out of the cabin. They were unaware of the FBI's presence. Without issuing a warning, an HRT sniper fired once, wounding Weaver. As the three retreated back toward the cabin door, the sniper fired again, thinking he had missed with his first shot. This second bullet went through a door, and hit Vicki Weaver in the head; it then passed through Harris's chest. Harris would survive, but Vicki Weaver, who had been standing just inside the door, out of sight, holding her ten-month-old-daughter, Elisheba, died on the spot.

With Weaver's son Sammy and Vicki now dead, and Randy Weaver and Harris wounded, what remained of the Weaver family stayed in the cabin for another ten days. When FBI headquarters instructed that negotiation efforts commence, Fred went up the hill in an armored personnel carrier and used a bullhorn just outside of the cabin to try to communicate, but they now refused all of his efforts. Based on what had transpired, they could only assume that the government was intent on killing them; not too surprisingly, they were reluctant to talk.

Eventually, former Green Beret James "Bo" Gritz, a heavily decorated Vietnam vet who had made a second career as a survivalist, conspiracy theorist, and liaison to various right-wing groups, appeared on the scene, offering to serve as an intermediary in an effort to secure a peaceful surrender. He convinced the team that he had enough in common with Weaver that he would be able to talk him out. Fred coached Gritz on the approach he should take, which was to convince those inside that they would not be harmed if they came out peacefully. Over a period of several days, with Fred's coaching, Gritz and Jack McLamb, another right-wing figure, helped convince Weaver and his family to come out by acting as their escorts down the mountain.

Harris surrendered first, followed the next day by Weaver and his three daughters. Despite all the violence in the first hours of this incident, once they established good communications, the situation was resolved without any further loss of life, a testament to the value of negotiations.

Weaver was charged in federal court with a variety of crimes, including murder, conspiracy, failure to appear, and making and possessing unregistered weapons. But given countervailing charges of government misconduct—primarily the use of excessive force—he was eventually acquitted on all counts except failure to appear. Ultimately, the federal government awarded Weaver $100,000 in damages and $1 million to each of his daughters.

Because of Hurricane Andrew striking Florida at the time, this infamous incident received only limited publicity at first, mostly in regional papers. However, news of the incident quickly spread to members of right-wing militias, becoming a rallying cry and recruiting tool for those opposed to government authority. It would be among the motivations for the 1995 Oklahoma City bombing that killed 168 people.

Equally tragic, the FBI made no immediate attempt to learn from its mistakes. The same inclination to use force, or "action imperative," would prevail with even more horrific consequences the next time the FBI was summoned to a major siege incident. This would occur only six months later with another group of people driven to extremes, gathered at a place with the inauspicious name of Ranch Apocalypse.

CHAPTER SEVEN

NEGOTIATING WITH
THE SINFUL MESSIAH

*There is nobody as enslaved as the fanatic, the person in whom one
impulse, one value, has assumed ascendancy over all others.*
—Milton R. Sapirstein

On February 28, 1993, I was with my family, just leaving the parking lot of our local hardware store in Virginia, when my beeper sounded. I pulled in to a Burger King parking lot and called my boss, Rob Grace, at Quantico. An armed force of eighty ATF agents had just that morning converged on the isolated compound of a religious group living in Mount Carmel, Texas, near Waco. The plan had been to execute a search warrant on the compound and an arrest warrant on weapons charges against the group's leader, Vernon Wayne Howell, also known as David Koresh. There were also past allegations of child abuse, so the plan included securing the group's children, then conducting a thorough search. But apparently the action had been carried out more like an assault than an investigation. As the lead ATF agent approached the entrance to Koresh's Ranch Apocalypse, all hell broke loose. Four ATF agents and several members of Koresh's group were killed.

When I arrived at the small airport in northern Virginia, I saw two FBI planes, one large and one small. I stood on the tarmac and watched as Dick Rogers, along with other senior FBI and ATF officials, boarded the larger one, an executive jet. I boarded the much slower propeller plane to which I was assigned.

Virginia to Texas is a long flight for a piston-driven aircraft, especially one that needs to stop in Little Rock on the way to refuel. As I flew west, it occurred to me that the FBI's travel priorities spoke volumes. The idea that the head of HRT needed to be rushed to the scene, while the head of the negotiation team could follow along later, was a clear indication of the mind-set after Talladega. The narrative that had emerged from that prison riot was that HRT had carried the day, to the exclusion of other components, and Dick Rogers's stock had never been higher. The disaster that followed from his preemptive actions at Ruby Ridge had done nothing to tarnish that image within the FBI, at least not yet. If anything, critical accounts of what had happened there created something of a bunker mentality among certain elements at FBI headquarters. For my own part, I was surprised that Rogers still had his job in spite of having overseen the debacle at Ruby Ridge. Then again, meting out punishment to the HRT commander would have been an admission of the gross errors of judgment that had taken place in Idaho.

At 10:00 p.m. Central Time, our small plane came down on the runway of a former Air Force base a few miles outside Waco. This facility was now Texas State Technical College, and it would serve as our command post. I entered the hangar and made my way past a massive C-5 military aircraft there for repair, then up a set of concrete stairs along one side. As I reached the top, I observed a large office in which FBI technicians were setting up telephone lines and computers. I continued on toward a smaller office in the rear where I was told I would find Jeff Jamar, the Special Agent in Charge of the San Antonio FBI office. Jamar was the FBI on-scene commander.

As I entered the room I saw a big man with broad shoulders, around six feet four inches tall, who had the tense and focused look of a pro football player on game day. Jeff Jamar had a reputation as a no-nonsense leader, and his demeanor was so intimidating that, as I would quickly learn, most of his subordinates tried to avoid him whenever possible. They also expended a great deal of energy speculating about, and trying to accommodate, his changing and often very angry moods.

I introduced myself, and he gave me a cordial but perfunctory summary of events so far. Dick Rogers and some of his tactical team had set up a forward command post just outside the Koresh compound, about eight miles away. He also confirmed that while ATF was still nominally in charge, the murder of federal agents was now a matter for the Bureau, not ATF. We were simply waiting for word from Washington that the attorney general had transferred authority to the FBI. The currently operating negotiation team was set up in an old military barracks building a short distance away, and Jamar deputized one of his assistants to show me the way.

As we walked across the base, the young agent briefed me on the overall mood of everyone involved. It was clear that the ATF personnel were in shock. He also shared some information about the group we were dealing with, who called themselves Branch Davidians.

In sum, David Koresh, born Vernon Wayne Howell, sounded like a charismatic con artist—perhaps more accurately described as an antisocial personality or sociopath. The Branch Davidians were a breakaway sect of the Seventh-day Adventist Church. He and more than a hundred followers had holed up at the ranch just outside town. Like Vicki Weaver, the Davidians believed in the book of Revelation's prophecies that the forces of evil will be unleashed during the "end times," and the righteous will have to do battle with them. In preparation, the Davidians had stockpiled automatic weapons and large amounts of ammunition, practiced defensive actions, grew their own food, and lived without modern amenities. Meanwhile, their unusual communal lifestyle also made them an object of curiosity and even suspicion among their neighbors. The Davidians were known to derive income from dealing in weapons. Koresh had a history of run-ins with the law, and there were persistent questions as to whether he was using his status as a religious leader to sexually exploit his followers, including young children. Koresh's charisma allowed him to gain control over people desperately seeking religious enlightenment. Despite having a learning disability, he had memorized large passages of the Bible at a young age and could string together seemingly unrelated verses of scripture to prove any point he wished. He told his followers that he was both the son of God and a sinner—the sinful messiah. He alone was able to drink alcohol, have sex with most of the women, have air-conditioning in his room, watch television, and avoid doing any physical labor at the compound. In essence, he told his followers to do as he said rather than as he did.

Toward the end of 1992, a UPS driver noticed the outline of grenade casings in packages he was delivering to the compound. He alerted authorities, and shortly thereafter, an undercover agent working for ATF infiltrated the Davidian community. He observed that the Davidians had modified certain weapons to make them fully automatic, which was not only a violation of federal law but also a clear sign of their belief that they had to prepare for Armageddon.

Whatever had led ATF to proceed with the aggressive show of force they had launched that morning, their hope for success had been based in part on the expectation of surprise. Informants had told them that the Davidians locked away their guns on Sundays, the first day after their Sabbath, and would be focused on working outside on a large addition to the compound.

But surprise was simply not in the cards. Early in the morning, television news teams from Waco had been on the road already, heading to the compound, known as Mount Carmel or Ranch Apocalypse. Who tipped them off to impending events? What is known is that one news crew asked directions to Mount Carmel from a rural mailman they encountered at a country crossroads not far away. What they didn't know was that this mailman was David Jones, the brother-in-law of David Koresh.

Jones quickly drove back to the compound and relayed this information to Koresh, who at the time was meeting inside the compound with undercover ATF agent Robert Rodriquez, who had rented a home nearby posing as a student and feigning interest in learning about the Davidians' beliefs. Koresh broke off their religious counseling session and told Rodriquez, "They're coming to get us, Robert." Rodriquez hastily departed and immediately reported the comment to his superiors at ATF. Though they had lost the element of surprise, ATF leaders chose to move forward anyway, a fatal error.

The exact details of what happened as the ATF tactical units approached the entrance to the compound are unclear. But a horrendous firefight broke out at 9:45 a.m. and continued for two and a half hours. By the time the shooting died down, four ATF agents lay dead and sixteen had been wounded. Five Branch Davidians were killed; many others had been wounded, including Koresh himself.

For Koresh, this action only confirmed his view of federal authorities as reckless oppressors. But perhaps its most ill-conceived aspect was that it played into Koresh's interpretation of biblical prophecy. The book of Revelation uses the term *Babylon* to refer to the earthly powers that oppress the righteous and with whom the righteous will have to do battle before the day of judgment. Here at the door of Ranch Apocalypse, in full tactical gear, were the "Babylonian" ATF agents. Rather than intimidating Koresh and his followers, the hostile display served merely to confirm for them that what the prophecies had foretold was at hand.

Shortly after the shooting started, Lieutenant Larry Lynch of the McLennan County Sheriff's Department received a call from Koresh, seeking to broker a cease-fire at the Waco Police Department where a rear command post had been set up. The cease-fire secured, the ATF agents were able to move forward and retrieve their casualties. In return, ATF agreed to call off the raid, withdraw, and stay off the Davidians' property. With live coverage on television, news of the incident quickly spread, and multiple law enforcement agencies, including the Texas Rangers and the Texas Department of Public Safety, rushed to the scene.

The FBI negotiation team had set up in a long, narrow barracks that looked to be of World War II vintage. Inside was a large open space, no doubt once filled with military bunk beds. In the rear was a small room where officers had positioned themselves for telephone communication with the Davidians. ATF had no trained negotiators at this time.

My first impression upon entering was that there were far too many men in this small space to carry out effective work. About a dozen ATF agents and others sat around in their blue tactical jumpsuits. With heads in hands and ashen faces, many of them looked like soldiers who had just survived an ambush, but without the consolation of victory. They appeared so tired and downtrodden that I was surprised they had not yet been sent home.

ATF supervisor Jim Cavanaugh was then functioning as the primary negotiator and was on the phone with Koresh. He introduced me to his ATF colleagues, as well as to some negotiators from the Austin Police Department who had also come up to help out. I also spoke on the phone with FBI Supervisory Special Agent Byron Sage, from the Austin

FBI office. He was still at the police department with Lieutenant Lynch; they'd been working all day negotiating on a second phone line in the compound.

Cavanaugh told me that tactical units had established an inner perimeter around the compound, with a motor home serving as a forward command post. In a slightly larger concentric circle, the sheriff's department and Texas Department of Public Safety had established an outer perimeter to control access. Beyond that second perimeter, the news media gathered in droves.

Cavanaugh described conversations to date with Koresh, which, after the cease-fire, had been perfunctory. He explained to me that they were using two phone lines to communicate with the compound, the one being handled at the police department by Lynch and Sage, which connected to Wayne Martin, an attorney and Davidian who conducted business from inside the compound, and the second reaching Koresh himself. I made a mental note to consolidate those lines when the opportunity arose. To gain control of the situation, we needed to control and limit all communication in and out. In time, we would want to install a military-style field telephone of our own, to avoid any problems should standard phone lines be cut.

The more immediate problem was that neither of these existing phone lines had been secured so that those inside could speak only with the authorities. Consequently, these lines were frequently tied up by news organizations attempting to land a big interview. Earlier in the day, the tabloid television show *A Current Affair* had convinced an operator to break in to an ongoing negotiation call so that their on-camera personality could speak with Koresh. Koresh had also used his phone line to call his mother and give her his last goodbye, something I would not have wanted to happen.

On the plus side, I learned that the negotiation process had already borne fruit. At 9:03 p.m., about an hour before I had landed in Waco, the negotiation team had delivered on a promise to have a local radio station recite a verse of scripture. In return, Koresh had allowed two children to leave the compound, and then another two, forty minutes later. Four down and perhaps a hundred left to go.

Byron Sage and I linked up in the early morning hours to consult with SAC Jamar. He said that a decision was forthcoming on changing lead agency status to the FBI. Rogers was already at the forward command post, and Jamar wanted our team to be ready to take over negotiations as soon as possible. I immediately recommended that we set up a negotiation operations center, or NOC, inside the hangar, in a separate space immediately adjacent to the FBI command post. I requested that technical personnel act quickly to capture the two telephone lines leading into the compound to thwart further media interference and other outside calls. I also requested authorization from Jamar to bring additional FBI field negotiators to Waco. As I saw it, the negotiation process could become quite complex and protracted.

"I think you're right about that," Jamar said. Then he nodded. "Bring in your boys."

I then asked about how we would coordinate our negotiation efforts with the tactical command. Jamar said that communication with Rogers's group should go through him, since Rogers was up forward. I should consult with Jamar, and he would communicate with Rogers. Again, this was a shift that should have alerted me to what was to come, since standard FBI protocol called for a closer exchange between negotiators and the HRT.

"To tell you the truth, sir, I'd much prefer that we all confer directly, which is the way—"

"I think we'll do fine with the procedure I laid out," Jamar said.

I looked at him, and his eyes made clear that our discussion was over.

I went back to the barracks, where Jim Cavanaugh and most of his team had been working since around noon. They asked me to take on primary negotiation responsibilities through the early morning hours so that they could get some rest. Rick Shirley, an experienced negotiator from Austin PD, and a few others, would stay on to assist me.

It was time for me to get on the phone and introduce myself to Koresh. Tired as they were, the ATF men were slow to leave, so to avoid any misunderstandings, I thought it best to be up front and provide some perspective. "If you guys are going to hang around, you have to understand that Koresh is really pissed at the ATF, and to some extent I have to run with that. I have to play up being FBI, not ATF, so if it sounds like I'm making you out to be the bad guys... well, it's just what I have to do. So I hope you understand why I'm doing it." I looked into each of the tired faces staring back at me. Cavanaugh concurred and most of the others nodded in agreement. At 12:20 a.m., just before the ATF team left, the Davidians released two more children (now six in total).

Cavanaugh stayed behind to introduce me to Koresh. He rang up the compound and, once he had Koresh on the phone, explained the transfer that was taking place. He then handed me the phone.

I took a deep breath and said, "Hi, David. This is Gary. I just got down here, and I want to make sure that you and your family get out of this situation safe and sound."

"Hey," he said. "Gary, huh. So who'd you say you were with, Gary?"

"The FBI."

"Hmm."

Koresh sounded tired as well. Obviously it had been a very long day for him. After introductions, we chatted for a while, and I asked him to tell me about what had happened. As he began to describe the raid from his perspective, I was struck by how willing he was to talk about what had happened, and by his relatively calm demeanor. He was angry, but it was a contained anger, directed at ATF. He seemed to be trying to make his case to me.

"I just don't get it," he said. "Why did those guys have to come in here shooting the place up? It just wasn't necessary...."

And then I heard him groan, which provided an opening.

"I understand you were hit by a bullet," I said. "You know, we can get you some medical attention right away, David. You just need to come out of there."

"I'm all right," he said.

"That's up to you," I said. "But if you come out, I assure you that every one of your people will be treated with dignity and respect."

"Yeah," he said. "We're not ready to come out."

Throughout the night, Koresh and I would speak on the phone every couple of hours. I had two basic objectives in continuing to call him back. First, I wanted to establish some trust between us. Second, I wanted to try to secure the release of additional children.

"You know, David, the FBI is in charge now. We weren't involved in the shootout. We're here for just one reason, and that's to reach a peaceful resolution. After that, we'll investigate what exactly happened and determine the truth. But first we have to end this standoff. Which is why we really need you to come on out peacefully."

Koresh continued to brush aside my requests for him to surrender, so I continued to press, but not too hard.

"You and I need to keep working to resolve this peacefully. You know, what would really help is if you let some more of your people come out. Would you be willing to do that?"

"I'll think about it," he said.

Just before dawn, he told me he would release two more children in the morning. At 8:22, he followed through on his promise.

The negotiation team had now secured a total of eight youngsters from inside the compound. It was becoming clear to me that we were not going to get any grand surrender right away or all at once, but we might very likely continue to get a few individuals out in periodic clusters.

Later that afternoon, at a quarter to five, the attorney general officially passed operational control of the incident to the FBI. We moved the negotiation team over to the FBI command post, which was now fully functioning. One of our first actions was to capture both telephone lines into the compound. Now when the Davidians picked up their phone, they got us and nobody else.

With full responsibility for the negotiation effort, I set up two teams operating in twelve-hour shifts, with me as the overall negotiation coordinator. Team leaders would be Byron Sage and Jim Botting, an experienced negotiator who had flown in from Los Angeles at my request. We also relied on Jim Cavanaugh from ATF, who had already developed some rapport with Koresh. My job would be to guide strategy, not to be the person on the phone. I also asked the Austin Police and McLennan County negotiators to remain on our team to assist.

As the incident progressed over the coming days and weeks, I would stagger my long, sixteen-plus-hour days over portions of both shifts. My goal was to maintain continuity and a consistent strategy in our approach, and also to act as a bridge between the two teams. Another large part of my job would be to regularly brief the man with overall responsibility, SAC Jamar, as well as the three other SACs who had flown in from New Orleans, El Paso, and Oklahoma City to assist in managing the incident.

Managing a crisis properly depends on managing information. In the NOC we posted situation boards on the walls that enabled everyone to stay up to date with critical information. An adjacent smaller room was for the exclusive use of the active negotiation team. Each core team consisted of five individuals. A coach sat next to the primary negotiator, monitoring the call and passing notes as required. Another negotiator operated the phone system and made sure the tape recorder was working properly for post-conversation analysis. The fourth team member served as the scribe, maintaining a log of key points in the discussion. These four negotiators and the shift team leader, as well as myself, were the only ones allowed in the room during live negotiations.

The remaining members of the larger negotiation team, as well as the profilers on hand to develop background information, were able to listen via a speaker setup in the larger adjacent room. Immediately after each negotiation session these two groups would sit together to assess the last call and prepare for the next. I made certain that nothing else was undertaken until these steps were completed. This was a hard-and-fast rule so that we would always be prepared for any unexpected next contact from the Davidians.

As the crisis continued, each day I would deliver an oral summary of each significant call to SAC Jamar and any other on-duty SACs, then follow up with written reports. We then faxed these summaries and our recommendations to experienced negotiators stationed at FBI headquarters back in Washington, D.C., who would present them and explain their meaning to senior FBI executives. I knew it was essential that our views reach senior management without any filters. Meanwhile, Rogers shuttled between the perimeter and the command post several times a day. I would sometimes see him in Jamar's office, but he rarely did more than stick his head into the negotiation operations center.

On March 1, at 4:48 p.m., Koresh released two more children, bringing to ten the total number of those who had come out. At 8:27 that evening, day two of the siege, the number rose to twelve.

Each time a child was to be released, the HRT liaison at NOC would radio the tactical agents just outside the ranch and advise them to move forward to pick up the released children. I would then dispatch negotiators to the inner perimeter, eight miles from our location, to pick up the children and drive them back to the NOC.

The children came out with notes pinned on them giving instructions as to where they were to be sent, mostly to relatives who were not Davidians. Our agents brought them into the NOC, and often a kid would sit in the negotiator's lap while he or she would call the compound to announce the child's safe arrival. To our surprise, Koresh allowed the parents to come to the phone each time and personally verify that their child was well and being treated with care.

We realized that these exchanges helped Koresh to retain his image as a caring and benign autocrat among his followers. I didn't believe he was allowing these children to leave out of genuine concern for their safety; rather his intent seemed to be to embolden the parents who stayed behind, freeing them from parental concern so that they would fight to the death for him.

At this stage of the ordeal we were still trying to piece together a complete picture of who was with Koresh inside the compound. By speaking first with the children and then with their parents, we were able to fully identify a large number of the adults. This contact also allowed us to impress upon the parents that we did not want to see any further harm come to anyone inside, to personalize ourselves to them.

At this point, we had brought out twelve children, already a far better outcome than one might have expected given the gun battle that had raged only a day before. But despite that progress, our agents' tenderness with the children, and our attention to the parents' concerns, all was not sweetness and light. The Davidians inside the compound had heavy weapons. Two of the ATF agents who died had been killed by a .50 caliber sniper rifle. The barren countryside around the compound provided nothing more than a few mesquite trees as cover, and thus the HRT teams had brought in armored vehicles from the army base at nearby Fort Hood out of necessity, for adequate protection against the Davidians' arsenal. While this was a reasonable precaution, the unintended consequence was to exacerbate the mixed message that permeated the entire undertaking. While negotiators tried to show understanding and find common ground, the tactical people couldn't help but present a warlike image that heightened the tension. An empathetic voice over the phone can only do so much to offset the powerful impression available to the subject's own eyes.

With this in mind, we redoubled our efforts to demonstrate peaceful intentions, as well as our resolve to assist the Davidians in coming out and rejoining their children. Our profilers' research told us that Koresh had for some time been preaching the necessity of martyrdom in the final confrontation with Babylon. The biblical imagery was now reinforced by his having been shot. In terms he could appropriate from the book of Revelation, "the lamb had been wounded." We tried not to give him any more evidence to use in convincing his followers that this was the ultimate showdown between the forces of good and the forces of evil. By appearing reasonable and willing to help, we tried to show that the FBI was not, as he might suggest, Babylon.

Before the siege, a documentary film about the Davidians had been produced by the Australian version of *20/20* as a result of child-abuse complaints made by two ejected Davidians from Australia. The film footage was instructive. They had filmed Koresh giving lengthy sermons to his followers at the compound. When our profilers brought these tapes in for us to review, the man we observed, with his silky smile, air of superiority, and emotionally laden sermonizing, came across as a slick con artist more than anything else. But we were detached law enforcement officers, not naive seekers after enlightenment. As we examined the faces of his followers, they appeared absolutely mesmerized, hanging on his every word. Comparing various statements he had made on these tapes, as well as statements he made to us, we could also see how easily he altered his stated beliefs to serve whatever seemed to be in his interest at the moment. If there had ever been any doubt, this persuaded us that arguing religion with him would be a fool's game. He may have truly believed that he had some divine mission, but in my opinion, he was using religion primarily as a tool for manipulating and controlling others. In addition, the local newspaper in Waco had begun running a series of articles titled "The Sinful Messiah," which provided more useful information about the Davidians and how they functioned.

During these first few days, we learned that Koresh's tenure with the Davidians had hit a rocky patch a few years earlier. He had pursued the elderly widow of Branch Davidian founder Benjamin Roden and wound up having a romantic relationship with her. This led to a confrontation for control with Roden's son, George, which culminated in a gunfight. Koresh was subsequently arrested and prosecuted for assault, but the jury found him innocent.

I discussed this with my negotiation teams, and as a result, our primary negotiators began to use that incident to remind Koresh that the court system could be fair. Henry Garcia, who had become our primary negotiator during the day shift, hit this theme hard. The American legal system had sided with him in the past, so there was no reason for him not to be able to expect a fair trial for the deaths of the ATF agents. At one point he said he would be willing to come out and be judged by what he called "your law," but he did not say when. Later that night, Koresh released two more children, bringing the total to fourteen.

At 10:06 p.m. on March 1, Henry was on the phone with Koresh when the Davidian leader made an offer out of the blue. If we allowed him to deliver a nationwide broadcast, then he and his followers would surrender peacefully. With a hand signal I encouraged Henry to pursue this in more detail.

"Okay, David," Henry said. "Let's see what we can do. What sort of message do you want to convey?"

"I want to speak about the book of Revelation," Koresh said.

Around the room, we exchanged knowing glances. Fresh on our minds was the 1978 incident in Jonestown, Guyana, when Reverend Jim Jones coerced over 900 of his People's Temple followers to "drink the Kool-Aid" that led to their deaths. The book of Revelation, with its focus on the apocalypse, could be a dangerous text in the hands of a charismatic and narcissistic leader.

Henry asked Koresh if what Jones had done was the kind of thing he had in mind—a farewell statement and then mass suicide.

"I'm not having anybody kill themselves," he said.

We told him that we would consider the idea, and the next day Koresh repeated his offer to surrender in return for airtime.

"So, David, if you just want to talk about the Bible, how about a tape-recorded message? Then we can review it and run it past our bosses."

"That's okay," he said. "I can work with that."

"And just one more thing. We want you to start out by saying on the tape that if the message is broadcast over nationwide radio, then you and all your followers will peacefully surrender."

"That's right," he said. "That's the deal."

I asked for a meeting with Jamar and the other SACs and brought with me profiler Pete Smerick from the FBI Behavioral Science Unit. We told them that we saw little risk in playing the tape, assuming that it did not contain any references to suicide. I made clear to the commanders that we had hope, but no guarantee, that Koresh would follow through on his promise.

"Why give him anything when there's no positive assurance we get something in return?" Jamar asked me.

I explained that this was not a typical bargaining interaction because we had so little leverage.

"The only thing Koresh wants from us is for us to go away. We're not going to do that. We can't bargain, since he doesn't want anything else. So really, we're not giving up anything."

I knew I risked losing credibility with Jamar if Koresh didn't follow through, but as far as I was concerned, we were putting nothing at risk. If it turned out that he was conning us, we would have demonstrated our goodwill, and the onus would be on him to demonstrate good faith in some other way.

Jamar gave his approval, and Koresh made the tape and sent it out for our review. As promised, the recording contained nothing more than a rambling sermon about the book of Revelation. We carefully listened to all fifty-seven minutes and found nothing in it that suggested it was a preamble for mass suicide. We even reached out to religious scholars at nearby Baylor University for their interpretation, and they, too, found nothing problematic.

At 8:15 a.m., March 2, Koresh released two more children, bringing our total to sixteen. He also released two women in their seventies who lived in a trailer adjacent to the compound. Unfortunately, though long-term Davidians, they seemed a little out of it and couldn't give us any useful information about conditions inside, or what, if anything, the Davidians were planning. At 1:20 p.m., following further negotiations, Koresh released another two children. That made eighteen children and two adults out. Each additional person released gave us hope that we were headed in the right direction.

That afternoon at 1:32, the Christian Broadcasting Network broadcast Koresh's tape nationwide, uncut, as promised. In subsequent conversations Koresh told us that he had heard the broadcast and was pleased with it.

Now it was time for him to deliver on his promise to come out peacefully.

With Jamar's approval, we worked out a plan whereby Koresh would be carried out on a stretcher by several of the Davidians. The others would then follow in small groups, marching to school buses that would take them to the receiving facility.

Koresh's number two man, Steve Schneider, would stay on the phone with us throughout the process to ensure coordinated movement. He would then come out last.

Koresh agreed to all these arrangements, and we brought up the buses so that they could be seen from inside the compound. HRT stood by, ready to secure the individuals. I asked Bill Luthin, the HRT liaison officer working in the negotiation room, to take special care to avoid appearing to manhandle anyone, as this would be watched by those still inside. Bill was very experienced and agreed to emphasize this point with HRT team members. We didn't want any misunderstanding that might short-circuit this peaceful end to such a volatile situation. Earlier, Koresh had told us that twenty children, forty-seven women, and forty-three men remained in the compound, and we wanted them all to make it out alive.

The negotiation team waited patiently, in radio contact with the frontline tactical people as the appointed time came and went. HRT reported no movement, so we called Steve Schneider.

"Steve, what's going on?"

"Everybody's lined up with their stuff, ready to go out," he said. He sounded confident, even relieved.

"What about David?"

"We're trying to get him downstairs on a stretcher, but the wounds make it tough to move him. He's hurting, you know."

"Yeah, we know. It must be tough. Just do the best you can."

We waited awhile longer, but still no one emerged from the compound.

We called back in, but this time Schneider's optimism seemed to have faded. Koresh was still coming, he told us, but this time his assurances sounded vague and unconvincing.

"Steve," Henry said, "you've really got to come clean with us. What's going on? We've delivered on everything we'd promised. Everyone's standing by."

"David just wants to give everybody a final Bible study lesson before coming out," he said.

This sounded like something Koresh would do, so we regained some measure of hope that things were still on track.

More time passed, and we called in yet again at 5:59 p.m., and spoke to Schneider. "The Lord spoke to David," he said. "The Lord told David to wait, not to come out."

Now we knew we'd been had. Funny how conveniently this divine intervention had appeared.

I slipped Henry a note, which he delivered verbatim: "But we delivered on our end of the bargain! We did everything you asked."

"I understand. But God has the final word."

"Steven, can you put David on the phone, please?"

"He's praying. He doesn't want to talk right now."

We were extremely disappointed, to say the least, but not totally surprised. As experienced negotiators, we were used to dealing with manipulative people, which is to say that we were accustomed to being lied to. These kinds of setbacks are a normal part of the negotiation process. It's important not to abandon the strategy just because Koresh had reneged in this instance. It's important not to overreact.

This created an immediate challenge. I knew that Rogers and Jamar would view it as a sign that Koresh was manipulating the negotiation team and that we were not being firm enough with him. Further, they would view it as an insult to their authority.

I went into Jamar's office to explain what had—or had not—

happened, and sitting in a chair in front of his desk was Dick Rogers. Both were visibly angry.

I reminded them that we had warned them that this kind of thing could happen, but that it shouldn't alter our approach. They listened, but I could see that they'd already decided that they wanted to punish Koresh. It became clear to me that their decision was based on a strong emotional response to what Koresh had done.

"This joker is screwing with us," Rogers said. "It's time to teach him a lesson."

"I don't think that's going to advance our cause," I said. "It doesn't matter if Koresh is jerking us around. The point is, we're getting people out of there."

Rogers and I were talking past each other, both trying to influence Jamar, but his body language showed he agreed with Rogers.

"My people can get in there and secure that place in fifteen minutes," Rogers said.

"Still too soon for that," Jamar said. "But I agree it's time to teach him a lesson."

I protested, saying we might well be able to get things back on track, but they were adamant, violating a core principle of the FBI negotiation program: never confuse getting even with getting what you want. Talladega had buoyed Rogers's confidence about what his team could do, but this was a very different situation; for one thing, they had guns, lots of them. For another, they had children inside. Philosophically, Rogers believed the best way to force them out was to tighten the noose around them, to apply increasing pressure until they capitulated. Yet I knew this approach would be counterproductive.

The very first thing I talk about when training new negotiators is the critical importance of self-control. If we cannot control our own emotions, how can we expect to influence the emotions of another party? But I also remind my negotiators that "negotiators negotiate and commanders command." It is the negotiators' responsibility to make the very best strategy recommendations we can, but to also know that the advice we give commanders will not always be embraced.

Despite my warning, Jamar ordered the armored Bradley vehicles to move onto Davidian property as a visible display of the FBI's power. I was concerned that this would only ratchet up the tension and damage our credibility.

That proved true in our next conversation with Schneider: he angrily denounced us for moving the armored vehicles forward.

"You promised to stay off our land," he said.

"But David promised to come out. It was a firm commitment, Steve. My bosses are angry and frustrated," said Henry.

"Honestly, we were going to come out, but what could we do? God told David to wait."

Koresh had conveniently used God as the ultimate trump card, but from everything I could tell, Schneider sincerely believed what he was saying. Under the circumstances, he had to hold his faith in what David had said about God. This firm belief shut down the conversation, at least temporarily.

When we spoke to Schneider the next day, now the fourth day of the standoff, he admitted that he was "personally embarrassed" that the Davidians hadn't followed through with the promise to come out. We hoped this signaled the opening of a wedge between Schneider and Koresh. Schneider was far better educated—he held a master's degree in divinity—and more articulate than Koresh, a high-school dropout. We had also learned that Schneider's wife, Judy, had become one of Koresh's concubines. Koresh had even fathered a child with her, whereas she and Steve had never conceived one. There seemed to be more than enough reasons for Schneider to harbor resentment that we could exploit. But that would require that Schneider had reserved some of his mind for independent thought. Of that there was no evidence.

The FBI and ATF leadership team began holding regular daily press conferences, with key remarks prepared by my negotiation team. Jamar ran these at first. Our team provided him with the daily talking points we wanted to convey, not just to the world but to the Davidians inside: all we wanted was a peaceful solution, and our primary concern was the safety of the children.

The scripted portion of the press conferences generally went well and served our objectives. We were less successful later when, during question-and-answer sessions, one or more of the FBI or ATF leaders would shoot from the hip. More than once during questioning by reporters, officials made offhand remarks casting doubt on the sincerity of Koresh's beliefs, with sarcastic references to his conversation with God. It then fell on our team to backtrack with the Davidians and explain what they meant. This did not help our cause.

As governments and corporations have learned through the years, it's far better to have a designated press spokesperson stand before the media rather than the boss. When faced with a tough question, the spokesperson can reply that he or she doesn't have the information sought but will follow up later. This provides much-needed time to formulate and deliver the best answer to the question.

It was also problematic that ATF officials continued to be involved in the daily press conferences. This undercut efforts to distance the FBI, and specifically our negotiation team, from this organization that the Davidians hated. Despite my repeated requests to remove the ATF from the press conferences, FBI officials in Washington preferred to try to underscore "unity" by keeping the ATF in the picture.

Once the Bradleys moved forward, I realized the internal battle over strategy was going to be as challenging as talking to Koresh. There was a growing disconnect between the strategy we were pursuing as negotiators and the thoughts of the tactical folks on the perimeter. The deeper realization was that Dick Rogers had not been chastened at all by the outcome of his rash orders at Ruby Ridge. Buoyed by Talladega, he was still committed to the tough-guy rule book.

Making matters worse, there appeared to be a growing misunderstanding at the forward position about what we negotiators were doing. Coordination between us and HRT was complicated by our separate locations; they were located just outside the Davidian compound, whereas we were eight miles away. I volunteered to brief the HRT operators as they were coming off or going on their shifts, but Dick Rogers declined the offer, saying it wasn't necessary and that he'd tell the guys what they needed to know. I was beginning to sense his personal frustration and growing discontent with the progress of the negotiations.

I also recommended that Rogers, Jamar, and I meet face-to-face at regular intervals in order to work out any strategy disagreements, but Jamar again declined to follow my suggestion. He said that the existing system, whereby I met with him and then he went forward and met separately with Rogers, was working to his satisfaction.

In truth, it contributed greatly to our problems.

Despite the growing tension with the Davidians, we were able to get back on track, and on March 3, the fourth day of the incident, at around four-thirty in the afternoon twelve-year-old Mark Jones was allowed to leave. At seven-thirty the following morning, his eleven-year-old brother, Kevin, followed. Our tally was now two adults and twenty children released, about half the total number of children thought to be inside at the beginning of the siege. Regardless of how else Koresh might be manipulating us, he was letting these children live, and that was a good thing.

At 8:41 on Friday morning, March 5, we negotiated the release of nine-year-old Heather Jones, the twenty-first child and twenty-third person overall to leave. Unfortunately, she would be the last person to exit for several days. It seemed that our continuing show of force had failed to make Koresh more compliant, and in fact had made him angry enough to break off contact.

Perhaps more than a lack of communication and poor coordination, fundamentally different views of how to resolve the matter began to erode the trust between the HRT and negotiation teams. Dick Rogers called me personally from the forward area one evening, enraged that the Davidians were pointing one of their .50 caliber sniper rifles toward HRT personnel. He angrily told me to make contact and tell them in no uncertain terms that they should remove the weapon immediately or be fired on. I instructed the primary negotiator to do just that. He spoke with Schneider and the weapon was quickly pulled back.

Days later I would learn that HRT personnel were absolutely livid that the negotiators had told the Davidians to pull back the heavy weapon. They preferred knowing where it was so they could keep an eye on it. I asked Lloyd Sigler, the capable HRT representative now working in the NOC, to explain to the HRT team members that we had been ordered by Dick Rogers himself to have the weapon removed. Lloyd passed on the information, but it never seemed to filter down to the team members. At no time did Dick Rogers ever explain to his own team, during or after the incident, that it was he who had ordered the weapon removed. Instead, HRT team members were left with the impression that we had undercut them.

Despite these problems, Jamar continued to approve my suggested initiatives to get things back on track with the Davidians. The next day, we offered to send in a suture kit to treat Koresh. To personalize ourselves as human beings, rather than as some faceless enemy, we included a brief videotape showing each of the primary negotiators who had spoken with him so far. Each one of us held up a photograph of our own family and stated how important we knew Koresh's large family to be to him. We each signed off by stating our strong desire to see everyone come out unharmed. This was unprecedented.

By Sunday, March 7, day eight, we found the negotiations with Koresh becoming increasingly challenging. His resistance to our efforts clearly increased; he began to subject the negotiators on the night shift to long religious diatribes, which only among ourselves we would call his "Bible babble." Our conversations to date had been pretty practical and secular in nature, but now his religious worldview came to dominate his side of the conversations.

We tried to discourage these long telephone conversations when we realized that they kept Koresh up all night, which meant that he would sleep much of the following day. When he was asleep, no one else inside the compound could authorize the release of any more children. We also knew that no children had been released while we had been talking about religion.

We would notice that while Koresh spoke in lofty terms of his religious philosophy, he occasionally digressed into decidedly less spiritual realms. One evening in the midst of one of these religious diatribes Koresh stopped and asked one of the negotiators what the team was eating for dinner. He was told by negotiator John Cox that they usually sent someone out to Whataburger, a nearby fast-food chain and the only place open late at night. In response, Koresh said, "Whataburger! That meat is terrible. If it turns out that I am the son of God, the world will find out about Whataburger." This did not sound to us like the comment of a man who truly believed in his own divine status.

Just after lunch on March 7, Koresh told us that he would send out another child if we could accurately tell him the meaning of the third seal in the book of Revelation. Aware of the limits of our own biblical knowledge, we again consulted religious scholars at Baylor University. Armed with what they told us about the most common interpretation of the third seal, we reported back. Koresh listened, then told us that we were not even close, but said nothing more. He made no effort to tell us how we were wrong, and he refused to release anyone. It's unlikely he would have agreed with any answer we came up with.

Koresh was regaining his strength and returning to his normal pattern of manipulating those around him, including us. While it might have been tempting to be confrontational with him, we continued to try to push toward our goal of getting people out. My task was not to settle scores with a sociopath but to save all the lives I could.

Soon after this we were presented with an unexpected opportunity. One of our negotiators heard a story on the then-popular Paul Harvey radio show about a fast-moving, guitar-shaped nebula blasting across the skies at thousands of miles per hour. Koresh was a guitar player and led a band made up of his followers, so we thought we could present it as a sign that it was time to come out.

The negotiator on duty called up Schneider and asked if he had heard about the comment on the radio. Schneider said that he had not, but he became very excited, speculating that this could be the sign that Koresh was waiting for, a message from God that they should come out. We contacted Paul Harvey's staff and requested that his show rebroadcast the report. After the rebroadcast we called back and asked Schneider if Koresh had heard it. Schneider sounded disappointed. They had listened, but Koresh's only response was to say, "That's not very fast." That was the end of that.

I was beginning to feel increasing pressure to show results if we were going to delay more aggressive tactical action. When Koresh indicated that the children inside the compound needed milk, we decided to call on McLennan County sheriff Jack Harwell to help work out a deal to get that milk to them. Harwell was not only a down-to-earth and straightforward law enforcement professional but an affable and easygoing man. He seemed to know how to talk to and get along with almost anyone. We felt that he might be able to serve as an intermediary and help overcome Koresh's resistance to our entreaties. Since the incident began, Jack had spent a great deal of time sitting in the negotiation room wearing his white cowboy hat, patiently listening to our conversations with Koresh.

In the fall of 1992, when accusations of child abuse had first been leveled at Koresh, it was Jack who met with him to discuss the issue. The gentle sheriff, who didn't even wear a gun, had been polite and respectful, and they seemed to have gotten along well. At one point Koresh had even said that he might well have surrendered had Harwell come to arrest him rather than the heavily armed men from the ATF.

A little after one on Monday afternoon, March 8—the ninth day of the siege—Jack called the compound, and the rest of us listened on headsets. Jack was magnificent. With just the right tone he was able to project his genuine concern. Koresh greeted him warmly; he obviously had great respect for the sheriff. Jack soon asked Koresh what he could do for the children, and, as expected, Koresh mentioned the need for milk. Jack told him he would make it happen. Even though we had been prepared to send in milk all along, having it appear to come from Jack would, we hoped, reestablish his bona fides with Koresh. It would also show he could get things done with the FBI. At 3:50 that afternoon, we left six gallons of milk just outside the compound.

A couple of hours later we were surprised to receive a videotape of Koresh, his wife, Rachel, and their children, and also some of the other children Koresh had fathered. We popped it into our VCR and observed him on the tape commenting about the tape we had sent, the one in which we talked about our kids. I had the sense that he appreciated what we had done and that this was his way of reciprocating. He even introduced us to several of his family members on tape. He also took the opportunity to show us his wounds. During the initial shootout a bullet had grazed his wrist just above his left thumb. He showed us where that same bullet had continued on and struck his left side, leaving a clearly visible bullet hole. He told us that the sutures we had sent in earlier had helped, and he thanked us for them. Using a faux John Wayne voice, he joked that the pain was nothing a tough guy like him couldn't handle. Koresh was idiosyncratic and unpredictable, but we seemed to have reestablished a kind of rapport. We looked on that tape as a very positive sign, and I conveyed this to Jamar.

But again, a moment of progress would be thwarted by the actions of our colleagues. At two-thirty the following morning, unbeknownst to me, Jamar approved a recommendation from someone to turn off all the power going into the compound. Coming as it did on the heels of the successful conversation between Koresh and Jack Harwell, the milk delivery, and the Koresh video, the timing could not have been worse. My team rightly felt that the rug had been pulled out from under us yet again. And so in addition to trying to convince Jamar to coordinate better, I also had to manage their growing frustrations. Even Steve Schneider questioned how he was expected to keep the just-delivered milk cold if the power was off. He had an excellent point.

Turning off a hostage taker's power during a siege can be a useful tool. Lack of electricity makes those inside less comfortable, which can sometimes make them more willing to compromise. But turning off power should never be done without weighing the pros and cons. This technique is also much less effective in a situation such as Waco, when all the subject wants is for us to go away. Moreover, the Davidians already lived a very spartan lifestyle; Koresh's quarters were the only part of the compound that had electricity anyway.

While I didn't know for certain, I suspected that Jamar's actions came as a result of pressure from Rogers. I imagined Dick asking how in the hell we could send milk to these guys without getting people out, particularly after Koresh had jerked us around.

I went to Jamar and expressed my grave concern that we were working at cross-purposes and that turning off the power was going to negate the progress we'd just made. He listened to my views but said that he saw no inconsistency between what we were saying and doing.

I couldn't for the life of me figure out how he couldn't see the inconsistency there, but I knew he wouldn't change his mind. To be fair, Jamar was under a great deal of pressure by this point, with a long and expensive siege going on, and he had the impression that Koresh was manipulating the FBI and that we needed to be more confrontational. But the result of this was that he was choosing to support both my recommendations and those of Dick Rogers, which would continue to put us at cross-purposes. I renewed my efforts to convince him that the more we tried to bully Koresh, the more he'd dig his heels in.

Seven hours after the power had been turned off, I was able to convince Jamar to turn it back on, just in time for the Davidians to watch the regularly scheduled 10:30 a.m. press conference with SAC Bob Ricks from the Oklahoma City FBI office. Of all the various FBI commanders who came to Waco, Bob took the most time to visit with the negotiation team and listen to the conversations we conducted with those inside the compound. He supported our efforts. We gave him talking points for these encounters with the media, and he was very good about getting them across in a natural way. Mostly, the idea was to take the main themes we had discussed with Koresh and Schneider on the phone, and to use television and radio broadcasts to drive these home to all the Davidians in the compound.

Throughout these days, we kept pushing for the release of more kids. Of the twenty-one released so far, the last had come out on March 5. On March 7, after we continued to press for more releases, Koresh had finally snapped at us, saying, "Hey! You don't understand. The rest of the kids in here are *my children*—they're not coming out!" We found this angry declaration worrisome, to say the least; we knew we had a major problem on our hands. The innocent children were always our primary concern; their parents had made their own choice to follow Koresh.

I now put in motion an idea that we had gotten from the Koresh videotape. I sent a team of negotiators to the Child Protective Services home where all of the released Davidian children were being kept. We had worked with Texas authorities to ensure that the children would be kept there in Waco awaiting their parents' surrender. We made clear to the parents that, contrary to their instructions, their children were not being sent off to live with relatives. Instead, they were waiting here for the parents to come out. I hoped that this fact would weigh on their minds and lead them to conclude that they had to go on living for their children rather than throw their lives away defending Koresh. We made a short videotape of all of the Davidian children in the home where they were being kept. We showed them playing, relaxing, and clearly being well cared for. We made arrangements to have the tape and still photos of the kids delivered on March 9 at 2:04 p.m.

One detail we had not noticed was a young boy named Bryan Schroeder sitting on the floor looking forlorn. His mother, Kathy Schroeder, was one of the most strident and angry women in the compound. She and her second husband, Michael, had lived there with three of their children: two boys from Kathy's prior marriage and their son Bryan. Michael was killed on the day of the initial shootout with the ATF, and Kathy was understandably bitter. All three children had left the compound, and Kathy's first husband, who had joint custody, came immediately to Waco to claim the two older boys. With the two older half brothers removed, this left young Bryan alone in the home with the other Davidian children. As the parents inside the compound watched the video, Kathy noticed that Bryan looked sad and lonely, and she became concerned.

At 10:25 on the evening of March 9, Koresh sent out another tape in response to ours. This tape showed additional Davidian families who were living in the compound, further helping us to identify individuals and better understand the relationships at work. This seemed to be the kind of positive exchange we were trying to promote.

The next evening, the power was shut off again, then turned back on in time for the next nightly press conference. In my view, turning the power off and on only served to demonstrate that we were trying to aggravate those inside, which is not helpful. Despite these less than ideal conditions, in an attempt to build on our earlier efforts the negotiation team filmed a second video of the Davidian children and sent that in as well on March 11, just after 1:00 p.m.

While we were attempting to build on the rapport we had established, the forward command continued on its separate and contradictory course. They requested additional Bradleys and some M1 Abrams tanks, the biggest and most imposing in the U.S. arsenal. These vehicles arrived at 9:30 that evening, after which Jamar made a rare visit to the negotiation room. Standing in front of a schematic of the interior of the compound, he enthusiastically cited statistics on the powerful armament: weapons capability, fuel capacity, engine power, weight, and size. Then, placing his finger on the map of the compound, he pointed out how an M1 was powerful enough to drive from one end of the long compound all the way through and out the other side without stopping. He seemed excited by the possibility.

The negotiators in the room were speechless. Surely he wasn't serious. Had he forgotten about the women and children inside? Having dealt with SAC Jamar repeatedly, I was somewhat accustomed to this type of bravado, but I could see the shock on the faces of the other negotiators. Jamar soon left the room, leaving a stunned group shaking our heads. For the first time, they understood what I had been dealing with.

Earlier on Thursday, March 11, Kathy Schroeder had called the negotiation team to complain about her son Bryan being left in the Child Protective Services home without his older half brothers. She said that she could see on the videotape we had sent in earlier that the boy was clearly upset. John Dolan, now the primary negotiator, patiently explained the legal issues that had forced us to turn over the two older boys to Kathy's ex-husband. Still, Kathy continued to rail at us.

As John listened to her, I wrote a note on a three-by-five index card and passed it to him. The note said: *Bryan needs a hug from his mommy.* John looked up at me, a big smile on his face, and nodded.

Kathy continued to vent her anger. Then John quietly and gently said, "You know, Kathy, I think what Bryan really needs now is a hug from his mommy." Kathy's silence spoke volumes. John waited, then built on the emotion he knew she was feeling. He talked about how the young boy needed her and how she was the only one in the world who could take care of him. By the time their conversation ended, he had convinced her to come out and give Bryan that hug. Without hesitation or equivocation, Kathy told us she would exit the next day. Koresh had repeatedly said anyone was free to come out at any time, but we were not convinced that he was not pressuring the adults to do otherwise. After the call, John gave me a high five and said, "You give good note."

At 10:41 the following morning, Friday, March 12, the thirteenth day of the standoff, Kathy Schroeder came out of the compound and surrendered to us. We immediately took her to a building nearby where her son Bryan was waiting for her. Once again, we had our video camera on hand to capture this emotional reunion of mother and son, hugging each other and crying for joy. The smile on little Bryan's face when he saw his mother brought tears to all our eyes.

We then arranged for a second delivery of milk to be sent in around three that afternoon. Two hours later, we put Kathy Schroeder on the telephone to speak with Steve Schneider. By this time she had visited not only with Bryan but also with all of the other children being taken care of at the Child Protective Services home. Kathy sang the praises of those caring for the children, providing reassurance to all the parents inside that their kids were well. She also spoke of the gentle treatment she had received at our hands. Steve Schneider seemed stunned, which was just the kind of reaction we were after. By being restrained and professional, we hoped to win them over, one by one.

At 6:00 p.m., a nineteen-year-old named Oliver Gyafras decided that he, too, wanted to come out. Both he and Kathy had each been forced to sit through a lengthy "exit interview" with Koresh before they could leave. During his talk with each of them, Koresh never told them they could not leave, but he reminded them that they were surrendering to the forces of evil that had attacked the compound and persecuted them for their religious beliefs. Fortunately, their desire to come out and live was stronger than any loyalty they felt for Koresh.

We had now brought out two non-elderly adults, both previously devoted Davidians. We believed that, after a certain number of such defections, even Koresh might come around, if only to salvage what he could of his leadership status. He seemed more committed to his followers' adulation than to any particular principle. I tried to explain to Jamar and the other commanders the nature of our "trickle, flow, and gush" strategy. I told them we were aiming not at a grand resolution strategy that would bring everyone out at once, but rather at a steadily increasing attrition of individuals leaving the compound. Our hope was that each subsequent release would weaken that much more the stranglehold Koresh held over the larger group.

At 9:15 p.m., we sent in a copy of the video showing Kathy's emotional reunion with young Bryan. We thought it sent a powerful message about embracing life. Two hours later, Steve Schneider told us once again that the forward command had cut off all the power. It was sad that we heard this from Schneider before we were notified by our own people.

On Sunday afternoon, despite the progress we were making through negotiation, Dick Rogers ratcheted up the coercive pressure by installing high-power lights aimed at the compound. This meant that our perimeter people could see the Davidians, but not the other way around. Was this a necessary protection, or another form of harassment?

We learned from our HRT liaison that on Monday morning, March 15, Jamar authorized the use of several armored combat engineering vehicles (CEVs) to clear away trash piles fifty yards to the rear of the compound. His rationale was that, conceivably, the Davidians could come out and hide behind those piles and fire on our agents on the perimeter. But the Davidians had not tried to exit the compound and had not fired on the FBI at any time. Where had this newfound concern come from? And why now?

Not surprisingly, the introduction of these heavy vehicles was seen by those inside the compound as being a decidedly hostile act. More than once, to our surprise, these huge machines severed the dedicated phone line installed to communicate with those inside. This forced us to set up a loudspeaker system to send messages and to alert the Davidians that the line had been cut and that we would supply a replacement.

Even with these setbacks, we were able to keep our efforts moving forward. The same day the CEVs showed up we had our first face-to-face meeting with the Davidians. At 4:20 in the afternoon, Byron Sage and Sheriff Jack Harwell went forward and had an open-air discussion with Steve Schneider and Wayne Martin just inside the perimeter. The primary item on the agenda was the safety of the children, and our desire to get them all out. This also allowed us to demonstrate our willingness to address their concerns about property seizure, continuing ministry in jail, preservation of the crime scene for their defense, and other issues of concern. These two were willing to talk about possibilities in a calm manner, but, unfortunately, both of them were loyal to Koresh and repeatedly made it clear that he alone made all the decisions.

On Tuesday, day seventeen of the situation, another SAC, Dick Schwein from El Paso, arrived to assist SACs Jamar, Ricks, and Dick Swensen. A caricature of the gung ho type, he wore a dark blue SWAT-type uniform (the other SACs wore casual civilian clothes) complete with a web belt holding a canteen. He also seemed surprisingly cavalier and flippant about the process. Once I heard him say in passing, "No use trying to talk to these bastards. We've got to just go in there and cut their balls off."

SAC Schwein contributed perhaps the single strangest element of the whole sad saga of the Waco siege: harassing the Davidians by blasting bizarre sound recordings—Tibetan chants, recorded sounds of dying rabbits (used by hunters to attract coyotes), Nancy Sinatra's "These Boots Are Made for Walking"—over loudspeakers. Schwein had picked up the idea from the U.S. Army. They had used such tapes during the Panama invasion, when they were trying to force General Manuel Noriega out of the papal nuncio's residence, where he had sought sanctuary. When I learned of this plan, again from our tactical liaison, I went immediately to Jamar and urged him not to allow this. I made the case that playing harassing music was not a recommended negotiation tactic, that it was not something taught by the FBI, and that it would send the wrong message to the Davidians, who were now starting to cooperate again. At best these tapes would be ineffective; at worst they would make us look foolish. But most fundamentally, what SAC Schwein failed to realize was that this technique had not succeeded in Panama, and it wasn't likely to work for us in Waco. Jamar assured me that he would speak to Schwein when he came on duty that night and make sure the tapes were not played.

Feeling somewhat reassured, I staggered back to my motel just before midnight. I took a shower, then turned on the television. There on the news, covered live, was the Davidian compound, brightly illuminated, with torturous sounds blaring over speakers. I was both embarrassed for the FBI and personally enraged. I immediately called the command post and asked to speak with Jamar, but he had gone for the evening.

The next morning I raised the issue with him again. Jamar was unaware that the tapes had been played. Evidently he had forgotten to speak with SAC Schwein on the matter, and he assured me it wouldn't happen again. But it did happen again—the very next night. When I confronted Jamar about this again, he shrugged off my complaint, saying that Schwein had nothing better to do on the night shift. He brushed it off as no big deal. It took several more nights before we were able to bring it to an end, and then only by going behind his back to appeal to leaders at FBI headquarters.

One of the most frustrating aspects of the whole affair was that many critics of the FBI's handling of Waco have blamed the use of these audiotapes on the negotiation team. They assumed the use of these tapes was part of our negotiation strategy, when nothing could be further from the truth. Again, the FBI was hamstrung by a failure to appreciate—and teach its regional leaders—the skills necessary for crisis management. That was coupled with an ingrained hubris that served to foster a false sense of capability and skill where in fact it did not exist.

When Steve Schneider next spoke with us, he asked in seeming disbelief what message the FBI was trying to convey to them with these sounds. Schneider said he had been working to convince more individuals to come out, but the tapes had put an end to it. Instead of being able to build on our success, we now had to dig ourselves out of yet another hole created by others.

Around 6:20 p.m., on March 18, day nineteen, matters went from bad to worse. Again over my protest, SAC Jamar authorized HRT to advance with the armored vehicles and knock down and remove four fuel tanks located on the right side of the compound. He also authorized them to remove a bus parked near the building. These removals were done recklessly, with no effort to minimize damage. It seemed that the FBI was deliberately seeking to irritate the Davidians. Some of my negotiators began to speculate that this was being done to deliberately undercut the negotiation process.

I went to Jamar again and reminded him that the fuel tanks had been there since the beginning of the incident and had not been seen as a problem before. I asked him why it was so critical to remove them now. His response was short, vague, and off the point—something about the Davidians being able to use the fuel to blow up our vehicles. Yet again, I suspected this idea had originated with Dick Rogers.

Even though Koresh was angry, he continued to take our calls. Henry Garcia, John Dolan, and the other negotiators continued to float the idea that if Koresh came out, he would be able to continue to meet with his followers while in jail awaiting trial. We reminded him that he might be found innocent in court as having acted in self-defense, an idea we didn't believe but hoped he might. Surprisingly, this possibility seemed to intrigue him.

We drafted a letter signed by Sheriff Harwell and SAC Jamar, which verified that Koresh would be allowed to meet regularly with his followers in jail while awaiting trial. We also sent in copies of national magazines that Koresh wanted to see, each with his photograph on the cover. Again his ego was coming to the fore, and again we tried to use this. We suggested that if he killed himself, he would receive only brief coverage, whereas if he was going through a trial, he would be in the media constantly.

We continued to pursue our negotiation strategy and once more things began to turn our way. At 8:00 p.m. on March 19, the twentieth day of the siege, Brad Branch and Kevin Whitecliff, both in their thirties, came out, bringing our total to twenty-seven. We had yet to achieve the tipping point that might convince Koresh to get out in front of where his followers were heading, but we were definitely getting back on track.

Two days later, seven more adults came out: Victorine Hollingsworth, Anetta Richards, Rita Riddle, Gladys Ottman, Sheila Martin, Ofelia Santoya, and James Lawter. These people had simply grown weary of the standoff and wanted to leave, further evidence that the "trickle, flow, gush" approach was working. When I reported to Jamar, he acknowledged this achievement but made clear that he wanted everybody out now. He apparently didn't value our incremental success. But once again, it was as if the command was purposely derailing our momentum. Three hours later armored CEVs were sent out again, this time to remove various items from the no-man's-land between the HRT perimeter and the compound. One such item was a beautiful, completely restored red Chevy Ranchero. In case Koresh wasn't getting the point as he watched from the compound, the CEV crushed the car flat as a pancake before dragging it off. To me this was the purest manifestation to date of the HRT's frustration, because it made absolutely no sense.

I couldn't believe they had done this when nine individuals had come out over the preceding three days. Were they blind to this fact? Once again I made the case to Jamar that positive behavior—the release of individuals—needed to be met with positive reinforcement, not humiliating punishment. This is one of the most basic tenets of psychology going back to Pavlov. If you want to train your dog to fetch a newspaper, you don't kick the dog when it brings you the paper. We had just kicked the dog for doing what we wanted. Despite this, at 10:12 a.m. on Tuesday, March 23, Livingstone Fagan came out, bringing the total to thirty-five. Two days later, on March 25, more clearing operations took place.

These acts of unnecessary exercise in pique—crushing a car and destroying other property needlessly—convinced me that our opportunity for meaningful negotiations had passed. Koresh quickly confirmed my intuition. Clearly angry, Koresh called the negotiation team and stated flatly, "No one else will be coming out." Jamar and Rogers's actions had finally put us negotiators in a hole so deep that we couldn't dig our way out. Steve Schneider got on the phone and pleaded with us to explain why things had suddenly turned so ugly when we had been working so well together. We had no good answer for him.

I had the same question for SAC Jamar. He looked at me with fire in his eyes and said that not enough people were coming out. We needed to punish Koresh for not moving fast enough. But I think the real story was that, with the FBI seemingly helpless to compel the Davidians to surrender, he was feeling the heat. The entire nation was watching, and the FBI was spending about $128,000 a day, a rate of expenditure that would add up to more than $5 million before all was said and done. This was a serious concern, but not as serious as the lives of dozens and dozens of men, women, and innocent children.

Venting my frustrations more strongly than before, I told him that I didn't think we would get anyone else out after these recent actions. He appeared unconcerned. I realized then that he had already determined what he was going to do.

I met with my team and told them that we were on a crashing airplane. We could parachute to safety or we could try to control the descent and minimize destruction on the ground. Despite their anger and disappointment, and despite the bad decisions coming down from our commanders, the entire negotiation team felt we needed to continue our efforts.

That night I received a call in my motel room from Rob Grace, my boss at Quantico. He thanked me for my work on the case but said it was time for me to step down as negotiation coordinator. Negotiators usually stayed on for three weeks, and I was well into my fourth. Only Byron Sage had been on the scene longer than me.

I have to admit that I was relieved, but I was also concerned about who would take over and how they would manage. Despite my many disagreements with SAC Jamar, I believe he is an honorable man who did what he thought was best. This could also be said of Dick Rogers, but he consistently failed to recognize the progress we were making. His aggressive approach continually undercut negotiation progress. It was his attitude that infected HRT operators at the scene, SAC Jamar, and some leaders back at FBI headquarters. (Later I learned that Rogers had complained that I was personally impeding HRT's efforts to take a more aggressive approach with the Davidians to resolve the situation sooner. That was certainly true enough.)

Rob told me that a high-level official at FBI headquarters wanted Clint Van Zandt, a former member of our unit, to replace me. I expressed deep concerns about this and recommended other negotiators I felt were better suited for the job. My main concern was that Van Zandt had a history of not being a team player. I also knew him to be a vocal born-again Christian, which is fine under normal conditions, but that might present issues when dealing with the self-deluded "Lamb of God." I worried that Van Zandt would attempt to try to convince Koresh to surrender by presenting his own competing interpretation of biblical prophecy. None of the thirty-five individuals released during the negotiation process so far had come out because of anything having to do with theology, and so I felt that attacking the group's beliefs was a dangerous way to proceed. Given Koresh's love of religious debate, such talk was far more likely to draw out the negotiations than persuade him to abandon his stand. Van Zandt was approved nonetheless, and when he arrived at the scene, accompanied by Rob Grace, the three of us met to formalize the handover of leadership. I expressed my belief that attempting to engage Koresh on religious issues was a dead end. Van Zandt assured both Rob and me that he would not try to inject his own beliefs into the negotiation process. At six in the morning on March 25, Van Zandt took over. No further Davidians would come out.

I had been at Ranch Apocalypse for twenty-six days, and I left exhausted, frustrated, and emotionally drained, but there was little time to dwell on any of that. Before the incident began, I had scheduled a trip to Amman, Jordan, for a negotiation training mission. I had a few days at home with my family before I had to leave again for the Middle East.

After I handed over the negotiations to Van Zandt, the situation in Waco deteriorated.

Despite his promises, Van Zandt did in fact spend many hours on the phone trying to convince Koresh that his interpretations of the Bible were wrong. Various negotiators on the team later told me of their frustrations with this nightly religious debate, which only served to keep Koresh awake all night, then sleeping all day.

I also learned that Van Zandt did not get along with SAC Jamar, who cut him out of the decision-making process. Byron Sage became the de facto team leader and through the remainder of the incident played the key negotiation leadership role in trying to save the lives of those who remained inside the compound.

Part of this effort was allowing attorneys Dick DeGuerin and Jack Zimmerman to speak on the phone and later go inside the compound to meet with Koresh. Their objective was to convince him that he had a valid legal defense against the charges that would be brought. Allowing defense attorneys to walk into an active crime scene did not sit well with the tactical team. When Sage accompanied the attorneys forward he noticed one of the Porta-Johns on which the words *Sage is a Davidian* had been scrawled into the accumulated dust, presumably by an angry tactical team member—a sign of continuing discontent and misunderstanding.

But the attorneys' forays seemed to offer some hope. Koresh told them he would surrender as soon as he wrote down his unique interpretation of the seven seals described in the book of Revelation. The lawyers appealed for time to allow Koresh to undertake and complete that effort, but after a number of days passed, it became increasingly clear that Koresh was again stalling. Days later, Steve Schneider confirmed that Koresh had not even started to write. For FBI decision makers, this was the ultimate confirmation that Koresh had no intention of coming out peacefully.

My own view is that Koresh was still ambivalent. Part of him wanted to live, and part of him was attracted to martyrdom. Despite his attorneys' efforts to convince him otherwise, he must have known that he was unlikely to avoid the death penalty for killing the ATF agents. This knowledge may have set the stage for the mass suicide he seemed to be planning. Consider that it was our formidable task to try to convince Koresh and his devoted followers to lay down their weapons and come out to face four counts of first-degree murder in the state that leads the nation in capital punishment.

The most appalling aspect of Koresh's narcissism and megalomania was that he seemed to have no concern for the innocent people who would die with him—he appeared to see nothing but his own personal drama.

Amid growing frustration, an FBI delegation flew to Washington to brief newly appointed Attorney General Janet Reno, but in fact it was more a sales pitch for one course of action than a complete presentation of all the information. Jamar brought Dick Rogers from HRT but no one from the negotiation team. The delegation expressed their legitimate concerns that the now significantly deteriorating sanitary conditions within the compound were endangering the lives of the children inside. They also made much of the suspicion that Koresh was sexually abusing underage girls in the compound. But even though this was alleged in past reports, and later confirmed by witnesses, we had no evidence that this was currently ongoing. And, if it was ongoing, why had it not been an issue over the preceding fifty days of the siege? Having provided a very one-sided picture of Waco as a crisis in need of immediate tactical intervention, Jamar requested authorization to use tear gas as a way to drive the Davidians out. Persuaded that children were indeed very much at risk, Attorney General Reno approved.

Just before 6:00 a.m. on April 19 the Davidians awoke to winds gusting at sixty miles per hour and a calm message from Byron Sage on the telephone.

He told Schneider that they were about to be subjected to nonlethal tear gas. It wasn't an assault, Sage told him, but everyone was being ordered to exit the compound immediately.

A minute later the Davidians threw the field telephone we had installed for them out the front door. There seemed to be no further need to talk. Sage then began to broadcast his appeals for surrender over the speaker system.

I was now back from Jordan and at FBI headquarters watching as the armored CEVs began pumping in the gas. Shortly after, those on the perimeter began to hear the ping of ricocheting bullets around them. The Davidians had begun to fire at them from inside the compound for the first time since the shootout with the ATF fifty-one days prior.

No one was coming out.

This was followed by a series of assumptions and decisions that would quickly bring the crisis to a head. Rogers speculated that the women and children were being physically blocked from leaving. And so Jamar ordered the CEVs to begin smashing into the compound's walls, opening up holes large enough that those who wanted to leave could do so.

Still no one came out.

As I watched, I wondered how the Davidians could see this as anything other than an assault. How on earth could mothers with children be expected to rush to safety toward armored vehicles when those same vehicles were punching holes into their home? An argument for inserting tear gas and letting it slowly do its work could perhaps be made; however, smashing holes in the compound constituted a dramatic escalation from the approved plan.

At 12:13 that afternoon, the FBI observed a curl of smoke emerge from the southwest corner of the building and soon more smoke and then flames. Hidden-microphone recordings, reviewed after the incident but not monitored live, picked up the voice of Schneider ordering a conflagration, and an HRT observer testified that he saw a Davidian pouring gas on piles of straw and lighting them. Stoked by the high winds, the fire quickly engulfed the compound.

Only nine of the remaining Davidians would make it out of the compound; the others were back in the center. Seven of the nine who came out that day had accelerants (fuel) on their clothing (sleeves and pant legs). One woman actually tried to go back into the burning compound but was tackled and brought to safety by a heroic HRT operator, Jim McGee. The crime scene examination that followed showed that most of the bodies were located in a central area where Koresh had assembled his followers to await their fate. The autopsy report suggested that some of the young children had been killed, presumably by their parents, to spare them the pain of burning to death. Koresh's body was found next to Steve Schneider's. Koresh had a bullet wound to the brain. Schneider had a bullet wound to the upper palate inside his mouth. It appeared as though Koresh had ordered Schneider to shoot him, after which Schneider killed himself. In all, seventy-five individuals died; an independent investigation would verify that the Davidians had started the fires that killed them.

As I watched the television pictures of the compound going up in flames, I felt sick to the pit of my stomach. I was as angry as I have ever been in my life. How could this have ended so badly? I was mostly angry at Koresh and the senseless waste of life he had ordered, but I was also mad that the FBI had not handled this as well as I knew we could have. I'm certain that with a little more patience and finesse we could have saved many more lives. I stood and walked out of FBI headquarters without saying a word to anyone. I didn't ask permission to leave; I just walked out in disgust and drove home. It was the saddest and most painful day of my career.

That day and into the night I called every individual on the negotiation team I could reach to assure them that what happened was not their fault and not their failure. I told them how proud of them I was and that their efforts had saved thirty-five people who otherwise would have perished. In fact, I'm as proud of the work of this team as I am of anything else in my entire career.

Waco was for the FBI a self-inflicted wound that would take years to heal. It caused the public to doubt the organization as never before, and once a reputation is tarnished, it's extremely difficult to regain the public's confidence. Some good would eventually come from it: several official inquiries and congressional hearings made clear that the negotiation and tactical teams had been at cross-purposes, and those sitting in judgment came to appreciate that the negotiation team had been on the right track and that Rogers and Jamar had got it wrong. Neither man was dismissed, however Waco would prove to be the effective end of both men's career advancement.

At the time of this writing, the FBI has not managed a major siege operation in over a decade. Few if any current top leaders in the FBI have even been present during a significant siege incident, and none has commanded one. It is my hope and desire that they will learn much by reading the account of what went wrong at Waco. If I anger some former colleagues with my candor and my effort to assist in this process, then so be it. The future of the FBI, its standing with the American people, and the maintenance of its hard-fought and well-deserved reputation cannot afford anything less than excellence in these matters.

CHAPTER EIGHT

PICKING UP THE PIECES

We seek the truth, and will endure the consequences.
—CHARLES SEYMOUR

The morning after the fire at Ranch Apocalypse, I was sent to the Southern Ohio Correctional Facility in Lucasville, where an inmate uprising had been going on for a little more than a week. Ordinarily, I was always ready to say, "Put me in, coach," but at this point, utterly exhausted and emotionally spent, I was hoping the incident would be over before I got there. Then again, I also needed to get Waco off my mind, and maybe this situation would give us a chance to get it right. Lucasville was a complex situation, though, with what in fact were three competing hostage situations taking place simultaneously.

I flew to Columbus, Ohio, where a local FBI agent picked me up and drove me to the prison, just north of the Kentucky border. After a two-hour trip through farmland, we saw the light gray buildings spread out on the edge of town. With its simple lines and no structure more than two stories, the prison could have been a typical American high school. Except, of course, for the double perimeter of ten-foot-high fences topped with concertina wire.

We pulled up to the administration building, which, again, had a driveway that looked suitable for parents to drop off and pick up their kids. Off to my right, just outside the fencing, I saw the twisted carcass of a state police helicopter that had crashed in the early days of the standoff—engine trouble. Fortunately, no one had been killed.

I got out and walked inside, where the wide hallways and linoleum floor extended the high school look and feel. But instead of football banners, the wall outside the warden's office displayed a photograph of bulky inmates working out with weights. The caption said, *What are you doing to stay in shape?*

My driver introduced me to FBI Cincinnati Field Office Assistant Special Agent in Charge Paul Mallett, the senior FBI official on the scene. In turn, he introduced me to the Lucasville prison warden, Arthur Tate, who had been an FBI agent earlier in his career and was very receptive to having our assistance and advice. Through our conversation, Art struck me as the kind of thoughtful leader you want managing a crisis. He told me that he very much wanted a negotiated resolution if at all possible. He wasn't just interested in punishing the inmates for what they had done; his focus and attention were on doing what was best to secure the safe release of his people and restore order to the facility.

Also present was profiler Larry Ankrom, an FBI colleague and good friend with whom I had worked at WFO and Quantico. Larry, who was from Ohio, had been in the area visiting family when prison officials asked the Bureau to supply them with a profiler. After the movie *Silence of the Lambs* came out, local authorities often asked for a profiler when what they really needed was a negotiator. Larry was an excellent profiler, but he also knew his limitations in the negotiation arena, so he had suggested that they send for me.

On the muted television set in the warden's office, left on to monitor media reporting of the situation, I faced the rebuke of a seemingly endless loop of footage from the Waco fire the previous day. Mallett and Tate both asked me about it, but I tried to get past their questions as quickly as possible. I told them that it had been the most difficult situation I had ever worked. I also said that it was a great tragedy that I wanted to help avoid here.

These men seemed both open and receptive to advice, which made them polar opposites from Jamar and Rogers. I couldn't help wondering how the standoff with the Davidians might have turned out differently if men like these had been in charge. The more immediate question was whether or not these men could maintain their demonstrated self-control long enough to peacefully resolve their own very complex situation.

The crisis had begun on Sunday morning, April 11, when inmates staged a fistfight in the prison's exercise area, an expansive series of playing fields. Inmates have endless hours to study how correctional officers respond to flare-ups, and they know that the guards in the yard don't carry guns. Typically, prisoners stage a scuffle, which forces the guards to converge. At that point the shanks (homemade knives) come out. The inmates overpower a few guards, then use their captives as bargaining chips to gain control over others.

Seven hundred inmates, roughly half the prison population, had been out in the recreation area when the first hostage taking occurred. Three hundred twenty-one of the inmates on the scene wanted no part of what was happening and retreated to the other side of the field, where prison authorities over loudspeakers instructed them to remain. The others went back into L Block and barricaded themselves inside with a total of eight correctional officers held as hostages.

The warden explained that the initial uprising, which occurred on Easter Sunday, was driven by several of the prison's black Muslims, who objected on religious grounds to a prison requirement that they be inoculated against tuberculosis. But this was merely the fuel tossed on a pre-existing tinderbox of grievances. After the firestorm broke out, other factions within the prison population took the opportunity to forward their own agendas. The two other principal groups in play were the Gangster Disciples, a black gang with no pretense of religious motivation, and the all-white Aryan Brotherhood. Given the dynamics within the prison, it appeared that each group felt the need to take their own hostages to, as they saw it, guarantee themselves a voice in any resolution that emerged. One faction barricaded themselves in the gymnasium, another in the cafeteria, the third in a classroom.

At dawn on April 12, prison officials cut off water and electricity. Later that day, correctional officers calling from the negotiation center in the main administration building contacted each of the three different inmate groups by telephone and negotiated the transfer of the bodies of the six prisoners known to have been killed during the initial riot. Correctional officers also moved into the yard and escorted away the 321 prisoners who had remained outside, then set about housing them in other units.

My first impression from that initial briefing was that Lucasville had a long history of overcrowding, as well as violence between inmates and staff and between the convicts themselves. The warden told me that negotiators had already heard a litany of grievances, including the desire to stop forced integration, the need to hire more black guards, the need to remove certain white supervisors, access to the media, relaxation of time limits on activities, and increasing recreational and educational activities.

"Those don't strike me as unreasonable demands," I said. "Which may improve the odds that we can negotiate our way to a resolution."

On the positive side, the warden and his colleagues told me, the white prisoners had released correctional officer Darrold Clark on the evening of April 15. In exchange, prison officials had allowed a live broadcast on local radio by an Aryan Nations inmate.

The next day, the Muslims requested a similar exchange. They released correctional officer James Demons, after which they were allowed to make a broadcast to air their grievances.

"We were pretty optimistic," the warden said. "But then, later that day, we found out that one of our guys, correctional officer Robert Vallandingham, had been murdered. We think an inmate just had it in for him from before the riot." There had been no demands made before his execution, so I suspected that was correct.

Then Warden Tate looked at me. "We're getting frustrated. If we thought the murder of Officer Vallandingham was the shape of things to come, we'd be ready to move in. It's important that we begin to make some progress on getting the hostages released. I'd like you to meet with our negotiation team, absorb what they're doing, and then make some recommendations. I'd like your help figuring out how we get ourselves out of this mess."

The negotiation room was a large conference area just down the hall from the warden's office. Glancing out the window, I could see L Block, a nondescript slab of concrete, some two hundred yards away.

The team consisted of eight Ohio correctional officer negotiators brought in from other facilities. All had received negotiation training but none had yet had any actual experience. They were being assisted by Dave Michael, the negotiator from the Dayton Police Department who had trained them. They had set up a dedicated telephone line for communicating with the inmates.

We went around the table and introduced ourselves. Michael was the only one who had ever negotiated an actual hostage incident, but they all seemed focused on the mission at hand and prepared to do what they needed to do. Michael himself seemed a bit aloof at first. I sensed that he viewed my arrival as threatening to his status as the most experienced negotiator on the scene, but once I established that I wasn't there to take over, he proved to be a good team player. I quietly listened as the team presented me with a comprehensive briefing on what they had been doing and how they saw the situation they faced.

When they were done, I told the team that as I saw it, our first task was to help these inmates figure out and clearly articulate what they wanted. It's hard enough to negotiate with one person when he doesn't know what he wants. At Lucasville, we faced three opposing factions that did not communicate well, had different agendas, and refused to cooperate with one another. In addition, no one group wanted to give up their bargaining chips—the correctional officers they held hostage.

"You guys know prisons," I started in. "But my experience with prison incidents tells me that inmates sometimes need several days to vent their emotions, exercise their frustrations, and generally act out. Perhaps they're finally getting to a point where they can be channeled toward a productive dialogue."

The correctional officers nodded in agreement.

"My hope is that we're nearing the time when they can settle down and make some better decisions. Maybe some cooler heads can start to step up."

"We need to find those cooler heads," Michael added.

"And find a way to encourage them along," I added.

The challenge I put on the table was this: how could we help the inmates get organized so they could figure out what they were after? Only when realistic concerns were on the table could we identify underlying needs and begin to structure an effective negotiation approach and then a reasonable resolution strategy. We knew we had to help them assemble a leadership team that we could negotiate with. We needed to focus on the most sensible of the inmates the team had spoken with so far, and to find ways to promote these individuals. Of course, this was easier said than done.

The primary negotiator was Dirk Prise from the Ohio Department of Corrections. His major challenge was going to be fielding calls from each of the three major factions.

"I've got individual inmates calling up at random to rant and rave," he said. "'I want my charges dropped.' 'I want to see my girlfriend.' 'I want to talk to Jesse Jackson.'"

"What do you tell 'em?" I asked.

"Mostly I say, 'I'm not authorized to do that.'"

I smiled at him. Dirk seemed far more affable and far less inflexible and authoritarian than some of the correctional officers I had known in the past. I felt he would do very well as the primary negotiator.

"Step one, I think, is to get beyond that. We need to give the inmates a sense that they've been heard. That will reinforce the idea that they can gain some concessions."

We began making a list of action points. There was bad blood between the inmates and the authorities. To overcome long-standing mistrust, we needed to introduce an outside intermediary who could facilitate discussions and serve as a neutral arbitrator. To begin having serious talks, we had to impose some structure. This meant encouraging each faction to list their concerns and have one individual as their representative to meet with us.

After Tate and Mallett agreed with our assessment, we sought an agreement to meet face-to-face with inmate leaders away from the larger prison population, so that they would feel no pressure to posture or perform. We proposed setting up two tables facing each other, one for the inmates and one for the authorities, on opposite sides of the inner perimeter fence. It took a while, but Dirk got the inmates to agree, in part by allowing them to feel that the format was their idea.

On April 21, the eleventh day of the incident, at 10:40 a.m., the selected inmate leaders, one from each of the factions, came out and sat down opposite officials of the FBI and Ohio State Police. Also sitting outside the fence was attorney Niki Schwartz, a well-known criminal defense attorney and former head of the Ohio chapter of the American Civil Liberties Union, who was serving as the neutral intermediary.

After a few minutes of preliminary discussion, the inmates agreed to having Department of Correction representatives, including Dirk Prise, come to the table to join in on the talks. Larry and I watched with binoculars through a window in a hallway near the negotiation room, eager to observe the body language. Everyone seemed calm and respectful—no grandstanding or obvious signs of anger. Maybe this could be the breakthrough we needed.

The lengthy discussion produced a cogent list of twenty-one demands, which Dirk carefully copied down for the record:

1. The prison will follow all administrative rules of the Ohio Department of Rehabilitation and Correction.
2. Inmate discipline will be administered fairly and without bias.
3. Complete medical attention will be given to the prisoners.
4. The inmate surrender will be witnessed by a religious leader.
5. The prison's unit management system (a policy to hear inmate complaints) will be reviewed.
6. The prison will review the *White v. Morris* federal case that permits prison cell integration.
7. All high-security inmates will be transferred out of L Block, as has been done in Cellblock K.
8. The procedure for early release will be reviewed and changed if warranted.
9. An attempt will be made to reduce overcrowding.
10. Policies involving inappropriate supervision will be rigidly enforced.
11. Medical staff will be reviewed.
12. Plans to install a new phone system will be speeded up.
13. Work opportunities will be evaluated and improved.
14. There will be no retaliation against rebelling inmates.
15. Policies concerning mail and visitor privileges will be reviewed.
16. Prompt transfer will be conducted for those eligible.

17. An attempt will be made to improve communications between inmates and officials.
18. Commissary prices will be reviewed.
19. The Ohio Department of Health will be contacted about tuberculosis testing.
20. The FBI will monitor prisoners' processing to ensure that their civil rights are upheld.
21. Prisoners' requests to be transferred out of state will be taken seriously if those inmates can prove an Ohio prison cannot provide a safe environment for them.

I was pleased that the inmates were now focused on reasonable and obtainable objectives, but this list of demands wasn't going to be an easy sell. The prison tactical teams were not in a conciliatory mood, especially after the murder of their colleague. Warden Tate had his doubts, too, until I pointed out to him the way each point was qualified with phrases such as "an attempt will be made," "will be reviewed," "will speed up," "changed if warranted," and "will be taken seriously." It was clear to me that the inmates wanted to end the siege and that we were hardly giving away the store or making promises that could not reasonably be kept.

With only slight modifications, the authorities agreed to these demands, and Tate signed a document to that effect.

When the inmates later asked if the agreement was enforceable, Schwartz told them quite honestly that it had no legal foundation. He quickly added, however, that based on his conversations with Tate, he was convinced that every effort would be made to honor the agreement and that each and every issue would be given full examination by the authorities. The inmates found this acceptable.

That evening, as a reward meant to reinforce the inmates' good behavior, correctional officers brought out a short ration of food and left the carts about a hundred feet from the L Block entrance. As agreed, the inmates left in exchange a videotape of the hostages that could be shown to their concerned families.

The next day, according to a protocol previously arranged, corrections officers delivered laundry bags to the yard for the inmates to use to carry out their personal belongings. Then at 3:55 p.m. the actual evacuation process began. We purposefully called it an evacuation, which sounded better to the inmates than surrender. The injured were the first to come out, four on stretchers and twenty-two walking. Two hours later, a group of inmates who had been identified by the others as predatory and subsequently isolated came out. After this, the rest came out in a trickle, a process that took many hours.

At 10:25 that night I stood at the window of the administration building and watched as three corrections officers, Richard Buffington, Michael Hensley, and Larry Dotson were walked out of L Block into the brightly lit prison yard. Five minutes later, Jeffrey Ratcliff and Kenneth Daniels came out. As they limped down the long hallway leading out of the facility, unshaven, their faces bruised but smiling, these released hostages were met by waves of applause from their emotional fellow officers, who lined the hallway.

Twenty minutes later, 407 inmates were in custody and the surrender was complete. L Block had been thoroughly trashed, with shredded mattresses and smashed television sets everywhere. While going through the debris, officers discovered the bodies of two additional inmates, the only remaining negative in an otherwise positive outcome.

Afterward, Tate and some members of the negotiation team received a number of harsh comments from other corrections officers who were angry over what had happened to Officer Vallandingham and frustrated by the lack of retribution. But if we had learned one thing from Waco, it was the lesson about not letting our own emotions overpower our responsibilities.

The negotiation team at Lucasville managed to save the lives of seven of the eight officers held. The other's death had not come as a result of failed negotiations. If those in charge had acted on the basis of their understandable anger over the death of their colleague, there would have been a great many more deaths to mourn. Their restraint paid off.

I flew home from Lucasville the next day. I felt good about the outcome and my small role in helping, but I was still thoroughly drained from the

Waco experience and I wanted nothing more than to spend some time with my family. Thinking about the death of Robert Vallandingham, I could only imagine the pain his wife and son were feeling. It made me appreciate all the more the fact that I was going home, and what I was going home to. At this time my kids were thirteen, eleven, and nine, and I wanted to be at their weekend soccer games, have dinner with them and Carol, see friends, and just be home to deal with everyday, normal "honey-dos."

While the successful resolution at Lucasville had offset some of my frustration about Waco, the reverberations of the events in Texas were far from over. Several television documentaries would attempt to assess what had happened, thereby keeping the issue in the spotlight. Some were accurate; some were sensationalized and filled with errors. And like Ruby Ridge, Waco also became a huge rallying point for domestic extremist groups and the far right wing.

In their comments, Republican congressmen railed against what they called the ineptitude of Janet Reno and Bill Clinton in dealing with the crisis. The Department of Justice and Treasury Department conducted separate inquiries and issued reports, mostly blaming David Koresh, and rightly so, but also questioning the FBI's aggressive and contradictory approach. ATF took the worst criticism for the ill-advised raid that sparked the standoff. The political leaders also raised questions about the appropriateness of the FBI's use of tear gas in a compound that held so many young children.

Meanwhile, conspiracy theories abounded. One held that the FBI purposely set the fires to kill all inside—this despite clear evidence that the Davidians had lit the flames. It was in the context of outrage over Waco that the Ruby Ridge incident was brought back to public attention as yet another example of FBI failure.

Attorney General Janet Reno publicly accepted responsibility for what had happened at Waco, an unheard-of act of honesty by a government official. Many praised her candor, but her political opponents sensed weakness and pounced. In reality, she had been brand-new to the job when she attended that FBI briefing with all the talk of children being sexually abused. I've often wondered what decisions would have resulted if a negotiation representative had been allowed to participate in the briefing on the final days of the siege to answer her questions and offer a somewhat different perspective on the existing risk to the children versus the risks of the planned operation.

Byron Sage, Jeff Jamar, Dick Rogers, and I were all called to testify before the House and later the Senate during congressional hearings. The lengthy and difficult task of assembling data on the incident fell mostly to Byron Sage, who gathered all the negotiation tapes, recommendations, call logs, and other information for the various inquiries.

The four of us shared a table with four microphones and faced our questioners, who grilled Jamar and Rogers on the decision making and the tactical operation. The criticism of their actions was so withering that there was no need for me to add my own broadsides. The format also called for us to respond to direct inquiries rather than to offer prepared statements. I used the opportunity to describe what we had accomplished on the negotiation front and articulate the strategy our team had pursued to secure the safe release of thirty-five individuals. The fact that the Bureau had failed to effectively manage the larger operation was painfully obvious to everyone.

This was my first congressional hearing, and I was not at all impressed with what I saw. In the hallways during recess, Democratic congressmen sought our help in formulating questions that would defend the Bureau against Republicans, normally supportive of the FBI, who seemed willing to throw the Bureau to the wolves solely for the purpose of embarrassing President Clinton—who as far as I could tell had very little input into the events at Waco.

Many congressmen, former pop star Sonny Bono among them, showed up in the room only when it was their time to talk. You could see them enter the hearing room and receive a quick briefing from a twenty-one-year-old aide before asking us their questions, often repeating the very same ones already asked numerous times before. It seemed that most were simply posturing for the cameras. Rather than a serious attempt at fact-finding, it seemed to be an opportunity for the members to score political points against each other.

After our testimony, the four of us went back to FBI headquarters to confer with the Bureau's legal counsel. Rogers, Jamar, Sage, and I were kept waiting for a while in a conference room. Neither Rogers nor Jamar was an expressive man, but they both nodded and thanked me for what I had said—or, more accurately, not said. While I fundamentally disagreed with Rogers's approach and Jamar's management of the incident, I believed both were dedicated public servants who had tried to do what they thought was best. They knew that I could have raked them over the coals. The truth was, I felt that I should emphasize the positive story of the negotiation effort without heaping scorn on the mistakes they had made. The evidence of their misjudgments spoke clearly enough.

Despite it all, I was heartened time and again to hear from a wide array of knowledgeable colleagues and experts in the crisis management and negotiation field that the negotiation team at Waco had it right, that the patient "trickle, flow, gush" strategy we pursued should have been supported and allowed to continue without the ill-advised tactical activities that led to disaster.

Louis Freeh became the new FBI director after Waco, and fortunately he was a vocal supporter of the negotiation process. He and several other high-level Bureau officials thanked me for my testimony. While I was completely honest in what I testified to, I didn't sell the Bureau down the river by emphasizing the negatives. It seemed to me that FBI leadership mistakes at Waco were by now quite obvious to all concerned.

All in all, there were five major investigations, the last of which was headed by former Missouri senator John Danforth. With the benefit of the passage of time and a calmer atmosphere, the Danforth Commission conducted the most comprehensive and thorough examination of the incident. Once again, the commission's findings correctly faulted many FBI management decisions while praising the undervalued and under-appreciated negotiation effort.

No FBI internal after-action meeting was ever held, so the rift that had surfaced between negotiators and tactical team operators was never adequately addressed and resolved. The lingering ill will would diminish with time, but it remained a sad situation for me.

Not long after the congressional hearings I went through a difficult period emotionally, moping around as I had never before done in my life. I was forty-three years old and had been in the FBI for twenty-one years. I had enjoyed a varied career that most agents would never know.

I still loved my job, but something wasn't right. I felt very sad. I also wasn't sleeping well, and I became so withdrawn that my wife became concerned and close friends began to ask me what was going on. I wasn't sure myself, so I didn't know what to say to them.

Eventually I talked through my state of funk with several negotiation colleagues who had also been at Waco. I learned that a lot of the negotiators from my team were having a tough time, too. Particularly supportive among my friends were John Dolan and Jim Botting, who had been a negotiator and a team leader, respectively, at Waco, and Dr. Mike Webster, the Canadian psychologist who had helped us develop much of the theoretical basis for our crisis intervention program and who specialized in counseling law enforcement officers. We talked on the phone regularly about work, and our conversations would naturally turn to these personal issues and how I was coping. I told them that I was in a total funk—low energy and not myself. I had been an informal counselor for dozens of law enforcement negotiation friends going through difficult times after tough incidents, never thinking I would someday need the same type of help. But I did.

Mike in particular was able to help me recognize and address my anger over what had happened at Waco and my frustrations over the failure of some FBI leaders to take responsibility for what had gone wrong. I felt like I was rowing upstream against the current of arrogance. Police agencies around the world took our negotiation training as gospel and followed our guidelines and recommendations to the letter, yet it seemed that within the FBI itself the negotiation program might be destined to remain undervalued and unappreciated.

As unlikely as it seems, the thing that snapped me out of my funk was more work. Some months after Waco, my longtime partner, mentor, and friend, Fred Lanceley, decided to retire. Ruby Ridge had been especially tough on Fred. The success of him and his team in negotiating an end to that tense standoff had never received appropriate recognition from the Bureau. SWAT gets the medals, but getting someone to surrender looks easy—until you have to convince a hostage taker to put down his weapons and come out.

I was promoted—put in charge of the entire FBI negotiation program and given the newly created title of chief negotiator. This would give me the opportunity to grow the FBI negotiation program and advocate on behalf of the strategies I had spent more than a decade helping to develop. These new responsibilities contributed greatly to helping me move past the funk I had been in. Simply put, I was far too busy to dwell on what had happened in the past. Almost every night calls came in asking me to assist with ongoing incidents or seeking guidance. It was a rare evening when I was not on the phone for an hour or more. Carol, for her part, pleased to see me happy again, never objected to my going to work and traveling, but she hated those calls interrupting our family life. She used to say, "If you're going to be working, then go to work. If you're going to be home, then be at home." She was right, of course, but the FBI had a way of demanding all you could give and then some.

Fortunately, the Waco experience also led to deeper reforms within the FBI. The FBI is an entrenched bureaucracy that tends to be resistant to change, but after Waco, the public criticism demanded it. Like me, Bob Gleason from our unit, now called the Crisis Management Unit (CMU), had long known that management was the weak link in the FBI's crisis response. Now he was tasked to put together an advanced crisis management curriculum for FBI leadership. I was assigned to develop a companion negotiation training curriculum for all potential FBI incident commanders. I later summarized this block of instruction in an article called "Negotiation Concepts for Commanders," published in the *FBI Law Enforcement Bulletin*. It remains one of the most widely circulated and heavily used negotiation training and operational guidance tools for law enforcement today. Bob and I gave this training to every SAC in the FBI.

Following a directive from Attorney General Janet Reno, I gave Leon Schenck, one of the newly assigned negotiators on my five-man team, the task of putting together the FBI Hostage Barricade Database System (HOBAS), bringing together a complete statistical summary of all such incidents based on FBI and police data we collected. Today HOBAS is the primary source of hostage and barricade data in the world and is nationally available to all law enforcement negotiation teams.

Eventually, Waco spurred Director Freeh to create the Critical Incident Response Group (CIRG), housed at the FBI academy. For the first time, this placed HRT, behavioral profilers, crisis managers, crisis negotiators, and some additional specialized components under one unified command. Henceforth, CIRG would manage all major sieges with the objective of ensuring proper coordination and management of the many skilled resources the FBI could bring to bear. The FBI would no longer simply rely on the capabilities or limitations of the local Special Agent in Charge.

Before these initiatives, very little high-quality training had been provided to FBI leaders. Too often, the Bureau assumed that because an individual had risen to a high rank within the FBI, he or she automatically knew how to manage a crisis. But few executives in the FBI, or even throughout the larger U.S. government, had the training or experience necessary to function competently in such situations. Sad to say, this remains largely true today.

In addition to providing this training, the FBI negotiation program was increasingly recognized by police departments around the country as the place to get expert negotiation assistance twenty-four hours a day, seven days a week. The FBI's negotiation expertise was increasingly in demand abroad as well. Between 1990 and 1993, we deployed negotiators overseas in response to the kidnapping of American citizens more than thirty times; the number of cases would rise to over 120 by 2003. Each deployment was time-intensive and operationally challenging, not only for the negotiators deployed but also for our unit at Quantico, since we actively deployed, managed, and directed the response to these cases.

In the years after Waco our hostage negotiation team established itself as a crucial component of the FBI's efforts at crisis response. While we received plaudits from Director Freeh and other senior officials, the best part of our job in those days was the feedback we received from American and foreign police departments that we'd helped in times of crisis. More often than not, we heard that our assistance had been critical to reaching a positive resolution. We knew our work was saving lives, and we got a tremendous amount of satisfaction from this.

The general public, of course, still associated the FBI with Waco, and it would continue to do so until we had a chance to show in a high-profile case that we'd incorporated its lessons. This chance finally came in 1996, in an incident that would truly test the patience of everyone involved.

CHAPTER NINE

A HELL OF A SIEGE

Perseverance is more prevailing than violence; and many things
which cannot be overcome when they are together, yield themselves
up when taken little by little.
—PLUTARCH

The day was warm and clear as we stood in an open field near Jordan, Montana, about four hundred miles east of Missoula. Up here near the Canadian border, the land seemed to go on forever, and yet it still seemed insignificant compared to the endless blue above, the rationale for Montana's nickname, Big Sky Country. My colleague and I wore short-sleeved shirts beneath our bulletproof vests, but we kept glancing back at the sky as though we feared this unusual feast of good weather would quickly evaporate, bringing back the gloom we had come to expect. June in Montana was so fickle that you could experience all four seasons in a single day. The rain was even worse than the snow because any soaking typically left the dirt roads rutted like an old washboard. One FBI SWAT team agent had already been killed driving too fast on the treacherous roads, trying to get to his shift on time.

Once a shoe or boot got sucked into the spring mud—called "gumbo" by the locals—usually nothing came back out but a bare foot. I'm sure anthropologists in the distant future will have a field day trying to figure out why so many single shoes and boots were found just beneath the surface of the earth near Jordan, Montana.

Dwayne Fuselier, standing beside me in the low brown grass, complained about having to wear the hot and heavy Kevlar, but I insisted we keep the vests on. I didn't want negotiation students to see me in a news photo not following safety regulations.

Several hundred yards behind us was an HRT SUV containing a sniper/observer team there to cover us if something went wrong. We were not armed, as agreed to by all parties, but we couldn't help but wonder if we could really trust representatives of the Freemen, a radical militia group, to leave their weapons behind as promised. I had personally observed that Russ Landers, one of their more hotheaded and intransigent members, had worn a gun to a prior meeting at this same location, even though all had agreed to come unarmed. I found little comfort knowing that, after the fact, our own marksmen would probably take out anyone who put a bullet in me. Still, the risk was reasonable and we were well covered.

In reality, we were more anxious about last-minute changes of heart than we were about potential dangers. The folks we were dealing with seemed to have great difficulty making up their minds.

A vehicle emerged from around a hill and drove toward us. The car stopped about a hundred yards from the cattle guard marking the edge of the Freemen's property, where we stood waiting out in the open. Edwin Clark got out of the car and walked toward us in an unhurried manner. Forty-six years old, five foot nine, 235 pounds, he wore a baseball cap, collared shirt, jeans, and work boots. He looked like the farmer and rancher he was, out on a routine errand. Was he about to say that he had convinced the others to end the siege, or was the momentum we thought we had rolling about to stall? Among the Freemen, Clark was the voice of reason we had been counting on to bring the others around. But we had been at this for eighty-one days now, the longest siege in U.S. history. At this point, everyone was so exhausted that, quite honestly, anything could happen.

The weather could not have been more different when I first arrived in Montana months earlier. I remember an extremely clear, extremely cold night in March with billions of stars; I was driving north from Billings with another FBI agent and a United States attorney who would be prosecuting the case against the Freemen. We were one of several groups who were quietly converging on Jordan, once described by *National Geographic* magazine as the most remote city in the continental United States. The nearest town of any size was Miles City, eighty-three miles away. I had been in Moscow the year before, teaching agents of the Federal Security Service, the successor agency to the Soviet-era KGB. If you had told me those were the steppes of Russia outside the car window that night, I would have believed you.

Our first goal that night driving up from Billings was to reach the Garfield County Fairgrounds, a mile or so outside of Jordan, without being noticed. A great deal of secrecy had gone into moving the personnel and equipment forward to implement our operation, code-named "Gray Sunset." A makeshift command post was to be set up in a couple of the barnlike cinder-block buildings located on the fairgrounds. The bulk of the FBI personnel deployed were waiting back in Billings to be called forward when needed. This included a large contingent of negotiators brought in from around the country.

Tom Kubic, the Special Agent in Charge of the Salt Lake City office, was in command of the entire operation. We were joined by Robin Montgomery. A well-regarded and steady FBI leader, he was also a Marine who had won a Silver Star in Vietnam. Robin was the SAC in charge of the newly created Critical Incident Response Group and my boss back at Quantico. While the SAC of CIRG would not be the final decision maker on the scene, his influence on all strategy decisions gave him de facto veto power over anything he deemed reckless. We would link up with Assistant Special Agent in Charge Roger Nisley, who had replaced Dick Rogers as the commander of the HRT. Unlike his predecessor, he struck me as very easygoing and levelheaded, with a healthy respect for the negotiation process.

It was still dark when we reached the fairgrounds. We pulled our vehicle into the largest of the fairground buildings and closed the door behind us to stay out of sight. It was unbelievably cold outside, but it was even colder inside. Now there was nothing to do but stamp our feet on the dirt floor and wait. Like most of the others, I had to retreat back into the car now and then to get warm. Maybe it was my Florida upbringing, but I never seemed to bring enough cold-weather gear on these operations.

A separate team of FBI agents had been working for months to get close to Leroy Schweitzer and Dan Peterson, the Freemen's leader and his number one assistant. An undercover agent had managed to insert hidden microphones in the Freemen's property, to assist in monitoring their activities.

While we waited at the fairgrounds outside Jordan, Schweitzer and Peterson were heading to a snow-covered hillside they had picked as the site for a new radio tower, which the Freemen hoped to use to broadcast their common-law ideology far and wide. Their driver was the man who had helped finance this project and had brought in the team of "construction workers" now standing by. He was also an undercover FBI agent.

Their car reached the top of the hill and parked. Schweitzer and Peterson got out to survey the large pile of metal poles and other materials lying on the ground. At that moment the workers—in reality, members of the FBI Hostage Rescue Team—seized both men, hustled them to the ground, then disarmed and handcuffed them. The two were then placed in separate vehicles and quickly driven away.

A short time later, the HRT team with the Freemen's leadership in custody arrived at the fairgrounds where we stood waiting. Federal law enforcement had definitely internalized the first and most basic lesson of Waco—the ATF's fatal mistake in not trying to arrest David Koresh when he was outside and away from his followers. Step one of our plan in dealing with the Montana Freemen was to place their leaders in federal custody. That goal was now accomplished.

The second step was to try to reach the rest of the Freemen and get them to surrender. Schweitzer and Peterson had been apprehended by undercover agents driving civilian cars. For the long ride to a holding cell in Billings, they needed to be transferred to a vehicle outfitted for transferring prisoners. Schweitzer seemed like a tough nut to crack, but SAC Kubic asked me to approach Peterson during that brief transfer and see if I could talk him into helping us convince the others to surrender peacefully. When it comes to trying to create any kind of dialogue with those in custody, it's often a negotiator who gets the assignment.

The cars carrying the two prisoners rolled inside the big fairgrounds building, and the two men were brought out in handcuffs. Peterson was wearing jeans, a baseball cap, and a jacket with a fleece collar.

I said, "Mr. Peterson, I'm Gary Noesner and I'm with the FBI. I'd like to chat with you for a minute."

He wouldn't so much as look at me.

The crotch area of his pants was soaking wet. Apparently the arrest had been a very big surprise for him.

The Freemen were yet another small, loose-knit group of individuals who, like Randy Weaver, held antigovernment right-wing views that led them to believe they were sovereign and a law unto themselves. They did not recognize the authority of the U.S. government in any way. Like other antigovernment groups, they refused to pay taxes, obey laws other than their own, obtain driver's licenses, or display tags on their vehicles. Like survivalist and militia groups elsewhere, they derived a large part of their income by filing false liens against anyone they considered a nuisance or a problem, particularly public officials. Using these bogus liens, the Freemen would then draw fraudulent certified checks. As a result, the Freemen had committed numerous acts of financial fraud, mail fraud, and wire fraud, using some of their illegitimate financial instruments to pay off IRS debts, purchase vehicles, and pay home, ranch, and farm mortgages. The financial loss to the victim entities was both real and substantial.

The Freemen had also threatened a federal judge, and at one point they brandished weapons as they took over a meeting of the Jordan city council. As a result of this widespread and continuing criminal activity, a sealed federal indictment had been obtained charging various individuals with a multitude of criminal violations. Local charges were also pending when the Freemen took refuge on a group of ranches owned by members of the Clark family, a remote stretch of property about twenty-five miles west of Jordan. Local law consisted of the sheriff, his undersheriff, and two officers of the Montana Highway Patrol—not a force large enough to take on a well-armed group of malcontents. Unfortunately, this understandable reluctance to confront the Freemen merely served to embolden them. These right-wing militiamen had begun to believe their own propaganda about not being subject to the law.

After local warrants were issued against them, the Freemen publicly

threatened to abduct Sheriff Charles Phipps and Garfield County prosecutor Nick Murnion, try them in common-law court for treason, and
hang them. They also threatened an ABC news crew that came to interview them, and stole their expensive camera equipment at gunpoint.

These acts had put the Freemen on an unavoidable collision course
with the government, which is when the local authorities turned to the
FBI for assistance. With memories of Waco still fresh and painful, this
time the FBI was going to do everything humanly possible to avoid a
violent assault.

For the past year, the Freemen had held weekly two-day seminars in
a classroom on the Clark ranch, teaching common law, how to file Uniform Commercial Code liens, and procedures for paying debts or pur-
chasing property with bogus certified checks. A brand-new and very
expensive motor home rested on the property, illegally obtained through
these fraudulent financial instruments. Approximately twenty-five individuals attended each class, and at the conclusion of each training session the attendees were each given a fake certified check signed by
Leroy Schweitzer. Of great concern was that Schweitzer was also identifying and trying to recruit individuals from these classes to assist with
his abduction plans against the sheriff and the prosecutor.

More than three hundred individuals had attended these courses,
most of them farmers or ranchers who had fallen on hard times and
were desperate for something that would help them keep their properties. Some had grossly mismanaged their financial affairs, borrowed far
too heavily, and now faced foreclosure. Sadly, these naive individuals
believed it when Schweitzer and the others said that they could rightfully ignore the federal government and live as they pleased. Many got
suckered into criminal behavior and would pay the price for it later.

The FBI obtained a warrant to conduct surveillance, which ultimately confirmed the continuing criminal activities of the Freemen. FBI
informants and undercover agents were assigned to the Freemen
classes, each making regular observations and securing information
that supported the criminal indictment eventually obtained.

In addition to Schweitzer and Peterson, approximately twenty-five
other individuals, adults and children, had taken refuge on the Clark
property. They had renamed the area "Justus Township" and posted

signs to let all know that this was a sovereign enclave. The word *Justus* had a double meaning: both "justice" and "just us." It was not a single property but rather five or six separate but adjoining ranches spread over a large geographical area. The individuals living on these sites often had different backgrounds, different interests, and different levels of commitment to the Freemen cause.

Long before we took any action, we held a series of detailed planning meetings. Steve Romano, my deputy in the unit, helped FBI investigators and profilers from CIRG put together a comprehensive playbook, including detailed background information on each of the Freemen, individual photographs, details of past criminal activity, personality attributes, and other relevant facts about their associates and activities. It also included information about likely intermediaries and family members we could use to influence them.

The next phase of our plan called for us to try to capitalize on the confusion and uncertainty that no doubt would overtake the Freemen when they realized that Schweitzer and Peterson were in custody. Our plan called for the opposite of an ATF-style frontal assault. Our intention was to call each of the five or six individual sites where the remaining Freemen were located, urging them to immediately and peacefully surrender. We hoped they would assume that arrest warrants were also about to be executed against their locations, but we wanted them to understand and appreciate that they were being given an opportunity to avoid a tactical confrontation. Waco and Ruby Ridge held out lessons not just for federal authorities but also for those who opposed that authority.

If this approach was unsuccessful, and we knew it might be, we were prepared to use intermediaries to speak directly to the Freemen on our behalf. What the Freemen did not know was that we had no intention of executing arrest raids at their homes. This was to be the smarter and more thoughtful FBI, very much aware of the paradox of power. We had no tactical perimeter set up around any of these locations. In fact, with our reserves being held in Billings, the FBI was nowhere to be seen. With no visible way to enforce the order, we were simply asking the Freemen to give themselves up at a designated location nearby.

The negotiators who called each of these locations identified themselves as FBI agents, then explained that Schweitzer and Peterson were now in custody. Sometimes those who answered the calls listened briefly, but most refused to speak with us at all, simply saying that we had no "venue" or jurisdiction over them, then hanging up.

We were not surprised by their response. Even so, it's much easier to go tactical after failed negotiations than to negotiate after failed tactics. I know of at least one case in which a police marksman missed when he took a shot at a barricaded perpetrator. It was then a major challenge for the negotiators to try to convince the subject that the authorities were really there to help and didn't want to do him harm.

The arrest of Schweitzer and Peterson accomplished its goal of removing a venomous influence, but the resulting leadership void presented its own problems. I'm convinced that if the ATF had removed David Koresh from the equation at Waco, Schneider ultimately would have cooperated and led everyone out. But the Freemen were a much looser group. Eventually, we would need someone we could negotiate with, someone who could influence the others. Here, as at Lucasville, part of our job was going to be creating a leadership structure.

"Justus Township" consisted of 960 acres of rolling farmland in a very remote and rugged setting. It was a forty-five-minute drive from Jordan, with its sixteen streets and 450 people. There were four main houses on the properties, in addition to four small fishing cabins. We set up observation points where we could watch from a distance, but we were careful to avoid any encroachment on their land—another lesson learned both at Waco and at Ruby Ridge. Most people view their home, no matter how humble, as their castle. For members of groups like the Freemen, this feeling is magnified, particularly where the government is involved.

FBI tactical agents and Montana Highway Patrol units, working as combined teams, set up a very loose perimeter to control who went in and out. They made a concerted effort to engage in friendly small talk with local citizens and tried to downplay the sense that a siege was under way. We allowed local ranchers to move through the roadblocks at the various strategic crossings near Justus Township, but no one was allowed onto the Clark ranch without our approval. FBI personnel wore "soft" clothing: casual work clothes rather than the ominous-looking black or military green tactical equipment usually worn by SWAT elements during a siege operation.

Ralph Clark, age sixty-five, and his brother Emmett, sixty-seven, were the elders of the group, living on the property in separate homes. They had gotten caught up in the Freemen ideology and had allowed Schweitzer and others to seek refuge on their land. Our undercover FBI agent said that Emmett didn't appear to understand the Freemen ideology but had embraced it and the group as a means to save his land, which had been foreclosed. Mostly he just wanted to be left alone.

In addition to the Freemen ideologues—Schweitzer, Peterson, Dale Jacobi, Rodney Skurdal, and Steve Hance—there were also Russ Landers and his wife, Dana Dudley, who were simply con artists and swindlers with a long string of charges against them. For them, the Freemen belief system provided a pretext to flout the laws they had broken. Another family, the Mangums, were also on the lam, fleeing outstanding criminal charges from another state. And of course there were the Clarks and the related Stantons, too.

Eventually, I brought the entire negotiation team up from Billings and we established our negotiation operations center in one of the fairground buildings. Before the larger team arrived, I spent the first cold nights in that unheated barn sleeping on a cot near the phone banks our technicians had set up. We wanted to have someone available at all times of the day if any of the Freemen locations called out to us, but they never did.

In time we brought in portable heaters, but they produced only enough warmth to prevent actual frostbite. When the rest of the negotiation team arrived a few days later, we moved in to spartan but warmer motel rooms in Jordan. Life became more bearable when hot showers and warm meals became part of the routine.

The primary locations on the properties were the school building where the Freemen classes had been taught; the residence of the Stanton family; the four fishing cabins; Emmett's residence; Ralph's residence; Ralph's trailer, where Landers and Dudley lived; and the house of Emmett's son Edwin.

Edwin's wife, Janet, a nurse at the local medical clinic in Jordan known to be uninvolved with the Freemen activities or ideology, simply went on with her normal life. We stopped her car the first day as she left the property to go to work, and we explained that we were trying to work out a peaceful resolution with the group. She was cordial but told us that her husband and the others refused to speak with us.

"I can't control these men," she said. "I don't know what to tell you. And right now I'd just like to get to my job."

We decided to permit Janet to come and go as she wished, believing that later on she might become a useful liaison between the outside world and the close circle in which the Freemen lived. Also on that first day, Clark neighbor Jeff Loomis visited the Freemen and then agreed to talk with us. He reported essentially the same thing that Janet had, namely, that the Freemen outright refused to speak with the FBI.

On the second day, a couple of members of the right-wing Montana Militia showed up at the command post and demanded to speak with the FBI and find out what was going on with the siege. We were under no obligation to explain ourselves to them, but rather than brush aside their request, Special Agent Tom Canady, the lead investigative case agent, and I were designated to talk with them and try to defuse any potential problems they might cause.

Tom and I met with the militia members at the Hell Creek Bar in Jordan that afternoon. The four of us introduced ourselves and then sat down at a booth in the back to have a cup of coffee.

The two militiamen were dressed for winter ranch work in jeans and heavy fleece-lined coats. They greeted us warily, as if this could be a trap and we might suddenly cart them off to jail. With narrowed eyes and jaws jutting forth, they also seemed primed for a confrontation.

I figured we had nothing to hide from these guys, so instead of playing tough or arguing, which evidently was what they'd expected, Tom and I tried to disarm them with openness and candor. They asked us why we were doing what we were doing, and we gave them detailed information about the Freemen's fraudulent and threatening activities. Tom described the outstanding federal charges that had been brought for bank fraud, embezzlement, aiding and abetting, conspiracy to impede or injure a federal officer, mailing threatening communications, mail fraud, interference with commerce by threat of violence, felony possession of firearms, possession of a firearm by a fugitive, and carrying firearms during a crime of violence. These were in addition to numerous state charges. I told them that we were trying to avoid the kind of outcome that had happened at Waco and Ruby Ridge, and that we planned to negotiate in good faith with the Freemen.

We wanted to make sure these men understood that we weren't in Montana to stamp out freedom of expression; instead, we were there to arrest individuals who had violated the law and threatened their fellow citizens. We explained that the Freemen's actions had left us no choice. We even explained the low-key approach we were taking, aimed at a peaceful resolution.

One of the militiamen asked if U.S. military personnel and tanks were being used to surround Justus Township. I knew that the Posse Comitatus Act, the law that prohibits the use of military forces to enforce civilian law, was very much a mainstay of militia ideology. I assured him that the military was not involved in any way, adding that in fact none of the authorities had set foot on the Clark ranch or other properties. I explained that only FBI and Montana Highway Patrol personnel were involved in the operation and that they were staying a safe and respectful distance away.

I offered to personally drive both of them wherever they wanted to go to see for themselves. No response. For each and every additional question they raised we answered respectfully and truthfully, effectively taking the wind out of their sails. We gave them our names and numbers and requested that they call us if they had any further questions, heard any rumors, or wanted to know what we were doing. We asked them to please explain all of these things to others in their group so they would know the truth.

As we left the bar, these men shook our hands much more vigorously than they had coming in, nodded, and made eye contact. They weren't saying it, but it appeared they appreciated the time we had spent with them. We never heard from the Montana Militia again.

If we'd disarmed at least some of our right-wing critics, we still had the media to contend with. Local and national television and print reporters began to descend in droves. Most were up front in saying they had come to witness another disaster like Ruby Ridge or Waco, but FBI media coordinators worked to dispel their prejudices. We did not want inflammatory coverage, and we certainly did not want to give them another tragic story to report.

Once it became clear that the Freemen were not going to speak with us, we moved on to the next phase of our plan, which was the use of third-party intermediaries.

As is usually the case in hostage/barricade/suicide incidents, we had a briefing book that contained whatever background information was available on the subjects. For Justus Township, that book included overhead photos of the land and houses and of each individual, as well as family histories that included marriages, relatives, and friends.

We had to be cautious in using intermediaries because the people most often in a position to help can be difficult to control. They frequently have their own agendas—a grievance, perhaps, or a desire to influence. Also, bringing them to the scene might expose them to danger.

Family members sometimes criticize police for not letting them speak with loved ones during a crisis incident. In truth, the police rarely know enough about the existing relationships between the perpetrator, family members, and friends to take the risk. In one case, a distraught husband found out his wife was having an affair, took her hostage, and threatened to kill her. After many fruitless hours trying to negotiate with the man, the local police sought out potential intermediaries. An individual came forward and claimed he was the perpetrator's best friend. He told the cops he was confident that he could talk reason to his pal. The police readily agreed to allow this man to make a telephone call into the apartment to speak with the perpetrator. When the perpetrator answered the phone and heard this man's voice, he exploded in rage and fired his weapon. The SWAT team immediately forced its way in, only to find both him and his wife dead. As it turned out, the man who had volunteered to call in was the wife's lover. It's important to fully interview such individuals and try to find out as much as possible about the existing relationship before deciding whether or not to use them as intermediaries.

With the Freemen we did not have a typical situation. We faced some self-deluded, hardheaded, and confused individuals who were potentially very dangerous but in our opinion not suicidal. Some had distorted ideological perspectives; others simply didn't want to face justice in the courts. The hard-core ideologues—Skurdal, Jacobi, Landers—believed that by avoiding talking with us they could deny FBI jurisdiction over them. The Clarks just wanted to keep their property and be left alone. Unfortunately, given their actions, this was no longer possible.

Within the first five days of the incident, my negotiation team identified, interviewed, coached, and deployed fifteen intermediaries. After we briefed them on what we were after and how to handle themselves, they then made their own way onto the Justus Township property and arranged to meet with their friend or loved one. This was done in a low-key, casual way that did not arouse anyone's suspicions, at least not at first.

After each visitor came out, we again met at the fairgrounds or the coffee shop to debrief them. We gained a clearer picture of what the Freemen were thinking, but otherwise, results were mixed. Sometimes the person would say, "I sat down with him for an hour and he wouldn't budge. He's dead set on hanging tough." At other times what we heard was, "I don't know...he seems a little worried. He may be open to coming out."

It was my sense now that we had to attack the Freemen's intransigence on two tracks. The first was to continue to use the intermediaries, appealing to specific individuals on a one-to-one basis. On the second track, we would identify and use people who were not personally connected to the Freemen but whom they would view as interested in discussing their political theories. These people would target the hard-core Freemen ideologues who clung to misguided beliefs about personal sovereignty. For this we called on Karl Ohs, a Montana legislator.

A staunch Republican who would go on to become lieutenant governor, Ohs was a close friend of Butch Anderson, the birth father of Val Stanton, one of the women living in Justus Township. Butch and Karl agreed to go inside to visit Val and the others, which they did repeatedly over a period of weeks.

A soft-spoken, intelligent rancher, Karl once rode his horse in to see the Freemen when the weather made the road impassable to cars. On horseback he looked exactly like the famous Marlboro Man. He had a genuine desire to help resolve this incident, and he would sacrifice a great deal of his personal time and energy over the course of the stand-off. Even though the Freemen continued in their refusal to meet with the FBI and periodically rejected other intermediaries during the ordeal, they always agreed to see Karl. I focused most of my personal attention on meeting with Ohs and coordinating his many visits. With his deep roots in this community, Karl was the best possible guide to the mind-set of these fiercely independent westerners, as well as a superb ambassador.

I also spent much of my time with the senior FBI management team on the scene, briefing them at our twice-daily management team meetings. Here, unlike Waco, all the component leaders met frequently to keep on the same sheet of music. It made a huge difference to have their support and buy-in, rather than resistance. We also made sure that one of the negotiators attended each SWAT team shift briefing. We wanted to make sure that the tactical units knew everything we were doing and why.

FBI director Louis Freeh's support for the negotiation process became very clear when he mandated that I should participate in all the daily teleconferences between him and on-site senior management in Jordan. So each day at the designated time, I would join the three or four Special Agents in Charge, along with HRT commander Roger Nisley, to participate in a telephone briefing for the director. We did not discuss Waco or Ruby Ridge, but those incidents were the subtext as we made every decision.

As the standoff continued and we reached the second week of the siege, a few of the midlevel managers began to voice concern that this situation was taking too long. Whatever their commitment to a survivalist mind-set, these Freemen were supremely self-reliant Montana ranchers, the kind of people who had elk meat in the freezer and vegetables put away from the summer. The whole time we were camped outside their land, they were free to hunt for game on that land. This was not a group that could be squeezed very easily for the basic elements of comfort and survival.

Some within the FBI began to wonder out loud if we had overlearned the lesson of past mistakes and become gun-shy, frightened to take decisive action. The FBI had been making these kinds of raids and arrests throughout our long history, so why should this incident be any different? I listened to some of this grumbling and wondered whether those who felt this way truly understood the implications for the FBI if this incident went the way of Waco and Ruby Ridge. A time might come when we had to take action to save lives, but we weren't at that point yet.

Director Freeh soon put a stop to such complaints. During one of our conference calls for the senior managers in Montana he said, "Gary, it's important for you to know that as your director, I am in no hurry to end this incident. I want to make sure that we take whatever time necessary to negotiate this out the right way."

He didn't have to refer to Waco directly. Waco was the eight-hundred-pound gorilla in every room we entered in those days.

When Director Freeh said this, I looked at all the faces around the table. My colleagues clearly understood that this was a new era in crisis management for the FBI. William Sessions, Freeh's predecessor at the Bureau, had been a very detached administrator, which had been part of the problem. Freeh was much more hands-on, decisive, and engaged. He was on the phone with us in Montana every day. The negotiators were now setting the direction and tone, and the director was squarely behind us. End of story.

On April 4, the eleventh day of the siege, Karl Ohs, after several attempts, was at last able to facilitate a direct meeting with the Freemen, himself, and three additional Montana state legislators. We had no expectation that this one conversation was going to resolve all the differences, but we hoped that it would at least help focus and refine the issues, which might then help us find some common ground.

A table and chairs were set up in an open area near a cattle guard at the boundary of the Clark property. The Freemen drove up the road, got out of their cars and pickups, and sat down. Then Karl and the other legislators listened as the Freemen ranted about the legal system and advanced their claim that the government had no jurisdiction over them. They said they wanted to have their rights protected in common-law courts, meaning that their cases would be decided by individuals who believed as they did.

As the legislators listened, they continually urged the Freemen to address these issues in federal court and to talk directly with the FBI to resolve the standoff. They even promised to hold a legislative forum on the common-law issues. The following day, talks continued in the motor home on the property, but little if anything was accomplished. The Freemen continued to insist that the federal government had no jurisdiction over them and that they had not broken any laws. They insisted that their financial liens and checks were legal under common law. They were also angry that the FBI had trespassed on their property to arrest Schweitzer and Peterson, the event that had triggered the siege. In addition, the Clarks were not willing to leave their land, and the others, their guests who had sought refuge there, were not willing to leave to face other criminal charges.

The only problem with our post-Waco restraint was that the Freemen knew as well as we did that the FBI could not risk another televised debacle. This meant that the threat of force, the key element used to encourage most negotiations, was effectively removed. With their wells pumping water and their freezers full of food, why not just wait it out?

In our briefing materials used to coach all the intermediaries, we outlined a long list of positive police actions we had taken—or not taken, as the case might be. We had them emphasize to the Freemen that the FBI had not trespassed onto Justus Township after the arrest of Schweitzer and Peterson, and that telephone calls into the locations were respectfully kept at a minimum or discontinued so as not to irritate them. We had made it clear that anyone was free to leave anytime they wanted. We had allowed medication to be delivered for twenty-one-year-old Casey Clark, the son of Edwin and Janet Clark. A large number of relatives and friends had been freely allowed to visit and call at their discretion. At the Freemen's request, the media had been kept far away. The Freemen had been allowed to meet with Montana state legislators, and through the legislators, the Freemen had received an unbiased report on the conditions of Schweitzer, Peterson, and Richard Clark, another relative and Freeman arrested separately, away from Jordan. Furthermore, we had not set up any high-power lights or broadcast any loud noises, and no individuals in Justus Township had been harassed in any way. Electricity and water service had not been interrupted. No press statements critical of the Freemen had been issued by the FBI. There had been no fly-overs by FBI helicopters. When lumped together, these made a compelling case in support of our position, but like the prisoners at Lucasville, the Freemen needed time to calm down and begin to think more rationally.

Justus Township neighbor Jeff Loomis became a regular contact. We had Jeff carry in a note that outlined three basic areas where we were willing to compromise:

1. We stated that we were extremely flexible on the mechanics of their surrender—the how, the when, and the procedure.
2. We were willing to make any arrangements suitable to the Freemen that would guarantee the preservation of their so-called evidence. This consisted of the voluminous common-law writings they had assembled that they felt supported their case. We promised to allow any mutually agreed-upon third party to safeguard these papers for their defense team to use in court.
3. We agreed to help facilitate the legislative forum agreed to by the Montana state legislators to address their perceived rights and legal position.

We hoped that by stipulating these commitments so explicitly, we would lend form and substance to the idea that this was the best deal they were going to get from the government. Unfortunately, the same three holdouts continued to obstruct any forward movement that the others might have accepted. Freemen Rodney Skurdal and Dale Jacobi clung to their common-law convictions and remained unwilling to consider any compromise. Russ Landers continued to object to any settlement that would end up putting him in legal jeopardy.

As he continued his own shuttle diplomacy, Karl Ohs was usually accompanied by Butch Anderson, Val Stanton's birth father. We had targeted Val as someone we might persuade to leave the property. We felt that if we could convince those who did not face charges, or serious charges, to come out, we would begin to erode the group's solidarity. Butch managed to find times to speak with Val away from the influence of the hard-core Freemen. While Karl distracted the true believers on larger issues, Butch was working on Val to come out.

On the twelfth day of the siege, those efforts paid off. Val Stanton decided to take her young daughter, Mariah, and walk out, the first major blow to the Freemen since the arrest of Schweitzer and Peterson. While we never felt Val or Mariah was in great danger, we were nonetheless relieved when they reached our side of the fence line.

Karl Ohs also focused his attention on Edwin Clark, who in his view was far and away the most reasonable individual among the Freemen. With this in mind, we had Ohs push the reluctant Edwin to assume a leadership role. He had the unique status of being the de facto leader of the Clark family, with special authority over the land and those living on it.

At one point, Edwin Clark relented and told Ohs that he was willing to meet with us. But then the other Freemen got Clark to change his mind. Edwin was a friendly and likeable individual, but he placed too high a value on consensus. Karl Ohs was extremely disappointed, and he told me he was losing heart.

"I don't know if these boys are ever going to come to their senses," he told me.

But then we got a break. Tom Spillum, owner of one of the two small motels in Jordan where FBI personnel stayed, was the stepson of die-hard Freeman William Stanton, who had been arrested long before the siege and was serving time in jail. Several of our negotiators had gotten to know Tom pretty well. We knew that he was in touch with his mother, Agnes, wife of the jailed Freeman, and according to Tom, she was torn about what she should do.

With encouragement from us, Tom began a series of telephone calls and visits aimed at convincing Agnes and her son, Ebert Stanton, to come out. It was Ebert's wife, Val, who had already departed Justus Township with her daughter.

On the eighteenth day of the siege, Tom at last prevailed, and Agnes and Ebert both decided to leave. In response to this second major blow to the Freemen's solidarity, the hard core of the group delivered an ultimatum: there would be no more unsupervised phone calls or other contacts with anyone outside.

For the next two weeks the siege continued unchanged. We had learned that leaving agents to work long hours in remote locations with no relief in sight could allow frustration to build up, so we rotated all FBI personnel, including negotiators, in and out of Jordan. My deputy, Steve Romano, came in to relieve me as negotiation team leader. Steve knew as much about the Freemen as anyone, and he and I shared a common philosophy and approach to the negotiation process. For the remainder of the siege we would alternate two-week stints in Jordan, trying to make the negotiation operations as seamless as possible.

This siege was shaping up to be one of a kind. Not only did we have a perimeter that was loosely defined, but there were no longer any telephone negotiations. All of our contact was undertaken through the various intermediaries, who were now carefully scrutinized by the Freemen. For safety reasons the intermediaries were allowed to travel in and out only during daylight hours, so other than an overnight skeleton crew, negotiation operations essentially shut down at the end of the business day. In at least this one respect, this was a very civilized operation.

Each morning we would leave our rather modest motel accommodations in town and drive out to the command post at the fairgrounds, where the government had set up a big communal kitchen to take care of us. We had three meals a day dished up by Forest Service cook crews. The menu, designed for wilderness firefighters, was varied and good but also extremely high in calories. No one lost weight during this operation.

These crews, like most everyone else in Jordan, were friendly and welcoming to the entire FBI team. They told us that they appreciated us moving against the Freemen, who'd been giving them problems for years. Around Easter the children from the local school delivered handmade drawings thanking the FBI for being there.

In addition to the fairgrounds, we had a second, albeit informal, center of operations at the Hell Creek Bar, where the negotiation team and other FBI elements would gravitate most every evening after dinner. The owner, Joe Herbold, who had only recently purchased the place, was a real people person, the kind of guy who might have been a successful negotiator. The bar had a bona fide Wild West swinging saloon door and a huge carved bar that must have been installed in the 1880s. On a normal Saturday night Joe might have a dozen customers come into his establishment, some of them fairly wild and woolly. (One night I sat and talked to a guy whose job was as a government coyote hunter.) Joe looked more like a guy who might work in a cubicle in Chicago or Seattle, but here he was, maintaining this frontier outpost. With the siege and all the new customers it brought in, his bar looked not only Wild West but gold rush boomtown as well.

Initially, there were three groups of patrons, each maintaining a respectful separation from the others: the regular local citizens, the deployed FBI agents, and members of the news media. After a few weeks, these groups began to mingle a bit and get to know one another. Joe maintained a strict policy of no shop talk, which helped maintain peace and civility. (As I said, with a little training he might have become an excellent member of our negotiation team.)

The Hell Creek was a great place to blow off steam. One evening I joined an impromptu concert with a local rancher playing the bass, a news media reporter on piano, and me playing guitar. It was surreal, to say the least.

As if to rescue the audience, a cowboy burst in the front door and loudly announced: "Two-headed calf." That was all it took. A couple of dozen bar patrons emptied out onto the dirt road where, in the back of his pickup truck, the proud cowboy displayed a stillborn calf with two distinct and separate heads. We all stood around the bed of his truck and looked on in amazement. A multitude of jokes about being "two-faced" quickly followed.

The people of Jordan were hardworking, law-abiding folks, and they were embarrassed by the unwanted attention the Freemen had brought to their town. During the siege, Montana had come under further scrutiny when the FBI located the source of a series of mail bombs that had killed three people and injured twenty-three. The man they arrested, Theodore Kaczynski, also known as the Unabomber, was a mathematician who'd soured on technology and had taken to living in a primitive cabin in a remote area between Missoula and Helena. The citizens of

Jordan had extra incentive to show the world that not everyone in Montana was alienated, armed, and dangerous. Local citizens started to appear on the streets wearing FBI T-shirts and hats they had bartered for with various agents. One cowboy who frequented the bar got one of my FBI negotiator's shirts in exchange for some pronghorn antlers. I'd say I negotiated the better end of the deal on that one. Then, on day thirty-four of the siege, after a long stretch of little progress, two uninvited people showed up at the fairgrounds and asked the state troopers guarding the perimeter if they could speak with the FBI. One of these was Bo Gritz, who had assisted in resolving the Ruby Ridge incident; the other was Randy Weaver himself. Gritz had already made a name as a spokesman for disaffected militia groups and as a liaison between them and the government. In militia circles, Weaver, of course, was a cause célèbre. We invited them in and sat them down to hear what they had to say. It turned out that these two thought they could get through to the Freemen where we could not.

I had not been at Ruby Ridge, so I did not know them personally, and I wasn't at all sure of their intentions. With his bushy mustache and weight lifter's build, Gritz came across as the former Green Beret that he was—bold, brash, confident, and self-assured. I also wasn't sure that he would be able to accomplish anything with the Freemen. On the other hand, I didn't see any particular downside to his intervention, assuming we could keep his ego under control and properly channel his enthusiasm. I was also concerned that our refusal to allow him to make the effort would be misinterpreted by the right wing as a sign that we weren't really committed to ending the siege in a peaceful way.

Weaver, on the other hand, was a soft-spoken man who seemed for the most part content to let Gritz do the talking. I asked him directly how he thought he could help.

He looked at me with sad eyes and said, "Maybe I can convince them not to make the same stupid mistakes I made. You can't get into a shooting war with the U.S. government and win. If I had it to do over again, I'd surrender. Then maybe my wife and son would be alive today."

His words hung in the air for a moment, and though I was surprised by his candor, I had no doubt he was sincere. I wondered if he was motivated in part by trying to bring meaning to the loss he had suffered. For sure, few other individuals could make as strong an argument for surrender as Randy Weaver himself.

After meeting Gritz and Weaver, I went to the FBI command team to discuss whether we should avail ourselves of their offer. Everyone agreed that we should use Gritz, but Weaver was a different matter. I tried to convince them that he, better than anyone else, would be able to explain what they had to lose. But my colleagues were adamant; they were concerned that involving him would subject the FBI to criticism. Perhaps even more than that, they believed it inappropriate to use him. They truly held Weaver in contempt for what he had done.

As a group, we called Director Freeh. He agreed with my recommendation to use Gritz but sided with the others in opposing the use of Weaver.

We had Karl Ohs contact the Freemen and ask if they would be willing to meet with Bo Gritz, telling them that Gritz had come on his own and wanted to speak with them. The Freemen said they were not interested, but Gritz—who some say was the real-life model for the movie character Rambo—would not take no for an answer.

We allowed him to go forward to the Freemen property line, and he was there only a short time before the Freemen came out to talk with him, then brought him inside.

Over a four-day period, Gritz met with the Freemen at the schoolhouse. Afterward, we learned that they never warmed up to him as they had with Karl Ohs—to the Freemen's taste, he was just too pushy.

When we debriefed him, Gritz admitted that he had made only limited progress in getting through to the men in Justus Township. He told us that he had taken it upon himself to scare some sense into them, and scare them he did. He said that if they continued to resist, the government would come in to get them in the dead of night. He told them there would be loud explosions and flashes of bright light that would disorient them. Then they would be dragged out in handcuffs through the mud and humiliated in public.

While I never would have endorsed this approach, I think it may have had a positive effect, at least in planting the idea that the FBI's patience was not endless and that a tactical assault was still a very real possibility.

After failing to barter the truce he was seeking, a frustrated Gritz appeared before the news media, where he harshly criticized the Freemen and questioned their motives. This exercise in pique undid whatever good Gritz had done, and the Freemen refused any further meetings with him. He and Randy Weaver left town in a rush and were not seen around those parts again.

After the Gritz initiative, we heard that there was going to be a rally in support of the Freemen in Jordan, but only eight individuals showed up. There were more reporters covering the story than there were participants. Gritz's diatribe may well have killed off whatever outside support the Freemen had once enjoyed. The news media—particularly the print media in Montana—were extremely critical of the Freemen and their ideology, and cartoons poking fun at the group began to appear in the state papers.

Family members were also unsympathetic. When we asked one to pen a letter to his brother, who was inside with his two sons, he wrote the following:

> *I can see why you would want to kill yourself. . . . If you must end your life, at least be clear about why, it's not about taxes or bad government or anything else. It is about the rottenness inside yourself. So go ahead and end it.*

As you might imagine, we chose not to send in this letter.

On day fifty-three, the Freemen requested and were allowed to meet with Charlie Duke, a right-wing member of the Colorado state senate well known in militia circles. Steve Romano and Dwayne Fuselier orchestrated and managed the encounter while I was back in Virginia. They met with Duke to brief him, after which the senator went into Justus Township. He emerged with the Freemen's authorization for him to act as their intermediary with the FBI. He even convinced them to meet face-to-face with us for the first time.

Once again, our agents set up a table and chairs at the same cattle guard where the Montana legislators had met with the Freemen.

Our objective was to listen to what the Freemen had to say and to schedule another meeting, and that was it. Some on-scene leaders were expecting more, though I felt that we should simply show our respect for them and indicate our genuine desire to help them out of this situation. But it was also essential to establish the prospects for a dialogue.

Steve and Special Agent Dwayne Fuselier represented the FBI at the table. If the Freemen who came had expected to find demanding and authoritative feds, what they got instead were two very reasonable agents who showed openness and concern. Over the course of the next six days the two groups continued to meet twice a day. The problem was, we simply didn't speak the same language or, you might say, even live in the same universe. For all our cordiality, anytime they got down to real discussion of the issues they would hit a roadblock. They would say the Freeman had to come out and face charges; the Freeman would counter that the FBI had no authority to demand anything of them.

The Freemen would not give up their insistence that they be tried by their peers in a common-law court. Steve and Dwayne suggested that the best course of action was for the Freemen to come out and tell their side of the story in an authorized court, but the Freemen weren't buying it. When I came back from Virginia, the management team was frustrated and met to discuss how to move things along. We decided that our best option was to create an illusion of impatience and mounting anger.

I have argued against showing a bellicose face when it contradicts and undermines the negotiations. But this was a case in which negotiation alone was not moving us forward. The best approach is always a carefully modulated combination of earnest talk backed up by the option of tactical intervention. Now we needed to reinforce that option.

Until this point, we had allowed reporters and television crews to cluster on a hill where they could observe and film Justus Township from a safe distance, but in full view of the Freemen. We now decided to move the media away, hoping to plant the thought that something was about to happen that we wanted hidden from the media.

We then brought several armored personnel carriers to the command post, spurring the media to report on their sudden arrival. The FBI actually borrowed two of these vehicles from local law enforcement, painted them black, and stenciled *FBI* in white letters on the sides. One of these trucks was in fact inoperable, but we were the only ones who knew that.

Then a team of agents went forward and constructed a new gate in a stretch of fence where there was not even a road—a fairly clear suggestion that something was up. Would the Freemen assume that we were planning to bring in more large equipment, maybe even assault vehicles? We hoped that was what they would fear. Also for the first time, we allowed an FBI helicopter to fly close enough to be seen and heard by those at Justus Township. We were careful not to fly over the property itself, but came just close enough to get their attention.

The next step was to cut off power to the ranch. Some local officials had publicly criticized the FBI for not doing this sooner, but what they didn't know was that we needed the power on, especially the power going into the schoolhouse, where one of the hidden microphones had been planted prior to the siege. We had picked up useful information by listening in, but at this point we were willing to sacrifice this access in order to gain the psychological effect of the power blackout.

Finally, and perhaps most important, I met with Janet Clark, the nurse who was still coming and going to her job each day, and explained that the situation had dragged on far too long. I told her that despite our past patience, we were not getting the cooperation we needed from her husband and the others. I told her that authorities in Washington now wanted us to resolve this matter with all deliberate speed. I never said we were going to launch an assault; I simply implied that something was going to happen soon. I was confident that Janet would pass this information on to Edwin, the husband she loved, who was inside with their son, Casey.

We did all this between days sixty-six and seventy-one of the siege. The news media unwittingly did their part, repeatedly issuing reports that the FBI seemed ready to move. At this time we also began to get word through various means that many of those on the ranch were growing as weary of the siege as we were.

As a result of these initiatives, on day seventy-five Edwin Clark for the first time mustered the courage to come out alone and meet with us. Through Karl Ohs, we had been pressuring him relentlessly to assume a leadership role in order to take control and preclude violence. Edwin sat down with Dwayne Fuselier and me in a motor home we'd deployed near the property. He was cordial and polite, but we could also see that he had a lot of responsibility on his broad shoulders, and he was fatigued. He voiced concern about his son, Casey, his father, Ralph, and his uncle Emmett. His father, especially, needed medical attention.

Edwin appeared to me to be a normal, hardworking guy who had made some bad decisions. Those decisions had led to circumstances that now had escalated beyond his control. He had no criminal record. He also didn't seem like someone foolish enough to really fall for the nonsense being spouted by the Freemen, yet here he was. He voiced his frustrations with the intransigence and indecisiveness of the others, but he still wanted to be respectful of their beliefs. Edwin also wanted to be hospitable to the individuals who had sought refuge on his property.

Over the next several days Dwayne and I met with Edwin at various times inside the motor home. At each meeting it became increasingly clear that Edwin was a likeable, down-to-earth guy. As was common among men in this region, he would engage in small talk with us before moving into substantive discussions. He told us about his love for hunting and about his collection of dinosaur bones, which he'd found on his property. I liked him, and this bolstered my desire to help make sure he and his family were not hurt in this siege.

At one such meeting he told us that he wished to come out, but that he needed to speak to Leroy Schweitzer to get his advice on how to proceed. He also indicated a desire to have the help of the Cause Foundation, a right-wing equivalent of the ACLU, known for defending the legal rights of right-wing extremists in trouble with the law. Earlier, the foundation had sent a letter offering its assistance, an offer we had passed along to the Freemen.

I told Edwin that enlisting the help and involvement of the Cause Foundation was not a problem. In fact, I told him that it was wise for him and the others to get legal assistance, which we had recommended all along. I told him candidly that a visit to Leroy Schweitzer in jail in Billings was going to be more of a challenge. We would have to transport Edwin to Billings, let him meet with Schweitzer, and then allow him to return to Justus Township. I told him that nothing like that had ever been done before. We didn't even know if Schweitzer would meet with him, or what Schweitzer would say.

I told Edwin that if I was going to support this unprecedented undertaking, I would need to know what he wanted to talk to Schweitzer about. Edwin said he wanted to get Schweitzer's instructions on how they should preserve their common-law evidence, the various papers and documents they believed validated their common-law rights. He also wanted to tell Leroy that he planned to surrender. I asked Edwin what he would do if Schweitzer instructed him to continue the siege and not surrender. Edwin looked me in the eye and said, "If that's what he says, then I'll have to make my own decision about what's the right thing to do." I was convinced that Edwin had made up his mind to surrender; he just wanted Schweitzer's blessing in order to feel better about it.

Based on that exchange, Dwayne and I met with the command team. As expected, there was no problem with contacting the Cause Foundation and allowing them to become involved, so we began making arrangements to bring them to Montana. Dwayne and I also strongly recommended that we fly Edwin to Billings to meet directly with Schweitzer. If Schweitzer opposed the surrender, I told the command team, then Edwin would most likely disregard those instructions and come out anyway. Edwin was clearly tired of the whole mess and wanted it over.

The on-scene commander, Tom Kubic, and CIRG leader Robin Montgomery agreed on both counts, which took a great deal of courage. Not only was this action unprecedented, but if something went wrong, the FBI would be roundly criticized.

On the seventy-ninth day of the siege, Edwin Clark left the property, secretly boarded an FBI plane, and flew to Billings, Montana, where he met in jail with Leroy Schweitzer. To our relief, Schweitzer agreed that it was time to end the siege; his only interest was that the government not be allowed to destroy the documents he believed would support their claims of sovereignty.

Three representatives of the Cause Foundation, director Kirk Lyons, Dave Holloway, and South Carolina attorney Larry Salley, soon arrived in Billings, where they, too, were allowed to meet with Schweitzer. Edwin was quietly flown back to Jordan and allowed to return to Justus Township.

With Schweitzer's blessing and the involvement of the Cause Foundation, we worked out the specifics of a surrender process. Five key issues were agreed to:

1. Karl Ohs would take custody of the Freemen's evidence.
2. The Freemen would maintain 51 percent control of their appointed counsel. (This was a nonissue, a concern based on their misunderstanding of the law. Suspects always retain 100 percent control over their own defense.)
3. The United States attorney would not oppose bail for Ralph and Emmett Clark.
4. The Freemen would be allowed to meet with one another in jail.
5. Their appointed counsel would be sworn in under common law.

The Freemen agreed to these points. We were cautiously optimistic.

On day eighty, the three Cause Foundation representatives entered Justus Township to assist the Freemen in assembling their evidence. These outsiders were extremely helpful in keeping the disorganized Freemen on task.

Later in the morning, Ashley Landers, daughter of Russ Landers, the fugitive from justice, suddenly walked out, suitcase in hand, and surrendered on her own. We had heard that she wanted to get out and away from her parents, and apparently she couldn't wait another minute. Shortly thereafter, Karl Ohs drove a rental truck onto the property and loaded up the Freemen's evidence to be secured for their defense in court.

On the eighty-first day of the longest siege in United States history, Dwayne and I stood on our side of the cattle guard in our short-sleeved shirts and bulletproof vests, waiting for the final word from Edwin

Clark. We watched as his car approached from the horizon on their side and came toward us along the dirt road.

Edwin stopped his car and turned off the ignition. As he got out and walked toward us, I could see a broad smile break out from under his bushy mustache. "Well, boys," he said, "we had a hell of a siege, didn't we?"

We shook hands, and I felt a tremendous sense of relief. As we had learned more of his story, both Dwayne and I had developed a bond with Edwin. I felt sorry for him, and I genuinely liked both him and his wife, Janet. I hoped that life would work out better for them in the years ahead.

The three Cause Foundation guys now came out and joined us to witness the surrender process. We all watched as the individual Freemen drove up to the cattle guard that marked the edge of the property. They got out of their vehicles, shook hands with the Cause Foundation representatives and Edwin, then crossed the cattle guard where Dwayne and I met them.

It had taken a very long time, but not a shot was fired. The Freemen's land would be lost and their lives would be changed, but they were alive, and if they so chose, most would be able to move on. I certainly hoped that would be true for Edwin and his family.

As we were ready to leave, I observed that one of the Cause Foundation guys had a tear in his eye. He had always considered himself an enemy of the FBI, he told me, but no longer. He also said that he was proud to have been a part of such a professional and creative operation, one that ended so well.

I glanced at Dwayne and saw that his eyes were welling up also. That's what made him such a good negotiator—the fact that he really cared.

Our success in Montana was a validation of what the FBI negotiation program stood for, what we had learned and practiced for over two decades, and what we had taught to cops around the world. The trauma of Waco and Ruby Ridge had been answered by handling this situation the way it needed to be done. As Edwin Clark said, it was indeed, in a very good way, a hell of a siege.

CHAPTER TEN

PREPARE THE MISSILES

Wise men talk because they have something to say; fools, because
they have to say something.
—PLATO

L ike almost every police group in the country, the Texas Rangers
had never run a major siege operation. Their inclination was to take
decisive action against criminals in the act of breaking the law. Even
though they'd been at Waco in a support role to the FBI and had witnessed the tragic ending up close, they remained a decisive and action-
oriented outfit. Yet they soon would confront their own major standoff
and have to make the tough choice between immediate tactical action
and more thoughtful negotiations.

In April 1997, almost one year after the Montana incident, I was back
out west, standing beside a motor home command post overlooking the
Davis Mountains of Texas, not far north of the border with Mexico.
Once again I was on the scene to try and coax a bunch of right-wing
separatists to come out from behind their barricade. Unlike the case
with the Freemen in Montana, this time we had a clear leader to deal
with. Unfortunately, he was not nearly as reasonable and likeable as
Edwin Clark.

Richard McLaren, self-proclaimed chief ambassador and consul
general of the Republic of Texas, the militia group in question, was a

pompous, self-important man with a passionate belief in the righteous-ness of his cause. He and his fellow Republic of Texas members were also known to be armed, and they were responsible for a recent kidnap-ping. This was only one of many reasons the Texas Rangers were not going to be nearly as tolerant of delay as we had been at Justus Town-ship.

Captain Barry Caver of the Texas Rangers was the overall tactical commander on the scene for the Republic of Texas siege, with sheriff's deputies, municipal police, correctional authorities, Border Patrol, and FBI agents there to help.

We had a ham radio set up on a table outside the motor home, and Caver and I, plus Ranger sergeant Jess Malone, stood in the desert twi-light and listened to McLaren's irritating, high-pitched voice. The Republic of Texas leader was broadcasting yet another of his requests for fellow believers from other right-wing militias to come to his aid.

McLaren's style on these transmissions was always overexcited, his manner of speaking rapid-fire, but this time his rhetoric grew ever more inflated with rage. I leaned in and listened more intently as he solemnly intoned, "Prepare the missiles." This message wasn't meant for his fol-lowers, I realized; it was meant for us. And in that instant, I knew our strategy was working.

"Prepare the missiles" meant that McLaren was desperate and scared. He and his men—our best estimate was that there were perhaps thirteen people involved—were known to have automatic weapons, but the idea that he would have missiles was preposterous. For days, via telephone, fax, and Internet, he had issued his "red alert." He had spo-ken freely to media outlets and declared war on the authorities. All of his statements had seemed cocky and self-assured, as if, based on his own assessment of the fallout from Waco and our patience in Montana, he was confident that the Rangers and the other officers from the Texas Department of Public Safety would not assault his position. His appeals for assistance had attracted at least one group of militia members, driving a car with its trunk full of weapons, who were arrested trying to come to his aid. But as he broadcast his latest appeal, McLaren sounded like a cornered man at his wits' end, no longer confident of anything. With daylight fading and darkness coming on, he seemed to be desperately posturing, trying to ward off any tactical action from the Rangers during the night.

Thirty-eight-year-old Jess Malone was the primary negotiator at the scene. In this collaboration, the FBI advisors were known as "the suits," and the Rangers were known as "the hats." Malone wore a white western shirt, white cowboy hat, and blue jeans with a custom leather belt and holster. From what I could tell of him, the western wear was not just a fashion statement. Muscular, tall, and tough-looking, Malone moved with all the no-nonsense authority you would expect of a Texas lawman.

Earlier, Jess had told McLaren over the telephone, "This has gone on a long time. We're getting tired and we're getting frustrated, and I have to tell you, the sooner you all come out, the safer it'll be for everyone."

Malone waited a beat, then added calmly, "We don't want to see anyone get hurt." His tone was nonthreatening, but of course his words held the unavoidable implication that failure to cooperate could lead to some very unpleasant consequences. Most important, he never provided McLaren the reassurance he sought that the Rangers would not attack. Operations might very well take place during the night. The authorities were determined to maintain measured control, but their patience was not endless.

My involvement with the Republic of Texas had begun two months earlier, in February 1997, when Davis County sheriff Steve Bailey asked the local FBI office to send experts to advise him on how to deal with McLaren and his followers. FBI profiler Al Brantley and I flew to Texas to size up the situation and offer whatever assistance we could.

Sheriff Bailey's team was understaffed and isolated, and confronted by a man who seemed to be just about as grandiose as David Koresh. The sheriff wanted to keep things in Davis County from coming to a head and slipping out of control. He wanted no part of anything resembling the debacle at Ranch Apocalypse.

Holed up in a house trailer that he referred to as "the embassy," McLaren had been making quite a nuisance of himself and, like the Freemen in Montana, spewing out hundreds of bogus liens against anyone who criticized him. He had even demanded that then governor

George W. Bush and other officials vacate their offices. Members of the Republic of Texas (ROT)—tax protesters, political extremists, and con artists—believed, like the Freeman, that they were not subject to any state or federal laws.

The ROT's principal claim was that Texas had been illegally annexed by the United States in 1845. Accordingly, the state was actually an independent, sovereign nation, and the federal government had no jurisdiction. Nor did the state government have any jurisdiction over the ROT because the politicians in Austin had subordinated themselves to Washington, rendering themselves impotent.

But McLaren's views were so radical that he'd actually been impeached from the ROT mainstream, after which he had retreated to his property not only to avoid being arrested on charges related to the bogus liens but also to rally support and gain sympathy by taking a stand. Day after day, McLaren railed over the Internet against all forms of authority, saying that any attack against him would set off the liberation of America from the "new world order." Like the Texas patriots at the Alamo, he vowed to never surrender.

With a little digging, what Al Brantley and I learned was that Richard Lance McLaren was a forty-three-year-old married Ohio native who had come to Texas from Missouri eighteen years earlier. The man who proclaimed himself chief ambassador and consul general of the ROT had not even been born in the Lone Star State.

Although McLaren and several of his fellow ROT members were under investigation for mail and bank fraud as well as conspiracy, there were no substantial federal charges against them, which meant there were legal limitations on the amount and type of assistance the FBI could provide. It was our shared view that any overt federal involvement would only make the situation worse by appearing to confirm McLaren's charges that the federal government was heavy-handed and oppressive.

Al's judgment was that McLaren was a man who mostly enjoyed being the center of attention, and I saw no reason to disagree. McLaren's inability to get along with others meant that he could only preside over a small group of weak individuals who passively allowed him to speak on their behalf. With his Koresh-like verbal ability, he frequently engaged in rambling lectures to show others how smart he was. Much of his current anger stemmed from being ostracized by the ROT mainstream. He had no history of violence up to this time, and when arrested previously he had not resisted. Bottom line, Al and I felt that McLaren was mostly bluster.

But if the authorities moved against him, McLaren and his followers would most likely defend themselves. To ensure against anything resembling the siege at Waco, the better idea would be to lure McLaren away from the property and away from his bodyguards—the leadership decapitation we had carried out in Montana. But Sheriff Bailey had only one full-time and two part-time deputies, so this was not going to be an easy strategy to carry out. Accordingly, the sheriff decided to watch and wait and hope for the best.

Having done the best we could under our limited mandate, Al and I headed back to Washington and the FBI academy.

On April 27, 1997, in the community of Davis Mountain Resort, Joe Rowe and his wife, Margaret Ann, were just about to eat a quiet Sunday lunch when three men and a woman, armed and dressed in military fatigues, burst in on them. The Rowes' property stood adjacent to land owned by McLaren's Republic of Texas, and the Rowes and the ROT had been engaged in an ongoing land dispute. For months members of the group had been patrolling the area and openly brandishing weapons, sometimes walking onto the Rowes' property. That morning, Joe Rowe called the sheriff to complain about an armed trespasser. Responding to the scene, Sheriff Bailey arrested a forty-three-year-old man named Robert Jonathan Scheidt. "Captain of the embassy guard" for the ROT, Scheidt was carrying two assault rifles.

The ROT's plan was to hold the Rowes hostage in exchange for Scheidt's release from the county jail. The ROT also demanded the release of Jo Ann Turner, an ROT member arrested in Austin the previous week in connection with the group's filing of bogus liens to obtain fraudulent loans.

It appeared that the sheriff's watch-and-wait tolerance had given McLaren the impression that he could get away with anything. Now the authorities had no choice but to act. State troopers barricaded the road leading in and out of Davis Mountain Resort and asked the more than eighty nearby residents to stay inside their homes. Those who chose to leave were allowed out, but not back in.

After negotiating for more than twelve hours, the Texas Rangers agreed to trade the Rowes for Scheidt. Joe Rowe, who had been cut by flying glass during the invasion of his home, had a heart condition, and the Rangers were concerned for his health. As Joe Rowe was taken to the hospital, the ROT gang retreated to their compound. Meanwhile, state authorities filed kidnap charges against McLaren and the other ROT members—Richard Keyes, Gregg Paulson, and Karen Paulson— who had committed the break-in and abduction.

While standard FBI procedure is never to exchange hostages, provide weapons, or furnish illegal drugs, we also leave room for flexibility, particularly when lives are at stake. This trade moved the Rowes out of harm's way, which meant that McLaren now had to be more concerned than ever about the potential for an assault since he no longer had them to use as shields. And even though Scheidt was out of jail for the moment, no one had any intention of letting him walk free.

The downside of the exchange was that McLaren claimed it as a great victory. It also fueled his grandiosity. He telephoned the media and said that he would not end the standoff until the authorities agreed to a referendum on Texas independence. "Maybe somebody will talk to us now," he said. "We've been trying for two years to get someone to talk to us." McLaren escalated even further, characterizing law enforcement authorities as "foreign agents" and demanding that the international court in The Hague recognize their legitimacy as a sovereign nation. As the hours passed he became increasingly agitated and his rhetoric more vitriolic.

I flew back to El Paso late Tuesday afternoon, April 29, and was told to check in to a motel and wait there. Profiler Al Brantley had come in just ahead of me and was already en route to Fort Davis in his rental car.

Meanwhile, McLaren's attorney, Terry O'Rourke, gave Captain Caver of the Texas Rangers some letters from McLaren that expressed some of the ROT leader's typically inflated concerns. McLaren not only wanted the Rangers and the other authorities to stay away, but he wanted to be dealt with as the ambassador of an independent country.

The conditions Caver offered were considerably less grand. Fundamentally, they called for McLaren's surrender. Not too surprisingly, the talks broke off, at which point I was told to proceed to Fort Davis.

The following morning, Wednesday the thirtieth, I got up early and drove to the forward command post, which was in a nearby fire department building. In my initial briefing I learned that a negotiation team had already been established, consisting of Texas Ranger Jess Malone, the primary negotiator who would speak to McLaren, and FBI negotiators Lane Akin and Carlos Conejo. Al and I were there to assist.

The Texas Rangers are known for acting decisively to enforce the law and restore order, a heroic reputation summed up in the adage "One riot, one Ranger." Accordingly, they were already voicing great frustration over their dealings with McLaren, and they were seriously considering a full tactical assault. Texas Ranger senior captain Bruce Casteel was the senior official at the scene when I arrived. He asked me what I thought would happen if they initiated tactical probes against McLaren. I voiced my opinion that ROT members would most likely respond with violence.

Before the siege, McLaren had been thought to have at most thirteen people holed up with him. We knew that Robert Scheidt was there, along with Richard Keyes and Gregg Paulson and his wife, Karen—the party that had invaded the Rowes' home. The rest of the cast of characters were Robert Otto, a bodyguard, who claimed to be a Native American and was also known as "White Eagle"; Evelyn Horak, McLaren's common-law wife; and Mike Matson. Beyond these, we weren't sure. McLaren, Otto, and several others were believed to be carrying semiautomatic weapons.

Given our lack of specific knowledge, I was concerned that we were moving toward a "linear approach" to incident management, which could lead to another debacle. It goes something like this: "First we try to talk them out, then if that doesn't work, we drop those ongoing efforts and tactically force them out." I suggested that the Rangers should consider the "parallel approach": authorities negotiate in good faith while simultaneously preparing for and showing their ability to undertake tactical action. Limited demonstration of tactical movement can help the negotiation process along by encouraging dialogue. Too little action can make the subject feel confident and secure, and thus less likely to negotiate in earnest. Too much action might trigger a firefight.

The Rangers accepted my suggestion and undertook an effort to be more visible to McLaren and the others at the "embassy." At the same time, they were careful not to encroach on ROT property or get close enough to trigger a violent response.

But McLaren now refused to speak with the Rangers. I suggested that we use the media to get our position out to the public. So far, McLaren was making all the significant statements, characterizing himself as a victim of federal intrusion and portraying the authorities as harassing him and his followers. I felt we could use the press to provide an accurate account of the situation, discourage supporters from rallying to his aid, and encourage McLaren to return to negotiations. The Rangers asked that I work with Department of Public Safety (DPS) press spokesman Mike Cox to develop a strategy. Mike had been plenty busy responding to endless media inquiries about McLaren, the ROT, and the charges pending against those hiding at the "embassy." He was now happy to use his microphone in a more proactive way.

We worked out the following points for Mike to deliver in his press conference:

1. "This is a State of Texas matter only. This is a case of Texas authorities trying to execute arrest warrants based on probable cause that crimes have been committed. McLaren and others have not been convicted of anything; they have only been charged and must appear to answer those charges according to Texas law and be tried by a jury of their fellow Texans."

Obviously, we felt this last piece was particularly important to help remove the argument that the big bad federal government was coming after McLaren for his beliefs.

2. "This is not a federal matter and should not be viewed as the U.S. government trying to move against the ROT. The DPS and Texas Rangers are in charge of this incident; the FBI is only here in an advisory role."

We couldn't deny that the FBI had some personnel on the scene, as this had already been widely reported. A total denial would be a lie.

3. "The ROT claims that people should be free in their homes, yet ROT members violently invaded a home and at gunpoint took two people hostage. The people of Texas expect law enforcement authorities to investigate and prosecute such crimes. Texas authorities are attempting to serve valid arrest warrants; they are not concerned about Mr. McLaren's political beliefs."

I hoped this point would elicit a response from McLaren, perhaps even bring him back to negotiations. I didn't think McLaren would want to be characterized as he was in our statement, which pulled the rug right out from under his self-serving interpretation of events. Right-wing movements always rail about the sanctity of individual rights, saying that a man's home is his castle and that no one has a right to come into someone else's home without permission. Yet here we were clearly showing that the ROT had violated this principle.

4. "Texas authorities have continued to undertake extensive efforts to open and maintain dialogue with McLaren. He has broken off contact. Texas authorities have shown patience and are committed to a peaceful resolution; we await Mr. McLaren's contact."

Again, this statement put enormous pressure on McLaren to reach out. The version of events he had presented to the media and distributed over the Internet was now a myth blown out of the water. Our statement served to make Texas authorities look rational while at the same time showing McLaren as obstructing efforts to reach a peaceful conclusion.

5. "We plan to serve the warrants."

And we wanted to make it clear that law enforcement was not going away.

While Mike Cox was preparing to give the press conference to deliver these points, the Rangers also dropped off a written response to McLaren's demands from the previous evening. This package included a letter from attorney Terry O'Rourke encouraging McLaren to come out. We also recommended that the package include a personal letter from Jess Malone, our primary negotiator, requesting that McLaren pick up the telephone to speak with him. We felt this would personalize Jess and demonstrate our sincere willingness to talk. Our earlier and repeated efforts to call in and speak to McLaren had been rebuffed.

Mike's appearance before the press received significant coverage, the overriding theme being that the citizens of Texas would demand that authorities bring to trial anyone who violated the sanctity of any citizen's home.

We didn't have to wait long for the ROT to take the bait. At about three that afternoon, Gregg Paulson phoned right-wing radio personality Doug Town. Based in Tampa, Florida, Town had already been on the phone with various individuals inside the ROT compound. Town contacted the FBI, and negotiators from my unit at Quantico spoke with him, trying to make sure that he understood that this was not another Waco, that the FBI was not in charge, and that we did not have a significant presence at Fort Davis.

At the request of negotiator Jim Duffy back at my unit in Quantico, Town set up a direct call between the ROT and negotiator Jess Malone. On that call, Paulson ranted about our characterization of him as having violently kidnapped the Rowes. In contrast, Jess maintained an easygoing, nonconfrontational manner and ran circles around Paulson. Jess carefully avoided getting into an argument. He also stressed the importance of keeping open a direct line of communications in the hope of achieving a peaceful resolution. Jess then asked Paulson if he and McLaren would, with a guarantee of safety and their right to return to the "embassy," be willing to come out for a "summit meeting." We knew the word *summit* would appeal to the ROT's sense of itself as a sovereign nation. Paulson went for it. He said he would call us back at seven-thirty that night.

This telephone exchange with Paulson reminded me that the authorities had so far not captured the ROT phone lines. Typically, one of the first things we try to do in a siege is isolate the phone lines so that the subjects can only speak with or through the negotiators—but the ROT still had unfettered access to the outside world. I suggested all efforts be undertaken right away to change that, meaning that whenever the ROT picked up the phone they would get us and only us. This would make the negotiators their sole broker for all communications, which was exactly what we wanted.

Unfortunately, this suggestion was misunderstood by someone on the law enforcement side. The result was a screw-up in which the ROT phone was cut off entirely. For some time we had been asking McLaren to speak with us, telling him he could do so whenever he wanted, and now we'd made that impossible. Making matters worse, the lines were cut just before the 7:30 p.m. call we had scheduled with Paulson.

Mistakes do happen during crisis situations, most often because the left hand of law enforcement doesn't know what the right hand is doing. In this case, someone may have been confused about the instructions, or may have simply assumed that we were following the policy of many police departments, which is to cut phone lines and power immediately when responding to an incident. I don't think authorities should ever do anything just because it's been done in the past. Each action has to be carefully considered in the context of the specific situation, with both the positive and the negative potential taken into account.

Similarly, some SWAT teams prefer that negotiators not make initial contact with the subject until the team has the perimeter effectively contained, which can take time. These teams are concerned that the subject may want to come out before a surrender can be accomplished in a tactically preferred manner. I've always believed that if someone really wants to surrender before we are fully ready, the officers on hand will somehow make it work, even if it isn't entirely according to the SWAT playbook. The notion of asking a subject to wait to surrender makes no sense to me.

In my opinion, the very first thing an agency should try to achieve is "verbal containment." This means establishing a dialogue, trying to keep the barricaded person calm, and explaining each of our movements in advance so that he does not see them as threatening.

Fred Lanceley used to tell negotiation classes that our job is not just about what happens over the phone line. It is everything the subject observes from his window as well as everything he hears on radio or sees on television. All of these stimuli have to be carefully controlled and managed in an integrated manner.

Unfortunately, we were now in a situation in which the press conference had set us up for progress, but we had no way to capitalize on it because we had no way to talk to the subjects.

At 10:00 Thursday morning I requested a meeting with Captain Caver. He was a tall, lean man, clean-cut with dark hair. By all appear-

ances he was approachable, laid-back, and easygoing. I'd never encountered him at Waco, but I knew that he, too, had been part of the law
enforcement team outside the Branch Davidian compound. I was hoping he had taken away from that ill-fated siege the same lessons I had.
Though he listened patiently while Al Brantley and I explained our concerns and made our recommendations, I could tell he was growing
impatient with McLaren and that he was leaning toward quick and decisive action.

I thought it would be appropriate to share my concerns with him
about any direct tactical action, so I took him aside and asked him a few
key questions. "What will you say to the widow of one of your Rangers
when you have to deliver the news that her husband has been killed
making this assault? If the widow looks at you with tears in her eyes and
wants to know if you had done everything possible to avoid putting her
husband in harm's way, will you be able to say you had? Will you be
able to say that you explored every possible alternative? If you can't say
yes to those questions, then perhaps you need to consider attempting
some other initiatives before you send your people into harm's way. I
believe we should try to reach our objectives without the use of force if
at all possible."

Caver looked startled. "What do you suggest I do?"

I told him I thought we might be able to undertake some incremental
actions that would encourage McLaren to negotiate with us in earnest to
avoid bloodshed. We could posture that we were going to assault him,
without actually moving in, to try to convince him to surrender.

"I'm open to your suggestions and will do anything reasonable to
keep my men safe," he said.

In this conversation, he also acknowledged that he had never been
told about the call scheduled with Paulson for seven-thirty the night
before. He said that cutting the phone lines had been his decision, but he
also said that he never would have done so if he had known about the
call. Inadvertently, we had experienced the same communications problems that had plagued us at Waco. Even a well-meaning and open-
minded commander can wind up spending more time with the tacticians
than with the negotiators, which means that they may not be fully aware
of the progress of the dialogue with those inside.

When teaching the FBI negotiation course, I would describe this as the "crisis within the crisis," emphasizing the critical need for negotiation leadership to have direct access to the on-scene commander. I used to tell my students that negotiating with an on-scene commander was often more difficult than dealing with the perpetrator. But Captain Caver made it clear that he wanted our input, and that he would do whatever he reasonably could to avoid an escalation to violence.

Shortly after our meeting, Caver directed that a telephone line be sent in to McLaren to support the reopening of negotiations. Two hours later Jess was able to reestablish contact.

McLaren was surprisingly civil, but he also complained that he had been trying to communicate but hadn't been able to get a call out. Jess Malone rose to the occasion, casually stating that there had been some problems with the telephone lines. McLaren then announced that he was sending out a "diplomatic pouch" with a letter we should read.

The pouch arrived around three in the afternoon. It contained a formal-looking ROT document written to look like a legal affidavit, along with a formal cease-fire agreement that McLaren had signed and wanted the Rangers to sign as well. This second document requested mediation by a neutral country. The inflated diplomatic tone was vintage McLaren.

About an hour later, the negotiation team met to formulate a response. The group decided to send McLaren a letter informing him that the authorities could not sign the agreement as drafted. The carrot included along with that stick was that the authorities would, however, honor their earlier promise of a humane surrender process.

This letter was delivered to McLaren at around eight that evening. At around nine, McLaren called Jess Malone and said that the letter was not what he had expected. He began to posture about his official standing as an ambassador of the ROT and rambled on in his convoluted way. After listening patiently to this for some time, Jess, becoming somewhat frustrated, responded, "You are not an ambassador." McLaren, who evidently did not appreciate the reality check, immediately hung up.

Late that evening, Paulson called Jess and engaged in a lengthy discussion. Paulson seemed scared, seeking reassurance that the Rangers would not be coming in during the night to get them. In keeping with our prepared strategy, Jess provided no such reassurance. Paulson's willingness to die for the cause appeared to be waning. We let him sleep on it.

At 9:05 the following morning, Paulson called once again. He told Jess that the only things keeping him from coming out were his honor and his duty. He said that he had written orders from the ROT command to defend their flag, and these were orders he could not disobey. I sensed that Paulson was fishing for help.

In keeping with my role as the primary negotiator's coach, I passed a note to Jess saying, *Let's find out who, besides McLaren, Paulson would accept orders from.*

The coach always sits shoulder to shoulder with the primary negotiator, listening on a headset while remaining absolutely quiet. Learning to write good notes that help the primary negotiator stay on track is an art unto itself. A well-timed note can make a big difference, allowing the negotiator to seize a sudden and unexpected opportunity that arises in the dialogue.

Jess asked Paulson about the ROT chain of command. Paulson said that President Boyce Halbison and Major General Melvin Kriewald were the only people who could order him to come out. It appeared that Paulson didn't know either of these individuals personally. He even had difficulty pronouncing their names as he shuffled through papers, reading from a list.

Getting Paulson to come out would be a real breakthrough. He could give us much-needed information about McLaren's intentions, accurately identify who was inside, and tell us what weapons they had and what defensive measures they had taken. It would also serve to loosen McLaren's control over the others inside the compound.

As soon as the exchange with Paulson ended, we immediately set about trying to locate Halbison and Kriewald. We hoped that their split from McLaren, and McLaren's subsequent embarrassing behavior, would encourage them to help us before he did further damage to the ROT's reputation.

A few minutes later, we learned that while we had been on the phone with Paulson, Robert Scheidt had walked down from the property and surrendered. He carried documents from McLaren, including last wills and testaments from those inside. I saw these wills as little more than a stunt to dramatize their willingness to fight to the death.

Shortly thereafter, Paulson called back and asked to speak to Scheidt. Paulson said that Scheidt had a code word that he was supposed to report back with, and tried to suggest that Scheidt had not surrendered but had been captured instead. Jess countered that Scheidt had walked out entirely on his own. Paulson's response was to call Scheidt a traitor.

We decided not to let Paulson speak directly with Scheidt, at least not until we knew more about why Scheidt had decided to come out. Had he been sent as a spy to report back on how many officers were surrounding them and where our command post was located? Was his surrender a test to see how well they would be treated? We simply didn't know. We came to believe that he had been sent out merely to deliver the wills, and that surrendering had been his own improvisation. With Paulson and now Scheidt losing heart, McLaren's control seemed to be waning.

At around two that afternoon, a letter arrived from Halbison ordering McLaren and all inside to surrender immediately. Jess made several attempts to call in and speak with McLaren after this, but was told McLaren was busy. The letter had clearly taken them off guard.

At 3:38, Paulson called Jess and said that the letter from Halbison was not the authorization he needed. He said that he needed a "proper" military order directly from Kriewald. We argued that Halbison, as the ROT president, was the commander in chief and therefore Kriewald's superior, but Paulson remained steadfast. Was he playing games with us? More likely, McLaren had raised this technical issue of chain of command, desperately trying to keep Paulson from bailing out. Meanwhile, we continued our efforts to reach Kriewald.

I felt it was time to inject a new element into our efforts, a nonaggressive yet highly visible tactical movement to create tension for those inside. We wanted to show McLaren and the others that we had the ability to bring this to an end whenever we wanted.

Captain Caver agreed, and at around six that evening, the Rangers and DPS authorities deployed a military construction tank, two armored personnel carriers, and more than ninety officers in vehicles to within a quarter mile of McLaren's position. With darkness coming on, this show of force would not be comforting. Obviously, if there had been hostages held by the ROT, such an initiative would not have been advisable. Trying to rattle an already unstable and cornered individual is too risky when hostages' lives are at stake. In this case, the tactical action initiated by the Rangers was meant as a carefully calibrated warning, meant to demonstrate the benefits of a negotiated resolution. And it got results.

McLaren immediately took to the ham radio asking for help from militia forces elsewhere. He also appeared to be broadcasting orders to his men on the perimeter, but we had no evidence that they even had ham receivers. That's when I heard him say, "Ready the missiles," and I knew he was running out of gas.

At around ten that night, McLaren's wife, Evelyn, placed a call to Jess. She said that she was afraid of our apparent intentions to escalate. "Can't you just give him what he wants?" she pleaded. Jess patiently appealed for her to use her influence with McLaren and the others to come out peacefully and avoid bloodshed.

Again, Jess was careful to avoid the term *surrender*. No one—least of all a rather pathetic individual with an inflated sense of self-importance—wants to be humiliated. I was always moved by General Grant's gesture to General Lee in allowing the Confederate leader to keep his sword during the surrender at Appomattox that ended the Civil War. That small but symbolic act cost Grant nothing, yet gained so much by allowing the venerated Lee to maintain his dignity and positively influence his loyal followers. Many of the individuals we deal with are hardly venerated warriors, but they are repeat offenders. If we treat them poorly when they surrender, they may not be so willing to cooperate with us the next time they're in a jam.

The next morning we got up early and drove back to the command post. It was only seven forty-five when Evelyn called to tell Jess that she had decided to come out. She said it would be at eleven or so that morning. Immediately I met with Captain Caver and urged him to make sure that his men treated her with dignity and respect. He promised that he would. Not only was that simply the right way to do things, but I wanted her to be able to speak positively to McLaren and the others about her reception.

At eleven-thirty she delivered on her promise, and Caver delivered on his. Evelyn came out, bringing with her a proposed agreement stating McLaren's terms and conditions for "surrender" (his choice of words). It seemed that he was still trying to save face. His proposal was written as a formal international cease-fire agreement between the ROT and the state of Texas. The district attorney and the Rangers reviewed the letter and felt they could sign two of the three pages, but they balked at the third page because it gave McLaren international recognition. I reminded everyone that while the path of deception is indeed a slippery slope, any document signed under duress had no legal standing. This helped convince the district attorney that Texas authorities could safely sign the proposed agreement without fear of legal entanglements.

We then sat down with Evelyn and made sure that she understood the gravity of the situation and the importance of convincing McLaren and the others to surrender. At around two in the afternoon she called and spoke with her husband. He asked for a code number, which she provided, apparently a confirmation that she had been well treated. She urged McLaren to come out, adding that she had learned that this would be the last chance for him to do so before the authorities launched an assault. She also told him that we had tanks and hundreds of officers assembled and were ready to come in with all necessary force.

Then she told him that we had agreed to sign the letter, but that there would have to be some minor changes. The changes we had made were mostly window dressing—we felt that if we simply signed his document without revision, he might smell a rat.

When Evelyn read the letter, McLaren seemed relieved. He asked her to reread several parts to him, then indicated that it was acceptable to him as amended. I was still convinced that he was eager to come out and that all this fine-tuning of the agreement was an effort to save face.

When Jess picked up the conversation with McLaren, he quickly transitioned into the process for a peaceful surrender. In such a situation, it's very important that both sides fully understand and agree to what, where, when, and how everything will happen. The two men agreed that McLaren and his bodyguard White Eagle would walk down from the property to the law enforcement perimeter and give themselves up. The remaining four individuals, fewer than we'd thought were there, would stack their weapons, stand by the ROT flag, and wait to be taken into custody.

At five-thirty that afternoon, seven days after the standoff began, McLaren surrendered. We had promised that he would be allowed to see Evelyn briefly when he was brought to the command post. This was a promise that we could stand behind.

When the tactical team moved forward to secure the ROT property, they found only Paulson and his wife waiting for them as agreed. Richard Keyes and another ROT member we had later learned was inside, Mike Matson, aided by the rough terrain, had managed to sneak through the law enforcement perimeter and escape. So now dog teams, riders on horseback, and helicopters all gave chase.

After three days, the officers with dogs began to get close. Matson told Keyes that he couldn't run anymore and that Keyes should go on without him. Keyes continued on foot as the officers closed in. Then Matson shot and killed a tracking dog, which prompted officers to return fire, killing Matson. Keyes made his way to civilization, where he was assisted by a militia group that transported him away from the Fort Davis area. On September 19, 1997, he was located by FBI agents and arrested.

While the ROT members may have appeared disorganized and incompetent, they had posed a very real risk to law enforcement officers as well as to their neighbors. A search of their property yielded a wide range of weapons. The ROT members also had set up explosive traps that might have harmed officers had they attempted to carry out the arrests by force. McLaren and most of the others were tried and convicted on charges ranging from engaging in organized criminal activity to burglary, failure to appear, civil contempt, aggravated kidnapping, and attempted capital murder.

There was little more for me to do out west. Al and I said goodbye to Captain Caver, Jess, and the others we had worked with, and headed to our rental cars. We wanted no part of any press conference. This was not a time for the FBI to be seen; our whole strategy had been to make it a local matter. As I drove to the airport, I smiled, thinking about one of my favorite TV shows as a kid—*The Lone Ranger*. I chuckled at the thought of someone seeing us drive off and asking, "Who were those masked men?"

CHAPTER ELEVEN

NO SHORTAGE OF CHALLENGES

The human race is challenged more than ever before to demonstrate
our mastery—not over nature but of ourselves.
—RACHEL LOUISE CARSON

The approach that worked so successfully in other standoff situations also was effective in a very different situation that took place in Puerto Rico in May 2000. Since 1941, the U.S. Navy had used the twenty-one-mile-long Vieques Island in Puerto Rico as a practice range for shelling and bombing, but over time the site had become more and more of a point of contention with the local population. According to the Navy, there was no alternative location that would allow them to carry out critical live-fire training. But when a security guard was accidentally killed during a bombing exercise in April 1999, protesters demanded that the Navy leave Vieques immediately. The cause had a great deal of political and public support in Puerto Rico and among some political figures on the U.S. mainland.

Despite a permanent court injunction against their trespassing, several protesters affiliated with the Vieques Fishermen's Association, the Puerto Rico Independence Party, and others occupied a portion of the island in the "live impact area," where the ordnance would land. The trespassers, thought to be about fifty individuals, set up eight separate camps scattered throughout the nine-hundred-acre site on the eastern tip of the island.

The Navy occupied 75 percent of Vieques's thirty-three thousand acres. A presidential panel had recommended that the Navy resume live-fire training but leave within five years. Pedro Rosselló, the governor of Puerto Rico, insisted that there be no further live-fire training at all and that the range be returned to civilian use. The Navy insisted that use of Vieques was an important matter of national security, and with that in mind, requested FBI assistance in removing the trespassers from the live-impact area.

The director of the FBI went on record with the attorney general stating that this was not a law enforcement issue and that the FBI should not be forced to make a tactical response. Despite that position, the FBI, along with the United States Marshals Service and the Coast Guard, were sent down to resolve this matter.

Everyone at CIRG viewed this as a no-win situation. The Vieques Island issue had galvanized the Puerto Rican people, and the island's three political parties, the Catholic Church, and university students were unified in seeking the cessation of Navy bombing operations. If the FBI removal operation was met with resistance and resulted in harm to any of the protesters, there would be huge political and reputational damage to the organization.

Despite those concerns, the CIRG deployed a large contingent of personnel, including negotiators and the HRT. We would use the Navy base at Roosevelt Roads, across the channel from Vieques, as a staging point. The action plan called for relying on the element of surprise to quickly gain control over the protesters and remove them from the live-impact area without incident. At least that had been the hope.

I flew to Puerto Rico to lead the negotiation team, deployed in the event of a standoff, but being there provided an unexpected pleasure. Captain Keith Naumann, the chief of staff for Rear Admiral Kevin Green, the senior Navy officer at Roosevelt Roads, was my best friend since childhood and had been the best man at my wedding. Admiral Green was the Navy's point man on the Vieques Island issue, so as his chief of staff, Keith was very familiar with the history and issues surrounding this problem. His background information and perspectives were very helpful to me. For the first time in our long respective government careers, his as a naval aviator and mine as an FBI special agent, these two boys from Atlantic Beach, Florida, were working together on a mission.

Keith told me that the Navy had threatened to close the entire Roosevelt Roads naval base if they lost the use of the practice site. Such a move would have a major economic impact on Puerto Rico. But apparently none of the politicians or protesters took the Navy's threat seriously.

The day before we planned to initiate the removal operation, a helicopter flew over the protesters' camps to help determine the number of individuals we would be confronting. This surveillance mission came back with some very troubling news: television camera crews were already set up at several locations. So much for the element of surprise.

Roger Nisley, now the SAC in charge of the CIRG, brought Chris Whitcomb and me into a meeting to discuss the implications of this new information. Chris formerly had been an HRT operator but now served as the CIRG media coordinator. We were all concerned that the protesters, knowing they were being filmed, would tend to act out and provide greater resistance than they might otherwise. This could only serve to inflame the political aspects of this confrontation.

I recommended that we revise the plan to have teams of negotiators lead, rather than follow each of the tactical teams as they approached the various camps. It would be the job of the Spanish-speaking negotiators to open up a peaceful and nonthreatening dialogue with the protesters, hoping to secure their cooperation in leaving, or at least in being taken into custody without any theatrics. We also agreed to have tactical personnel wear ordinary clothing and to advance toward the protesters "slow and easy" rather than "hard and fast."

Roger's embrace of this new approach demonstrated a willingness to think outside the box. The operation was less than twenty-four hours away, yet we were suddenly changing the plans we had developed over many weeks.

The next morning various FBI teams assembled and set off for Vieques. As planned, the teams arrived at each protest site simultaneously; stepping ahead of each team in a slow and confident manner were two Spanish-speaking negotiators, several of Puerto Rican ancestry.

They projected genuine respect for the protesters and an understanding of their cause, but also inserted just the right degree of firmness.

Treated this way, the protesters remained calm and fully complied with our directions. Many of them later commented that they were genuinely surprised by and greatly appreciative of the calm and professional way the FBI removed them from the island. Even better was the fact that the news media filmed this evidence of a "kindler and gentler" FBI removal operation. This no-win situation had suddenly become a big win for the FBI.

At the front gate of the Vieques live-impact area, a large, angry group had assembled, along with several television news teams, to protest the removal operation. FBI negotiator Liane McCarthy, a fluent Spanish-speaker from the FBI Boston office, and Henry Nava, a fluent Spanish-speaking negotiator from the FBI San Antonio office, calmly stood in front of this crowd and patiently explained what the FBI was doing and how we were doing it.

Back in Washington, Attorney General Janet Reno watched a live television broadcast as Liane and Henry expertly controlled the large crowd and calmed their anger. This was the type of news coverage the attorney general enjoyed seeing, and she conveyed her personal appreciation to Liane and Henry.

The Navy was also extremely grateful. The entire operation was a huge success, and the verbal skills of the negotiators supporting each tactical team had been the key element. Predictably, because no one was killed and nothing was burned down, this news event quickly fell off the national radar screen. But I couldn't have been more pleased and proud of my negotiation team.

Despite the overwhelming success of this operation, the issue of Vieques never really went away. Under heavy political influence the Navy eventually was forced to give up their target range, and true to their word, they shut down the Roosevelt Roads naval base as well. Puerto Rican politicians were shocked and dismayed at the closing of the base and the significant loss of jobs and local revenue that resulted. Several said they had wanted the Navy out of Vieques only, not Roosevelt Roads. It seems they wanted to have their cake and eat it, too. Perhaps they should have listened to the Navy sooner.

The results the FBI had begun to achieve in the 1990s, with skilled negotiation being applied in crisis situations, brought us significant international attention over the years. The purview of FBI negotiators was now global, with increasing levels of work outside the boundaries of the United States. Particularly challenging were cases in which American citizens were kidnapped abroad. In all, we would work on more than 120 international kidnappings, in addition to other incidents, often painfully aware that outside the United States we had far less control over how the situation would be handled. And outside the United States, the lessons learned by the FBI had not necessarily penetrated to all of the foreign governments involved.

The longest siege of my career began on December 17, 1996, when fourteen members of the Túpac Amaru Revolutionary Movement (MRTA) invaded the residence of the Japanese ambassador in Lima, Peru, during a party honoring the sixty-third birthday of Emperor Akihito.

The guest list meant that they took as hostages six hundred high-level diplomats, government officials, military leaders, and business executives, as well as Peruvian president Alberto Fujimori's mother and sister. The United States ambassador to Peru, Dennis Jett, had left the function just before the terrorists gained entry, but seven other U.S. diplomats were not as lucky.

When news of the incident reached Washington I was immediately deployed to Lima aboard a U.S. military aircraft along with other representatives of the multiagency Foreign Emergency Support Team (FEST). On the long plane ride to Lima, I discussed the dangerousness of the situation with Alanna Lavelle, one of the experienced negotiators assigned to my team at Quantico. In addition to being a great negotiator, Alanna also spoke fluent Spanish. Only a few months earlier, during a kidnap case in Ecuador, she had posed as a family friend and expertly stretched out the telephone calls with the kidnappers. This allowed the Ecuadorian authorities to trace the calls, locate the kidnappers, and then rescue the victim, John Heidema, a fifty-four-year-old American computer scientist. He had been taken hostage while vacationing in the rain forest with his daughter, who smartly feigned an asthma attack, which convinced the kidnappers to leave her behind. Her father was held for over thirty days in difficult conditions before he was rescued.

When Alanna and I arrived in Lima we met with Ambassador Jett, who expressed grave concern about the Americans and other hostages due to the MRTA's violent history and instructed me to make an assessment of the situation and keep him informed.

As I was leaving his office I received a message that someone from the British Embassy wanted to see me. It turned out to be Mike Dixon, the head of Scotland Yard's negotiation team, a good friend with whom I'd worked on other cases. We were soon joined by Dale McKelvey from the Royal Canadian Mounted Police (RCMP), who, like Mike, had attended my negotiation course. We would form a kind of ad hoc team, sharing information and making strategy recommendations to our respective governments, to be passed along further to President Fujimori. We would meet daily in my hotel room to exchange information about what we had learned and what recommendations we would make.

The MRTA's primary demand was the release of four hundred of their members being held in Peruvian jails. Another major problem we faced was that President Fujimori had risen to power on his tough stance against the MRTA and the Sendero Luminoso (Shining Path). These were both Marxist terrorist groups whose actions had led to thousands of deaths over the years. Mindful of his domestic constituency, President Fujimori refused to communicate with the terrorists, despite the fact that several hostages had been unilaterally released with messages saying the MRTA wanted to talk with the government.

Fujimori's apparent refusal to open a dialogue with the MRTA demonstrated that he had not heard of the concept of verbal containment. He was taking a serious risk by not attempting to open such a dialogue, as the MRTA might begin executing some of their hostages at any time to force the issue.

From what we could gather, there was no clear command structure controlling the various government elements surrounding the residence. To make matters worse, President Fujimori made frequent bellicose statements to the press that merely served to agitate the terrorists inside.

Also, the government's failure to control the perimeter around the Japanese ambassador's residence would cost us an opportunity to gain vital information. Just a few days into the crisis, the MRTA unilaterally released large numbers of hostages. When the hostages emerged from the residence, the multiple Peruvian police units surrounding the residence simply sent them home. No one intercepted them to conduct a debriefing. We lost a chance to find out how many terrorists were inside, what weapons they had, what they were saying about their intentions, and how they were treating the hostages. Management of this siege was turning into a three-ring circus, with Fujimori as the inept ringmaster.

Luckily, one of the released hostages was Anthony Vincent, the Canadian ambassador. He volunteered to become an intermediary between the terrorists and the Peruvian government. Working through the RCMP, our ad hoc international negotiation team was able to rely on the ambassador to inject our assessment and advice into the process.

The head of the Peruvian office of the International Committee of the Red Cross (ICRC), Michel Minnig, was also released. Acting more on his own than under guidance from Fujimori, he returned to the residence to deliver food and water to those still being held. He would return every day to bring more food and take out the trash, and he soon began to carry messages directly from the terrorists to the government. When I learned that he was doing this without guidance from the government, I set up a meeting with him in order to find out more about what he was doing. While his insights were interesting, he made it clear that his role with the ICRC prevented him from playing any role other than a humanitarian one.

While Fujimori allowed this contact to take place, he still distanced himself from direct involvement. Leaving the ICRC to operate on its own was hardly the ideal way to manage contact with terrorists during a siege, but it was the best thing we had going.

Through this ICRC effort, and partially because of space restrictions within the residence, the terrorists began to release additional hostages, including all the women. This allowed them to better manage the one hundred or so captives who remained. They were not physically abusive to the hostages, but toilets began to overflow, and in spite of Minnig's efforts, food and fresh water were in short supply.

After the first week, the MRTA released more hostages, including all the remaining American diplomats. We were delighted, but we recognized that this was, in fact, a smart strategic move on the part of the MRTA. By releasing all the American victims, they hoped to eliminate the potential for the United States to use its own tactical forces to conduct a rescue mission.

During the second week Monsignor Juan Luis Cipriani joined Ambassador Vincent in an attempt to mediate the crisis. Ambassador Jett made an appointment for me to meet with Cipriani to provide him with some ideas on how he might enhance his efforts as an intermediary. At my meeting with Cipriani, I stressed the importance of patience and keeping the dialogue open. I recommended that he always set the next meeting time with the MRTA before ending the current contact. I thought he also might be able to explore creative ways to address the MRTA's demands for prisoner release, such as sending some to a third country. As I discussed these and other suggestions, he and his assistant furiously scribbled down every single word. When I was done, he put his pen down, looked up at me, and said haughtily that he had already thought of all of these things.

With the American hostages released, I returned home just in time for Christmas, but kept in daily contact with other deployed FBI, RCMP, and Scotland Yard negotiators for the remainder of the ordeal. Monsignor Cipriani's efforts yielded little, and I soon became convinced that President Fujimori wasn't seriously pursuing a peaceful resolution, supporting limited negotiation contacts only as a means to buy time while preparing his commandos for a tactical assault. And in fact engineers were already at work, excavating tunnels that led underneath the street and into the residence.

Several of the hostages later commented that the MRTA could hear that tunnels were being dug—they just didn't know what to do about it. As a diversion meant to mask the sounds, Fujimori ordered loud military parades with marching bands to roll by on the street in front of the residence. During one of the parades a soldier riding in an armored vehicle stuck his middle finger in the air aimed directly at the terrorists. In response, an irritated MRTA terrorist cranked off a round from his AK-47, the first shot fired since the residence was taken over. A news videotape shows a bullet striking and ricocheting off an armored personnel carrier just inches away from the gesturing soldier. Everyone ducked for cover, and the parade quickly came to an end. Had that soldier been hit, the shot might have prompted an immediate assault with significant loss of life.

Through all of this the MRTA remained firm in its demands for the release of incarcerated terrorists, something Fujimori resolutely refused to consider. We were lucky that the MRTA did not start executing hostages to press their demands.

The FBI's advisory role expanded into a new arena—garbage collection. One of our agents suggested that we start to examine all the trash being carried out by the ICRC after each food delivery, looking for messages as well as any other clues to what might be going on inside. This job was extremely unpleasant and ended up being something the Peruvians didn't seem much interested in doing. So highly skilled FBI agents donned gloves and masks and did the job for them, finding a number of important handwritten notes from hostages, including one asking the government to acknowledge receipt of their notes by having the military band play a certain song. After many days, they were able to make this happen to let the hostages know their messages were being received.

In addition, one of the Peruvian hostages had been able to keep his cell phone hidden, and he periodically transmitted information. Further insight came through several hidden microphones that were secretly introduced into the residence. The single most salient fact picked up through these efforts was that every day at a certain time most of the young MRTA terrorists played a game of indoor soccer in a residence living room that had been cleared of furniture.

Weeks and then months passed with little progress. It was taking a long time to dig the tunnels. Finally, on April 22, 1997, 126 days after the siege had begun, military commandos placed a large charge of explosives inside a tunnel directly underneath the living room. They detonated it as the daily MRTA soccer match was in full swing, instantly killing many of the terrorists. Peruvian commandos then stormed the residence from multiple points of entry, killing the remaining terrorists and freeing the hostages.

Although one hostage, two commandos, and all of the terrorists died in this rescue, seventy-seven hostages were rescued. Time purchased through delays, more by luck than design, had enabled the commandos to devise and execute their plan with precision—another testament to the value of stalling for time.

Later, critics of the government made the accusation that several terrorists were summarily executed after surrendering, but that was never proven, and in any event there was no sympathy for them among the Peruvian public. The whole nation rightfully took pride in what they saw as a brilliant rescue. Fujimori was the hero, and he was videotaped in the news triumphantly touring the just-cleared residence, looking down at the bodies of terrorists.

I worried that other governments would examine this incident only from the narrow perspective of the successful outcome. My main complaint about Fujimori was that he placed all his eggs in one basket—the tactical rescue. Without ongoing negotiations to keep a lid on the tension, the MRTA might have initiated violence at any time. Had they done so, there would have been no way to quickly and safely intervene to save hostages. Fujimori and his followers saw him as a masterly tactician. Perhaps, but he had also been very, very lucky. It would be foolish to expect other terrorists to be so patient.

Could meaningful negotiations have resolved this situation without any loss of life? It's hard to say. However, I know that there will always be terrorists who, when given an option, will choose life over death. It's the job of the negotiation team not only to buy time but also to genuinely attempt to convince those wavering extremists to pursue a course of action in which they and their hostages can survive. While we always prepare for the worst, we still try to pursue the best outcome we can.

One positive outcome of the Peruvian incident was that Canadian, British, and American negotiation teams agreed to come together to conduct an after-action review at a conference I organized in Alexandria, Virginia. This led to an agreement to continue working together on other international negotiation matters. Our core group continued to meet annually, and I eventually expanded the group to create the International Negotiation Working Group (INWG), which now includes more than fifteen countries from around the world. This group, in turn, inspired me to try to enhance further the FBI's level of support for domestic police negotiation teams throughout the country. With that goal in mind, in 1999 I invited seven experienced police negotiation colleagues to the FBI academy for a conference. This gave rise to a national coordinating body, the National Council of Negotiation Associations (NCNA), to assist the various regional organizations around the country already serving police negotiators.

One of the early achievements of the newly formed NCNA was to ratify a set of negotiation guidelines that I drafted. With minor modifications these NCNA guidelines became, and remain today, the national standard. Endorsed by the NCNA member organizations representing several thousand law enforcement and correctional negotiators in the United States and Canada, they have codified the underlying philosophy and recommended negotiation approaches for all types of hostage, barricade, and suicide incidents.

Now for the first time, negotiation teams could provide their incident managers with nationally approved written guidance on handling critical events. This ability empowered and supported negotiation teams by allowing them to argue to incident commanders that their departments' handling of any situation would be assessed according to how well they followed the NCNA guidelines. I'm pleased that these same guidelines have been used to successfully defend police departments during several wrongful death lawsuits around the country.

In April 1998, the FBI elevated the FBI negotiation program and established the Crisis Negotiation Unit (CNU), with me named its first unit chief. More important, this promotion elevated me to the same rank as the Assistant Special Agent in Charge of the HRT. With ten full-time negotiation supervisory special agents and three support staff, we managed the training and deployment of more than 350 negotiators assigned to FBI field offices around the country, responding to law enforcement negotiation needs at home and abroad.

Our two-week negotiation training course was now known as the National Crisis Negotiation Course (NCNC). Police officers from around the globe continued to request opportunities to attend this prestigious program. We could only conduct a few classes each year, so we never had enough slots to satisfy the requests for attendance.

Unfortunately, I had to fight internal budget wars each year in an attempt to maintain funding. CNU had raised the profile of the negotiation program around the world, but within the FBI, getting the necessary budget dollars for training, or even finding available classroom space at the FBI academy, was never easy. I don't think that FBI officials at the highest levels ever fully appreciated or understood the significant national and international goodwill this training program brought to us, a situation I'm afraid persists to this day.

Over the last several years of my FBI career, overseas kidnappings of American citizens increasingly demanded a significant amount of my time and energy. There was rarely a time that my FBI negotiation team was not actively deployed abroad. In 1990 I had flown to Zaire on one of the FBI's first overseas kidnap cases and helped secure the release of American Brent Swan from the terrorist group FLEC-PM. In the first years of the new millennium, we were engaged in trying to resolve the kidnapping of oil-field workers by Ecuadorian guerrillas, as well as an incident in the Philippines in which the victim was a young man traveling to meet a young woman he had met online, whose relatives turned out to be terrorists who saw the young American as an opportunity for revenue. In another Philippine incident, the kidnap victims were missionaries.

On May 27, 2001, missionaries Martin and Gracia Burnham were celebrating their eighteenth wedding anniversary at the upscale Dos Palmas resort on Palawan Island, having saved just enough for a one-night stay. Terrorists from the Abu Sayyaf Group (ASG), Islamic separatists who operated primarily in the southern Philippines, chose that same night to travel across the sea by speedboat from their base on Basilan Island to gather up hostages at the resort.

Martin and Gracia were part of a group of eighteen people seized that night and whisked back to the ASG stronghold. The group included another American who had been on vacation when captured, Guillermo Sobrero. He was reportedly wounded during an early skirmish between the ASG and the Philippine military. After one month, unable to keep up with the frequent movement and forced marches dictated by the ASG in order to avoid Philippine military actions, he was beheaded. Most of the other hostages were eventually ransomed by their families. However, to protect its missionaries from kidnapping, the Burnhams' sponsoring organization steadfastly refused, as a matter of policy, to pay the $1 million ransom the kidnappers were demanding for the couple.

The ASG was ideologically aligned with Osama bin Laden, so I was deeply concerned about the fate that awaited Martin and Gracia. I quickly deployed a team of negotiators to the Philippines. For many months we tried to develop and maintain contact with the band of terrorists holding them. We eventually exchanged several text messages with the kidnappers. The U.S. military was also providing significant assistance to the Philippine military in support of their search efforts. Teams of FBI negotiators rotated in and out of the Philippines every three weeks.

Well into the Burnhams' captivity, we attempted to mount a sting-type operation by offering to pay a $300,000 ransom. Our plan was to pay the money, secure the safe release of the Burnhams, and then sweep in to destroy the ASG element and recover the money. The ASG agreed to our offer and the plan moved forward, but then they kept the money and didn't follow through with the promised release. At least the funds allowed the ASG to purchase much-needed food and supplies that Gracia later said helped them during a very lean period in their captivity. But then the group disappeared deeper into the jungle, and the already long and painful plight of the Burnhams continued. I spoke with my deployed negotiators almost every day during this yearlong case, always attempting to develop approaches that would establish dialogue with the ASG. Limited negotiation via text messaging was the best we were able to do.

Just days after the one-year anniversary of the Burnhams' capture, a Philippine military unit located the ASG camp where they were being held, and initiated a rescue operation. Tragically, the assault included indiscriminate shooting, which resulted in Martin's being killed, not by the ASG but by the rescuing forces. He was hit by three gunshots to the chest and died at the scene. Gracia received a gunshot wound in the right thigh but survived. A Philippine nurse also being held hostage was killed as well. Gracia was rescued by Philippine soldiers and taken to Manila for medical care.

Those who believe that military action is the only strategy against terrorism should view this sad ending as a cautionary tale for what can go wrong when bullets start to fly. The tactical capability of law enforcement and military units in the developing world is often limited. Unfortunately, bullets cannot tell good guys from bad guys. The ASG contingent and its leaders who held Martin and Gracia were later hunted down by the Philippine military and destroyed.

On July 25, 2002, Gracia traveled to the Washington, D.C., area and kindly appeared before the team of FBI negotiators who had been involved in trying to secure her safe release. It was a bittersweet meeting, with all in attendance thankful for her survival but deeply grieved by Martin's death. As I listened to Gracia recount her ordeal, I was yet again reminded how very important the work of our negotiators is, and how close to the line between life and death we usually operate.

In January 2002, my unit also provided significant assistance after the kidnapping of *Wall Street Journal* reporter Danny Pearl. We were never able to sustain a meaningful dialogue with his captors, but the limited contacts we did have assisted FBI investigators in identifying those responsible through their use of an Internet café in Pakistan.

CHAPTER TWELVE

BEING OUR BEST
WHEN OTHERS ARE
AT THEIR WORST

If you can keep your head when all about you are losing theirs...
—RUDYARD KIPLING

Having joined the FBI several days after my twenty-second birthday, I often joked that my parents had given me to the FBI as a child. The FBI had never been a job to me; it was a calling, an honor, and a privilege. Being a special agent wasn't just what I did for a living, it was who I was. It had been a demanding ten-to-twelve-hour-a-day commitment, working nights and weekends and often being away from my family, but the rewards had far outweighed the burdens.

By 2002, I had achieved most of my goals for the FBI's crisis (hostage) negotiation program and felt it was the right time to retire, and by the beginning of fall I had the necessary paperwork all filled out and submitted. But just like in all those pulp fiction detective novels, I had one more case to work.

This final case would be very different from anything I or anyone else had ever worked. We were dealing with an unknown adversary engaged in a rampage that terrorized everyone within a large metropolitan community over a period of several weeks. This incident filled the news as nothing before ever had.

It all began at 5:20 p.m. on Wednesday, October 2, 2002, when a bullet flew through the front window of the Michaels craft store on Georgia Avenue in Wheaton, Maryland, a suburb of Washington, D.C., fortunately not hitting anyone. Forty-four minutes later, fifty-five-year-old James D. Martin was walking across the parking lot at the Shoppers Food Warehouse not far away when a bullet struck him in the chest, killing him. What was going on? Was this the action of a lone madman, or perhaps the work of a group of violent Islamic terrorists attempting to strike fear in Americans in our own homeland? No one claimed credit for these shootings and no one knew the answers to those questions.

Over the next two days a total of six individuals in Maryland and Washington, D.C., were felled by a sniper's bullet. There was no apparent pattern to the shootings and no indication of any grievance against these seven individual victims, who were white, black, Hispanic, and Indian, male and female, and ranging in age from twenty-five to seventy-two.

Every law enforcement officer in the metropolitan area was in a state of high alert. Citizens in the area were panicked; parents, particularly, were worried about the safety of their children as they traveled to and from school and even as they sat in the classroom, but on October 4, police announced that the schools were safe and that parents should continue to send their kids to class. Then on October 7, a thirteen-year-old boy was shot and seriously wounded at Tasker Middle School in Bowie, Maryland.

It seemed as if the shooter was listening to the news and responding to what was being said. At one point an "expert" suggested that the shooter would likely stay near his own familiar area of comfort; the shooter's next victim was about sixty miles south, in Fredericksburg, Virginia. On another occasion a retired FBI profiler suggested that the shooter was apparently not a skilled marksman, since he had shot several victims in the torso and not the head; the next victim died of a bullet to the head. Her name was Linda Franklin, and ironically she was a support employee of the FBI.

My family was as worried as anyone else. My twenty-two-year-old daughter, Kelly, had driven away from the parking lot in Fredericksburg, Virginia, just a short time before a forty-three-year-old white female was shot in the back while loading packages into her car. My other daughter, Katie, age twenty, attending Mary Washington College in Fredericksburg, regularly filled up her car at the same Exxon gas station where fifty-three-year-old Kenneth Bridges was shot and killed on October 11. My son, Rusty, eighteen, had been named homecoming king at Robinson High School in Fairfax, Virginia, where we lived. Like any proud parents, my wife and I looked forward to seeing our son honored in the homecoming parade that would culminate at the football stadium. But like so many schools in the area, Robinson was forced to cancel all outdoor activities.

Yet these were minor concerns compared to the grief that the sniper was causing so many families in the Washington, D.C., area. Because several victims had been shot while fueling their cars, some gas stations hung large drapes near their pumps so that customers would not be scared away. People crouching down while pumping gas became a common sight. There were thousands of stories of individuals and families changing their routines and exercising high levels of caution in every aspect of their daily lives.

The FBI and ATF, along with other local, state, and federal agencies, quickly set up a task force to help identify, locate, and apprehend whoever was doing these shootings. The public came to know Chief Charles Moose of the Montgomery County Police Department as the leader of the investigation. In reality, there was a triumvirate of sorts in charge, consisting of Chief Moose and senior representatives of the FBI and ATF. This group attempted to bring some structure and coordination to the challenging task that was facing the many agencies working over a wide area encompassing Maryland, the District of Columbia, and Virginia.

As head of the Crisis Negotiation Unit within the Critical Incident Response Group, I had assigned the agents in my unit to geographic territories that matched up with FBI field offices, with one supervisor assigned to several regions to provide support. Vince Dalfonzo was responsible for Maryland. He happened to be a Baltimore native, so I attached him to the joint command post that had been established in Montgomery County. Vince joined a multiagency negotiation team that had been assembled in the hopes of drawing the sniper into a dialogue. That team also helped craft the daily press messages from Chief Moose and the other leaders. Until we could establish a direct dialogue with the sniper, our only means of communication was through these daily statements. It was important that the authorities avoid saying anything that might agitate the sniper and prompt him to kill again. A large team of negotiators from the FBI and other involved agencies stood ready to open a dialogue with the shooter if we could successfully get him to contact us.

On October 7, the sniper had left a tarot card near Tasker Middle School, where the thirteen-year-old boy had been seriously wounded. Written on the tarot card was "Mr. Policeman, I am God." The negotiation team expended much effort trying to interpret this message, but we also realized that its mere existence could be useful. If we kept the card secret from the press, we might use it to verify that we were talking with the real sniper if he contacted us. Unfortunately, this information was leaked to the press in a matter of hours.

On October 17, a man claiming to be the sniper called the public information officer for the Montgomery County police, saying, "I'm God." The three-minute call consisted of a very angry man demanding, "Don't you know who you're dealing with?" The caller also made reference to a crime in "Montgomery," which we assumed referred to the shootings in Montgomery County, Maryland. Later the sniper would call the police again and was quickly put through to the negotiation team room. FBI negotiator Marina Murphy took the call and attempted to draw him into a dialogue, but the caller seemed to become scared, and he simply hung up.

The next day, October 18, the sniper contacted a priest in Ashland, Virginia, Monsignor William Sullivan, the pastor of St. Ann's Church, and again said, "I am God." He also referred once more to a crime in "Montgomery." Unfortunately, the monsignor did not report this call to the police initially, believing that it was a prank call.

Officers and agents were busy chasing down more than sixteen thousand leads and following up on more than a hundred thousand phone calls to a telephone tip line. Despite their efforts, on Saturday, October 19, a thirty-seven-year-old man was shot in the abdomen in the parking lot of a Ponderosa Steakhouse in Ashland, Virginia. He was critically wounded but survived. A search of the crime scene revealed that the sniper had left a note in a wooded area from where the shot was fired.

Wrapped in plastic and tacked to a tree was a four-page message, the cover sheet of which said, "Call me God," along with, "For you, Mr. Police" and "Don't release to the press." The letter demanded that $10 million be wired to a stolen platinum Bank of America Visa credit card. The account number and PIN were included. The note said, "We will have unlimited withdrawal at any ATM worldwide." Despite this demand, I didn't believe the crime spree was about money. There had been no demand for money up front, and if money is what you want, there is no need to keep killing people before you've made that demand.

In his note, the sniper complained that the authorities had made it hard for him to make contact to begin ransom negotiations. He denounced the operators of the tip line, saying that he had called four times and been taken "for a hoax or a joke." He went on to say that "your failure to respond has cost you five lives" and "your children are not safe anywhere at any time."

Most unusual was the sniper's demand in the note that the police announce that they had "caught the sniper like a duck in a noose." It made absolutely no sense, but that was what he wanted us to say. After analyzing this demand, the negotiation team drafted the following message for Chief Moose to deliver in response: "You asked us to say, 'The sniper has been caught, like a duck in a noose.' We don't understand why you want us to say this, but we know it's important to you. That is why we are saying it now, to stop the killing."

In one of the rare instances in which profilers and negotiators disagreed, the FBI profiling team argued against making any such statement, believing that it would simply empower the sniper. Now working at the command post, I countered that the sniper was already feeling very empowered and that our failure to attempt to address this demand could prove fatal for more victims. Both Jim Cavanaugh (my ATF colleague from Waco) and Chief Moose expressed their agreement with me, but when I went home and turned on the television to watch the chief make our recommended statement, he omitted the critical portion. I later found out that SAC Gary Ball, the head of the FBI Baltimore office and the senior FBI official managing the incident, had sided with the profiling team and blocked the reference to "a duck in a noose." I was furious.

Chief Moose did issue a direct appeal to the sniper through the news media, saying, "We do want to talk to you. Call us."

Following up on the earlier call to the monsignor, investigators discovered that the sniper's reference to "Montgomery" concerned an unsolved murder-robbery on September 21 at a liquor store in Montgomery, Alabama. It turned out that a gun magazine had been left behind at the crime scene with a clear fingerprint. When the FBI ran that fingerprint, which was on file owing to an earlier juvenile offense, it led us to a young man named Lee Boyd Malvo. FBI agents sent out to investigate his background quickly discovered that he had spent the previous few years with an older man named John Muhammad. With their first solid bit of evidence, agents quickly turned up the heat to locate these two.

At about six in the morning on October 22, the sniper shot and killed Conrad Johnson, a thirty-five-year-old bus driver, as he stood in the doorway of his bus near Silver Spring, Maryland. He was the thirteenth person shot, the tenth to die. The sniper left a note near the scene saying that he was angry with the police for not doing what he had asked, which was to announce that the sniper had been caught like a duck in a noose. I took no pleasure from the fact that this validated the position I had advocated: if we had included the sniper's wording as demanded, we might have prevented the death of Conrad Johnson.

Meanwhile, investigators traced John Muhammad to Tacoma, Washington, where he and Lee Boyd Malvo once lived. In the backyard of Muhammad's former residence they found a tree stump where he had practiced shooting. In the stump they recovered metal casings that matched those found near the scene of the sniper killings. Police then learned (and made public) that Muhammad and Malvo were driving a Caprice. On the twenty-second, the night of the Johnson killing, an alert citizen spotted the vehicle in a rest area off a highway in Maryland. Members of the HRT approached the vehicle and arrested the two sleeping suspects.

Malvo and Muhammad were both convicted of murder. Muhammad was given the death penalty; because of his youth, Malvo was given multiple life sentences. Why had they undertaken this killing spree? It turned out that Muhammad's divorced wife and children lived in the

D.C. area. Authorities learned that Muhammad hoped to add her to the list of those killed by the sniper, thus making her death appear random and certainly not related to her ex-husband. Muhammad's ultimate objective was to regain custody of his children. Malvo, the younger accomplice, was just a pathetic figure who had been captivated and manipulated by the older Muhammad.

So, in essence, my career had come full circle. Just as with Charlie in Sperryville and Mario on Amtrak, I was once again confronting men whose extreme violence was driven by nothing more than their inability to cope with various stresses and emotional frustrations in their lives.

At the time of the D.C. sniper incident, I had been in the FBI for thirty years, and the FBI's chief negotiator for the past ten years. I had been eligible for retirement since turning fifty two years earlier, but I didn't feel quite ready at first, and the events of September 11, 2001, prompted me to stick around a bit longer. I wasn't sure if I could make any further contribution to the war on terrorism, but it just didn't seem to be the right time to leave the FBI. By 2003, though, I was ready. My three children were all in higher-education degree programs, and the reality of three tuitions provided an incentive for me to start drawing my pension while also taking on another job. I had grown weary of the administrative side of being a unit chief in a big bureaucracy, too. Fighting for budget dollars and manpower needs and attending endless meetings had never been my favorite things.

So January 3, 2003, became the effective date of a decision that had been a long time coming: the official end of my FBI career. The Bureau had sent me to all fifty states and to more than forty countries. Steve Romano took over the helm at CNU and carried forward the great legacy of the FBI negotiation program. John Flood would eventually take over when Steve retired.

I started this book with a case in which I recommended using deadly force. At first glance, this may seem strange in a book that argues for the primacy of negotiation. But as I hope I've made clear, there are times when we must conclude that negotiation isn't enough. In Charlie Leaf's case, I believed that he simply wasn't going to let Cheryl go; even if we managed to stall him for a bit longer, at some point he would very likely kill her and perhaps little Charlie. When negotiators start a dialogue with a threatening individual, we immediately begin to track the progress of our efforts. Has he become less angry and more willing to discuss reasonable alternatives to violence? Has his emotional equilibrium returned to a more normal state? Has the negotiator been able to establish a level of rapport that will enable him or her to begin to positively influence the behavior of the individual? In the overwhelming majority of cases the answer to these questions is yes, but there will always be times when the risks increase, when you have to move on to a tactical rescue. As I did in Sperryville, at this point the negotiator assumes a key role supporting the tactical operation by providing the time, intelligence, and opportunity required for success.

If I've gained any wisdom in my FBI career, it has come from recognizing the degree to which everyday life can mirror the dynamics of the destructive standoffs I faced in my FBI job. Each of us is called upon to negotiate stressful situations in business, social encounters, and family life time and again. From what I've observed, the happiest and most successful people tend to be those who are able to remain calm at these difficult times and put aside emotions such as pride or anger that stop them from finding common ground. We all need to be good listeners and learn to demonstrate our empathy and understanding of the problems, needs, and issues of others. Only then can we hope to influence their behavior in a positive way.

You might even say that all of life is a negotiation.

EPILOGUE

When I retired from the FBI I went to work for Control Risks, the premier kidnap-response consultancy in the world. My primary role was to assist clients in preparing for and operationally managing the kidnapping of one of their employees or family members to achieve the best outcome possible. My travel schedule increased significantly as a consultant, but I found I enjoyed the comparative freedom from the bureaucratic burdens that came with being a unit chief at the FBI.

However, my operational work was not over. From 2003 through 2008, I worked a lengthy and very complex kidnap incident involving three American defense contractors who were seized by a terrorist group, the Revolutionary Armed Forces of Colombia (FARC). This case received significant interest and active participation from a host of agencies within the U.S. government. It was among the most difficult I ever worked, and once again, dealing with parties other than the kidnappers often created a crisis within the crisis.

The government is staffed with many hardworking and capable individuals. It has tremendous resources and can be of great assistance in these matters, but it also has the capacity to make matters unnecessarily complicated. The government did much good in supporting Colombian military intelligence-gathering that eventually proved to be key in this incident. But constricted thinking and outdated policy guidelines often proved to be an impediment to creative problem solving that might have helped achieve an earlier release for the hostages.

Despite a number of government mistakes, after five and a half years of captivity the hostages were rescued by the Colombian military and returned home safely to their families. Working this case alongside the government, but this time from the perspective of the victims' families and employers, provided me with additional insights into what I see as shortcomings in the way our government sometimes responds to terrorist situations.

Even among government leaders, the word *terrorism* evokes a great deal of emotion. This response can often lead to constricted thinking. The fact that a hostage is taken and held by a terrorist group isn't the most important factor to consider when developing an effective resolution strategy. What's more important to understand is what the terrorists are trying to achieve. If money or some other tangible item is their goal, then a classic negotiation strategy can be employed, usually with great success. However, if the demands are political, then the situation is infinitely more complicated and challenging, but not necessarily hopeless. Such cases require great patience and creative thinking. In 1990, we secured the safe release of Brent Swan from terrorists in Africa, not by paying the ransom they sought but by providing office and medical supplies as an alternative. This creative and flexible approach worked. Often tactical intervention is necessary, but not in every case.

Unfortunately, many government officials do not appreciate the different and nuanced aspects of terrorism. Instead they simply react to the word *terrorist*, concluding that the demands must be political and therefore, they must respond in a firm, unyielding, and inflexible manner. This one-size-fits-all reaction may not be the best response to the kidnappers' true motivations or allow for thoughtful consideration of the wider range of resolution strategies that might be possible. In reality, most kidnap victims don't care if they are taken by criminals or terrorists, held for money or for political objectives. They and their families simply want them to be free, and I believe everything reasonable should be done to make that happen.

There is no legal prohibition against a U.S. family or corporation paying a ransom in a criminal kidnap case. However, if an American is held by a group on the State Department's terrorist list, paying a ransom may violate the prohibition against providing material support to a terrorist organization. Congress intended that prohibition to apply to organizations raising funds in the United States for terrorist groups abroad.

It was never envisioned to apply to kidnap cases. In my opinion, it should never be used to prevent a family or corporation from securing the safe release of a loved one or employee taken hostage, as some in government have tried to suggest.

In the days following September 11, 2001, there was a hard and noticeable turn toward use of the military as the exclusive response mechanism for dealing with such situations. Many officials felt compelled to repeatedly declare that the United States would not negotiate with terrorists. These strong declarations have helped promote the use of military action as a response to any crisis. As the saying goes, if you've got a hammer, you tend to think everything is a nail. But saying we will not negotiate with terrorists has never been shown to protect American citizens from being kidnapped abroad. In fact, Americans remain among the most sought-after individuals to kidnap.

I concur that the U.S. government should not make substantive concessions to terrorists. (I am not speaking of families or employers here.) However, this should not be interpreted, as it so often is, to mean that U.S. authorities will not hold discussions—that is, negotiate—with terrorists. I'm confident that the FBI would indeed attempt to actively negotiate with terrorists holding hostages on an aircraft at JFK Airport. To do otherwise would be dangerous and foolish. But negotiating with terrorists doesn't mean we will comply with their demands. It is counterproductive to restrict ourselves from opening a line of communication with the hostage takers simply because they happen to be terrorists and we feel a need to appear and sound tough. This is what President Fujimori did in Peru, and he was lucky he avoided a total catastrophe. I look at the recent effective efforts of the U.S. military in Iraq to reach out to extremist factions and even bring some onto our payroll as a tool to stop violence. Such creative and effective negotiations save American lives. I believe it is sufficient to say that it is our policy as a nation not to make substantive concessions to terrorists.

It is certainly true that payment of ransom to a criminal or even a terrorist group in order to secure the safe release of a hostage serves to encourage further kidnappings. But what is the alternative? Do we allow a hostage to languish in the jungle for years or be killed? Simply put, in an overwhelming majority of kidnap cases, no ransom payment means there will be no release, plain and simple. In my view, our efforts should first and foremost be focused on the safe release of the hostage. After that, we can and should vigorously pursue the kidnappers in order to bring them to justice, or when appropriate use our military capabilities to punish them for having taken an American hostage. We should continue to track them relentlessly. Only when terrorists learn that there will be a price to pay for holding Americans will this crime be reduced or eliminated. But we should not let our desire to punish terrorist kidnappers cloud our judgment and restrict our options. Saying we refuse to negotiate simply does not make the problem go away.

I know from firsthand experience that the current worldwide terrorism threat is both real and substantial, and that we must remain prepared to deal with this problem through a wide array of response strategies. Recently, Somali pirates have engaged in a broad campaign of hijacking ships in international waters to secure ransom payments. In these cases, ransom payments may be required on humanitarian grounds to secure the safe release of the crews and ships involved. However, that action should be closely followed by the full force of military operations. The pirates will stop their hijacking spree when they begin to suffer the consequences of their actions, no sooner. Capturing boats loaded with kidnappers and letting them go because they've not yet attacked a ship does nothing to discourage this terrible crime. I firmly believe in negotiations, but that does not preclude strong punitive military action when necessary. Yet we need to understand that when it is appropriate to conduct negotiations as a strategic tool, such an effort should not be viewed as a decision to acquiesce to terrorism.

The world's positive perception of America took a sharp decline in recent years. Some believed that we were acting with arrogance and disregard for the views of others, that we rejected cooperation with the international community and would go our own way. Fortunately, that trend seems to have abated.

Diplomacy and negotiation are allied skills. The process of listening carefully to others, acknowledging their points of view, and crafting appropriate strategies enables us to positively influence their behavior. We need to do a better job of understanding that others may see the world and its problems differently than we do. That doesn't necessarily mean that they are right or that we are wrong; it's just a different perspective that needs to be understood and acknowledged.

I was pleased to read not long ago that Robert Gates became the first secretary of defense to say that the United States needed more diplomats and the funding to support their activities. It speaks to his appreciation of the fact that the "hammer" alone will not solve all of our problems as a nation. We must have a wide range of tools available in our toolbox, including negotiation, and learn to use them appropriately. As with law enforcement SWAT teams, U.S. military power should be used only when we are left with no recourse, and not simply because we can. Whenever possible we should follow Martin Luther King Jr.'s advice to "pursue peaceful ends through peaceful means." Force should always be viewed as the least desirable and last option.

My thoughts and observations are based on almost three decades of directly dealing with terrorism around the world. I am not opposed to the use of force when necessary. My recommendation to use deadly force to save lives at Sperryville and my support for the HRT's assault at Talladega are two dramatic examples of that. I've also had the great honor and privilege to work with the U.S. Army Delta Force and the U.S. Navy SEALs on both exercises and real-life operational deployments. I'm a great supporter of their dedication, capabilities, and commitment to saving American lives. Further, I also happen to be the very proud father of a Navy SEAL. Yet, I know that it's absolutely vital that government leaders not use these brave soldiers and sailors, and the tremendous capabilities they represent, unless it's absolutely necessary.

The 2002 Moscow theater incident, in which a tactical action to dislodge Chechen terrorists led to the deaths of 129 hostages, the 2004 Beslan School incident in the Caucasus, when 334 hostages died, including 186 children, and the botched Egyptian rescue attempt in Malta discussed earlier, show the continuing danger of trying to resolve situations through force alone. Just because a situation may appear nonnegotiable shouldn't mean we don't try to negotiate.

None of the U.S. military counterterrorism teams has negotiators; that role is reserved for the FBI. But if the leaders who dispatch our military don't think negotiators will be required in a terrorist incident, based on their preconceived notions about terrorist behavior, they won't deploy them. That would eliminate the use of one of our most important and successful tools.

I also remain concerned that leaders in our government today still have, for the most part, insufficient experience in managing a major siege incident. The FBI has not handled one in more than a decade. The public assumes the required skills to manage a crisis incident are inherent within the organization, but are they? Past crisis management training exercises have concentrated on assembling resources, sorting out jurisdiction, establishing joint interagency command posts, deploying improved computer programs to track intelligence, and linking communications capabilities. All of that is important, but it does nothing to actually prepare an incident commander or key decision maker for the most important task he or she will face: determining how to effectively communicate with the terrorists. There will be much we will need to understand. What are their goals? What have they demanded? What do their actions and behaviors suggest to us? How do we effectively communicate with them in response to their demands? How do we forestall violence? How do we buy time to better prepare for possible tactical intervention? How can the negotiators assist the tactical forces that may have to intervene? These are some of the critical questions that need to be addressed, yet no management training program that I know of adequately addresses these questions.

I believe it's time for our nation to become better prepared for a terrorist siege event. The terrorist attack in Mumbai, India, in late November 2008 should serve as a warning that a similar incident could happen here in the United States. If it does, will we have the right resources and capable managers to effectively resolve the crisis with the least loss of life possible? The terrorists have to be good only once to do serious harm. We have to be good all the time.

ACKNOWLEDGMENTS

Without the hard work, dedication, and vision of the hostage negotiation pioneers in law enforcement who came before me, this book and the story it tells would not be possible. Their efforts in the negotiation field helped start this important discipline down the path to become the true profession it has become today. My own growth and development as a hostage negotiator were greatly influenced by these forward-thinking individuals, as well as the many skilled police and FBI negotiators around the world whom I worked with through the years. I will forever be in their debt. I continue to be in awe of their dedication to saving lives in the most challenging of situations.

I want to thank the FBI for giving me the opportunity and great honor to serve my country for over thirty years. I will always appreciate the unique opportunity I had to travel throughout the United States and a good bit of the world on so many challenging, interesting, and varied assignments. Few others in law enforcement will ever have such opportunities. I will always be proud of having been an FBI special agent and for all that stood for. The FBI's motto, Fidelity, Bravery, and Integrity, meant much more to me than just words.

Special recognition goes to Fred Lanceley, who was my mentor and partner during my early years as an FBI hostage negotiator. Fred's insightful analysis of hostage, barricade, and suicide incidents was a great influence on my own thinking. His review of the section of this book on the Ruby Ridge incident was most helpful. I would also like to thank Lt. George Bradford (retired), of the Washington Metropolitan Police Department, for his friendship and support during my early fieldwork as a negotiation practitioner. The entire MPD negotiation team that Lt. Bradford led was instrumental in helping me first put theory to practice. I would also like to give thanks to my old friend and negotiation colleague Jim Botting, FBI Los Angeles (retired), who has been and remains today a great source of wisdom, support, and friendship. Also, Dr. Mike Webster, my Canadian psychologist friend, has inspired me both professionally and personally for almost two decades.

It's appropriate that I recognize the members of the original FBI Critical Incident Negotiation Team, of which I was honored to be a part. This small hand-picked group of select FBI negotiators contained some of the best agents the FBI has ever produced. You know who you are. No crazier, more outrageously funny, more talented, and more resourceful group of FBI agents was ever assembled. Despite their zany antics, their manifest skills and abilities influenced countless law enforcement and correctional negotiators across this nation.

I am proud to have led the FBI negotiation program for the last ten years of my career. Being named the first chief of the FBI Crisis Negotiation Unit was a singular honor that will remain my proudest career achievement. The opportunity to advance the negotiation profession from that leadership position was something I will always cherish and appreciate. As chief of the CNU, I viewed my most important task as directly serving the training and operational needs of the FBI's 350 negotiators assigned throughout the field. Serving this special group of individuals was both an honor and a privilege.

It's important that I thank the many FBI agents and support employees with whom I worked during my various career assignments. You are too numerous to mention, but there are no finer or more dedicated public servants than these individuals. I've also been extremely fortunate to work alongside many skilled negotiators involved in the International Negotiation Working Group and the National Council of Negotiation Associations. I was proud to have played a role in helping form these important professional organizations that continue to promote the negotiation profession far and wide.

This book began as an idea many years ago. In exploring the process of writing a book, I reached out to my friend Peter Bergen, who has written several books about Osama bin Laden. Peter's insights and suggestions were most helpful to me. His most important recommendation was to work with literary agent Tina Bennett. Without Tina's encouragement, support, and guidance, this book would never have been written. I would also like to thank William Patrick for his excellent work helping to edit the original lengthy manuscript. Bill's skill and talents were of extraordinary help in organizing the material that went into this book. My editor at Random House, Tim Bartlett, was also an enormous help in crafting the kind of book that I wanted to write. I thank him for the many hours he spent with me on the phone going over the material. His patience and thoughtful suggestions were key factors in achieving the final product.

I also want to recognize my former FBI colleague and dear friend Steve Romano, who graciously read over the manuscript to ensure its accuracy. His attention to detail is legendary and his insightful suggestions were a big help to me. Former FBI colleague Byron Sage was also kind enough to provide assistance by reading over the Waco chapter and providing me with critical feedback. It's also an honor to give special thanks and recognition to Cheryl Hart Frappier, whose personal ordeal and courage are written about in the first chapter of this book. She kindly reviewed the Sperryville chapter and provided important insights that will help the reader better understand the ordeal she experienced. I'm continually inspired by her heroic story of survival.

Having a loving and supportive family is the key to my success in life. This book is dedicated to my wife, Carol, but I was never more grateful for the investment of college tuition than when my daughter Katie Salzman used her English degree to proofread the early chapters put together by dear old dad. She offered many helpful suggestions and provided me with a much needed critical review of the book's tone and content. Katie, her younger brother, Rusty, and her older sister, Kelly Brady, remain the true joys of my life. No father has ever been more proud of his children and their successes in life. I also want to thank my sister, Nancy Kennedy, for always encouraging and supporting her little brother. It's also appropriate to thank my oldest and dearest friends, Keith Naumann, Larry Collins, Tom Broner, and Bill Strate, for forty-five years of camaraderie and endless laughter.

Finally, I want to recognize Bill and Doris Noesner, my wonderful parents. I only wish they were alive today to read this book. I hope they would be proud of it and what it stands for. It could never have been possible without their enduring love and constant support. Starting out with good parents has been the best good fortune in my life. I recommend it to everyone.

PHOTO: © LYNLEE WASTIE

GARY NOESNER retired from the FBI in 2003 following a thirty-year career as an investigator, instructor, and negotiator. An FBI hostage negotiator for twenty-three years, he spent ten years as the Bureau's chief negotiator. Following his retirement from the FBI, he became a senior vice president with Control Risks, an international consultancy. Noesner has appeared on numerous television documentaries produced by A&E, the History Channel, Discovery, TLC, and National Geographic. He is the founder of the National Council of Negotiation Associations, which represents numerous organizations and thousands of law enforcement negotiators worldwide. He speaks at law enforcement and corporate events and continues to consult part-time.

garynoesner.com